LONGING for RUNNING WATER

Ecofeminism and Liberation

IVONE GEBARA

FORTRESS PRESS
Minneapolis

LONGING FOR RUNNING WATER
Ecofeminism and Liberation
Translated from the Portuguese by David Molineaux

Cover design: Mike Mihelich
Cover image: *Light Patterns on Water* by Alex L. Fradkin. Copyright © 1999 PhotoDisc. Used by permission.
Author photo: © 1990 Mev Puleo. Used by permission.
Interior design: Judy Gilats

ISBN 0-8006-3183-8

Manufactured in the U.S.A.   AF1-3183

                                   4   5   6   7   8   9   10

CONTENTS

PROLOGUE

As the deer longs for running waters . . .

My personal experience is totally urban. I was born in the very large city of São Paulo, Brazil, and have always lived in cities, although for the last twenty years I have lived in their poor, outlying areas. I like cities because I know how to get along in them: They have always been my living space, and it is in the urban context that many great legacies have been passed on to me. I like the city because it is a visible space for human creativity, a place of great artistic expression, of many ethnic groups and varied customs. I like the city because it is a place of challenge and of manifold questions, even if the answers almost always remain tentative.

My experience of jungles, rivers, and seas—and of animals, even pets—is very limited. I know the names of very few plants, flowers, and birds, even though I appreciate, respectively, their fragrance and their songs. I confess that I have always been sheltered from the cold, the wind, and the rain; and that my feet have always been well shod to protect me from insect bites and cold. In fact, I was brought up with some fear of animals, birds, and insects. I was afraid of small mishaps like soiling my feet or injuring myself on some discarded object, and big things like drowning in the sea.

I have, however, always appreciated big trees, above all fruit trees, as well as gardens, flowers, nicely cut grass, and the fragrance of the earth, especially after the rain. But these were invariably encountered "from afar," as if they were exceptional phenomena, like paintings, to be examined once in a while; they were "objects," things, occurrences outside myself. Even though I enjoyed the sen-

v

sations they offered me, they seemed to have a life totally distinct and independent from my own. To sum up, then, I acknowledge the poverty of my experience with the world of nature and of animals!

The fact that I am writing a book about ecology, environment, or the earth from an ecofeminist perspective does not mean, as some would expect, that there has been some great turnabout in my life— particularly with regard to my daily habits. I haven't gone out to live in the country or bought a farm or planted a garden—or even begun to raise domestic animals. I remain an urban woman, but I now have a different perception of things—a bodily perception of the unity and interdependence of all living things and a growing awareness that we are one body with the whole universe.

In adopting an ecofeminist perspective, which is a combination of social feminism and holistic ecology, what I have changed is my point of view: my way of looking at the world, at people, and at events.[1] I have abandoned my exclusively anthropocentric (human-centered) and androcentric (male-centered) view of the world. I have begun, then, to feel the life within me in a different way. Through ecofeminism, I have begun to see more clearly how much our bodies—my body, and the bodies of my neighbors—are affected, not just by unemployment and economic hardship, but also by the harmful effects the system of industrial exploitation imposes on them. I have begun to see more clearly how the exclusion of the poor is linked to the destruction of their lands, to the forces that leave them no choice but to move from place to place in a ceaseless exile, to racism, and to the growing militarization of their countries. To defend the unjust monopoly of a minority, the poor countries have become more intensely militarized: They arm themselves to kill their own poor. I have come to see how much all this fits in with the inherent logic of the patriarchal system—especially in its current form, which can be called "economic globalization," and is a global order, or rather a global disorder.

According to this system's well-worn logic, nature is entirely separate from the human and is dependent on the human will. Women, too, are identified with nature, both in their reproductive functions and in their role as "nurturers" in the broadest sense of the word; the work of providing for children is primarily, although not exclusively, a feminine one.

All this has led me to seek, reflect on, and to some extent even live out the spirit of a different kind of culture, different forms of relationship, and a different theology—one that goes beyond the antitheses and hierarchies to which we're accustomed, beyond a sort of divorce between life's material and its spiritual grounding.

I also recognize how slow this process is, and that it does not always move along with linear continuity. I feel myself to be in a reeducation process, a process that is beginning to affect many aspects of my life and that invites me to relate to all living things in a way that is very different from the way I learned in my own cultural tradition.

And so I am creating an urban ecofeminism, one that has little contact with the world of the forests, with the mysteries of the jungle, with the power of rivers and waterfalls, and with the eruptions of volcanoes. I am creating an ecofeminism based on the experience of those who have diminishing access to green things and clean water; of those who breathe an ever greater amount of the air pollution that has spread everywhere. My ecofeminism is pregnant with health: not health as we understood it in the past, but the health of a future that promises deeper communion between human beings and all other living things. My ecofeminism is shot through with the staunch conviction that beauty is important in healing people. It might be the beauty of sounds, of colors, of words, of faces, of food and drink, or of embraces. Like my friend Rubem Alves, I too can vouch for "salvation through beauty."

Before closing this prologue, I would like to acknowledge a debt of gratitude to many authors. Most of them are from the North, the North that has engaged in so many campaigns of domination and destruction, the North that keeps on subjecting people and regions to its greedy and exploitative projects. But in the very midst of that empire of profit, prophetic voices have composed an alternative song, one that is being heard also in the South. I feel myself to be in a communion of thought, and of sisterhood and brotherhood, with Rosemary Radford Ruether, Delores Williams, Dorothee Soelle, Sallie McFague, Thomas Berry, Brian Swimme, Maria Mies, Mary Hunt, Alice Walker, Edgar Morin, Eugen Drewermann, and so many others. They have opened new horizons for me. They have helped me, from within my own context, to think through the issues they have raised there, in the North, within that context. But these topics belong not only to the North. They are key issues for all of humanity and for all women who agree that there must be new forms of relationship among them, among all men and women, and with the entire earth. Their questions are contextual, but they take on planetary significance in the light of the process of raising our voices against the globalization of the economy, of politics, and of the culture in which we live.

Many authors from the South are also present. They will appear here and there in my reflections. Out of modesty, I won't be forever quoting these figures, whose work is daily bread for all of us here but whose contribution has been invaluable; without it, I could have done nothing. As readers, they will see that they are cited throughout these reflections.

There is much of them in me, but the composition and rhythm of this text are often my own. Each of us has his or her own specific way of speaking and feeling. In my daily life I inhabit a world far from that of philosophical and theological scholarship. From that world arise many questions in addition to the often unanswerable ones of my companions in the North and the South. In the final analysis, the notes used in playing the one great symphony of the universe are the same, even if it can be performed in a great multitude of ways.

I am also grateful for the courage of the many feminists and the few ecofeminists of Latin America. Women in struggle: tireless, passionate . . . "conspiring," inspiring, raising their voices in search of new alternatives and ways of living with dignity. They, too, are present in these pages, along with the members of the many women's groups I have been blessed to meet in my Latin American travels. To all of them I express my gratitude and my warm affection.

Finally, I am extremely grateful for the lives of the great number of anonymous women who cross my path daily. With some I stop and exchange greetings, impressions, and comments on the many events of daily life. With others my encounters are longer and more frequent. Most of them pass me by, however, rushing to work or walking slowly with heavy loads of laundry on their heads. They pass me as they pull their kids along by the hand or carry them in their wombs. . . . And their lives silently challenge me. The violence in which they live violates me, and often I don't know what to do either to help them or to bear my own "cross" of privilege—because to eat and drink, to have friends, and to reflect on life are privileges on a planet where the number of those excluded from them increases daily. And this privilege opens up a historical responsibility, a responsibility in love, not only for my own life but for the lives of so many persons.

This book is no more than an attempt. It seeks to contribute to the restoration of Earth's dignity, of the dignity of women and men alienated from Earth's body and their own bodies and often struggling against both, waging wars of conquest against them, dividing what ought to be united.

This book is an invitation to reflect together about ourselves and about new ways of expressing love, a love that is far broader than the defense of our own little slice in the larger pie of this world. It is a love that includes us all, because at bottom we are all part of this same pie, the one pie offered as "food and drink" for ourselves and for all living things.

"Take and eat, all of you: this is my body and this is my blood." We are food and drink for one another. We are one another's body and blood. We are one another's salvation. For this reason, I will try to take a few steps with you, dear reader, so that these convictions can become ever more flesh of our flesh. "Take and eat": I offer myself to you in the hope that this food may do you good and nourish all your hopes.

INTRODUCTION

≈

Like many others, I have become more and more concerned over ecological issues in recent years, at least in theory. I have seen how much society and culture are part of the ecological system, and consequently how much political, economic, social, educational, and religious issues are all related to ecology and to the stability of the ecosystem. In practice, however, I often feel constrained by the struggle for survival in which innumerable people in my country, especially women and children, continue to be immersed. And the survival struggle is always there, inviting us to take whatever steps are possible: to be converted, in a way, to the concreteness of daily life, to the reality of immediate need. So ecological problems urge me to search for a more inclusive style of thought, so that bit by bit people can feel the real connection between the issues of work, unemployment, hunger, and pollution, on the one hand, and the patriarchal image of God on the other.

Like most Latin Americans, I also inherit through my education an eminently anthropocentric, or human-centered, cultural tradition. It is very hard to develop alternative behaviors and educational processes that can lead us to greater solidarity and communion!

I feel, based on my own experience, that ecological and feminist proposals that do not arise from the concrete needs of the various popular groups do not have much coherence. I sense also that the solutions put forth by the established powers are not always likely to be accepted, because often they fail to address the people's most urgent needs.

In the northeastern Brazilian neighborhood in which I live now (and it is out of the perspective of my neighborhood that I write this book), the word "ecofeminism" is not part of people's vocabularies. The same goes for many other words we use in intellectual circles. So, although many of the women who are my neighbors have inspired my writing, they will not be my first readers.

I sense that ecofeminism is born of daily life, of day-to-day sharing among people, of enduring together garbage in the streets, bad smells, the absence of sewers and safe drinking water, poor nutrition, and inadequate health care. The ecofeminist issue is born of the lack of municipal garbage collection, of the multiplication of rats, cockroaches, and mosquitoes, and of the sores on children's skin. This is true because it is usually women who have to deal with daily survival issues: keeping the house clean and feeding and washing children.

Women and men struggle to survive, and they struggle a great deal; but they don't always make the connection between the chickens they sell on the corner, the dirty water that runs in the streets after streetcleaning, and their children's health. The street often turns into a public garbage dump. On the inside, their houses are generally neat, but the street, the collective space, is practically a no-man's-land. Because the poor have almost no access to public services, they do not care for public space as if it were their own, as if it were something a poor person could consider "mine." They know just how little the public spaces are really theirs, and by defiling or neglecting them they reproduce, on a small scale, the neglect they themselves suffer.

Further, the whole issue of public and private space opens up for reflection here. Within a traditional feminist perspective, we might say that public space has been men's domain and private space has been women's. Today, however, it isn't possible to argue this in any absolute sense. More and more often, it is women who are hired for certain public cleanup jobs, so they clean not only private space but also public space. At the same time, men are most adept at getting things dirty and failing to clean them up. This includes the production of nuclear waste, the accumulation of which is becoming alarming and distressing.

But the issue is not just the way gender is expressed in public and private spaces. It is more than that: It is an issue of social class, and of people's increasing exclusion from some spaces. The space in which the poor live out their lives, whether they be men, women, or children, is a poorly cared-for space, a space that is ignored and neglected.

Rich neighborhoods are cleaner and better cared for. Public services there, including sanitary services, are more efficient. However, it is not the rich who clean up: They do not have to deal with dirt and grime. It is the poor whose task it is to clean the houses and streets of the rich—and often, too, to assist them in their personal hygiene. The spaces of the rich are cleaned by the poor, and most especially by poor women, who continue to endure the disregard and invisibility that patriarchal society has imposed on them. Here we enter fully into the logic of the capitalist system, with its narrow exclusiveness, as well as the logic of hierarchical patriarchy and of class, race, and gender privilege.

This micro-example leads to a macro-understanding of human life as it is lived out in all our social institutions. In countries in which there are a frightful number of impoverished people, as is the case in Latin America, one can see how the places that are littered with garbage are also the places where the poorest people live, and among them are the most marginal of all: blacks and American Indians. The rich throw their garbage in the spaces used by the poor: Cities often open garbage dumps right where the poor build their homes. In areas in which there is no drinking water, in which air pollution is most dense, and in which health problems abound, the poor jostle one another for a few square feet on which to live.

We know that most of the waste is not produced by the poor. They are not the owners of polluting industries, of nuclear power plants, or of the military headquarters at which wars are planned; neither are they the principal consumers of canned and packaged goods. However, the poor are the first to be hurt by the various kinds of waste that are produced. It is true that the poor do generate a small amount of garbage, and that it ends up all around them; but it is virtually impossible for them to change the rules of a game created by others, a game that requires material wealth to live in places far from the garbage one produces.

The destruction of the rain forests goes hand in hand with waste production and the expansion of polluting industrial zones. Referring to the Brazilian government, Leila da Costa Ferreira says, it "still plays no part in the creation of policies to conserve biodiversity and social diversity, to protect indigenous lands, or to settle conflicts in mining areas."[1] Sensitivity to ecological issues is still very limited, and existing ecological organizations are fragile and vulnerable. Something similar can be said of the discourse and practice of the churches regarding this issue.

Within this context, I often ask myself what contribution ecofeminist reflection can make in Latin America. What is its usefulness and what are its objectives, given the concrete social and religious contradictions we face?

As I have gotten a feel for the world out of a broader perspective than that of my own neighborhood, my first impression has been of signs pointing to a qualitative change in our times. I see initiatives designed to break the frightening cycle of destructiveness in which we find ourselves. I see signs of a break with the patriarchal system that enslaves nature, women, men, and marginal populations, forcing them all to conform to a hierarchical pattern of relationships. I also see signs of the reemergence of "differences," exceptions to hierarchical models, and this reemergence surely points to the growth of a new sense of the meaning of our collective existence. All these indicators deserve to be underscored: They point to a qualitative change in perspective, and as such they are signs of a new hope.

In many parts of Latin America, the feminist movement is growing, especially the popular feminist movement. The name it is called by doesn't matter. Often the word "feminist" is not used, but the fact is that women are beginning to be concerned about what is happening to society in general and to themselves in particular. Many groups are struggling for women's dignity and for their self-esteem, and for a more open attitude on the part of civic and political organizations. As I see it, this already constitutes a break with the hierarchies supported by patriarchy and a move, on the part of women, away from political silence. In addition, ecological movements appear to be growing in popular circles, and take forms that probably would not be recognized by First World ecologists. The first thing these movements talk about is not how to save the earth and its rain forests and rivers, but how to live on the land; how to love it, and how to build a house on it. It is hard to try to save the earth when your relationship with it is marked by conflict, and when you spend your time just wishing for a piece of it—an urban lot or a patch of land in the countryside on which you can live. In the world of the poor, the ecology issue surfaces first of all in the form of demands for land reform in the countryside and the redistribution of urban lots in the city.

All this makes clear who is most responsible for the catastrophic destruction of the ecosystem. The poor do not destroy natural springs or watersheds; these have long since been taken away from them. The poor don't use powerful electric saws to cut hundred-year-old trees, because they don't own chainsaws. If they do so at all, it is as hired labor, as impoverished workers—and they do so to earn their bread and beans.

In the struggle for land and for a dignified life, the women of Latin America and their sons and daughters have moved up to the front lines. It is they who have the most to gain from these battles, because in a certain sense they are the ones who, on a daily basis, maintain the fragile balance of family life.

These popular movements are surely significant, because they alert us to the fact that life is an interdependent process; that the survival of one group depends on that of another, and that on them depends the survival of the earth and of all living beings. Not a few indigenous and African American groups are seeking their autonomy and their own identity. They are struggling to break with white arrogance and to get a hearing for their condemnation of whites' unlimited power and greed. Even if up until now their achievements have seemed insignificant, they are exposing the racist foundations of our white western system and the complicity of the major religions in perpetuating violence and discrimination.

In the light of these encouraging signs, and to further the process of seeking a new world order that is in harmony both with the planet and with the cosmos, ecofeminists are attempting to discern signs of hope. They do not invent new theories for the poor, much less for their liberation. All they try to do is to understand what is happening and, on the basis of this understanding, to dialogue with others who are willing to do so.

This is no new ideology. Rather, it is a different perception of reality that starts right from the unjust system in which we find ourselves and seeks to overcome it in order to bring happiness to everyone and everything.

Despite our lack of clarity and the tentativeness of our actions, I propose to examine the broad issue of ecofeminism from a philosophical perspective as it is related to Christian religious experience. I think it is always important to understand our need to refashion our beliefs and their particular formulations in each new moment of history. There is a connection—one that is not always visible—between certain religious doctrines and the destruction of the ecosystem. And because this is so, to change these doctrines is to open a path toward resurrection, toward social and ecological justice.

Our religious writings almost always seem to be trying to stand apart from any complicity with destructive processes, as if they were "oases" of purity, goodness, and freedom: privileged domains in which the air is pure and justice is possible. From this perspective, religion appears to have been born of another world: a world of perfection that is somehow above this one and superior to it. Religion itself seeks to perpetuate this illusion and fails to see the negative consequences of this attitude in contemporary life. We are not always interested in raising critical issues that might change this way of looking at things, because this would bring about considerable insecurity and weaken the foundations of many kinds of power we currently enjoy.

My task will be to point to the possibility of reinterpreting some key elements within the Christian tradition for the purpose of reconstructing Earth's body, the human body, and our relationship with all living bodies. I will not try to rewrite traditional theology; that would be both arrogant to attempt and impossible to accomplish. All I hope to do is put forth a few reflections in an attempt to show the urgent need to change our theological constructs in the new era that is emerging. It is no longer possible to separate the religious sphere from that of scientific discovery, as if they were two entirely different discourses. Neither is it possible to think of women and men as religious beings independent of the religion that is embodied in the earth and the cosmos.

Many others before me have attempted to reinterpret the Christian tradition in the light of the challenges of their own historical moments. This, too, is just one more attempt to understand our heritage in the light of a broader shared history; at the same time, it reflects my desire to reinterpret the meaning of our lives as a part of the great life process in which we are all immersed.

If all of humanity, the inhabitants of the entire earth, were to take on the task of saving their own lives along with the life of the earth, world religions would inevitably make this project their own. And as they became converted to this urgent and fundamental cause, they would have to modify some of their intellectual constructs along with the power structures that uphold them.

Patriarchal religions have always been marked by an incredible and paradoxical duality of perspective. They preach domination over the earth while at the same time exhorting us to loathe matter and struggle against the body. They preach love and peace while at the same time urging hatred and violence against those who are "different." To at least admit the existence of this ambiguity is the first step toward refashioning our beliefs within a perspective that allows us to treat all living things with respect.

Marcel Gauchet, in his book *Le désenchantement du monde,* predicted the crisis that would beset religions of transcendence.[2] The model that leads us to look for the grounding of this world somewhere outside it—and seeks assistance from supportive divinities—would appear to be destined for oblivion. Gauchet believes the same fate also awaits a certain style of understanding and organizing national states. The viewpoint I plan to develop will attempt to present the crisis affecting these transcendent models of religion in the light of the environmental crisis and of the current crisis in relations within the human community. All this is aimed at pointing up the urgency of acquiring a new understanding of the role of our religions, and, consequently, of our theologies, which are discourses that articulate our deepest beliefs. Theology will have to carry out its social role with greater humility and openness. Its truths will always need to be open-ended. They will be mere approximations of the Divine Mystery: attempts to grasp the meaning of our existence, if only in a tentative way. We will need to leave behind absolute statements and "ex cathedra" truths, and learn to live in

the midst of the extraordinary changeability and mysterious fragility—and our comparative ignorance—of the very Being in which we
have our being.

The Latin American theology of the last thirty years has shown
relatively little interest in feminist or ecological issues. (I am not
making an absolute statement, because in the last two or three years
some significant writings have appeared.)[3] I am not saying this to
criticize my colleagues; it is merely a statement of fact. I think the
Latin American context in the 1970s and 1980s, the years during
which liberation theology developed, simply did not allow for the
emergence of these topics.

Our theological tradition was at that time strongly influenced
by nineteenth-century rationalism and by the struggle to transform
economic structures, but it failed to relate the oppression of the
poor to the broader issue of the destruction of earth-systems. In the
same way, it failed to identify the direct or indirect legitimation
that patriarchal religions bestowed upon the mechanistic domination of the world and the manipulation of human beings. Today, of
course, many voices have been raised in the churches, both in
defense of the poor and in protest against genetic manipulation
and similar practices.

In the meantime, we fail to see that we often formulate our
protests from within this same hierarchical power system, without
altering our understanding of the human person, of God, and of
Jesus. We continue to accept the traditional monotheism and
anthropocentrism that have characterized and structured Christian
tradition. So we could say that, although the topics being discussed
today are somewhat different, they are still dealt with from within
a philosophy and a theology that justify the manipulation of life
while at the same time urging its defense. I have experienced this
ambiguity in my own life and will deal with it in my first chapter,
which focuses on epistemological issues, or issues related to our
ways of knowing.

Throughout the book, my approach will be emphatically philosophical and theological. I will try to uncover the thought structures
and understandings of human life that are implicit in the way the
Christian tradition is used interpret reality. We have done little of
this work in Latin America, and less still in the light of feminism

and ecological challenges. My reflections will be an attempt to offer some introduction to these very extensive topics.

I must underline the extent to which this work is limited by my personal experience and tradition. I offer no reflections on the African religious world or that of indigenous peoples. I have to recognize the limitations of my own knowledge regarding these cultures; I want to affirm also the importance of allowing these groups to offer interpretations of their own realities. I feel that in Latin America we too often seek out elements from various cultures and attempt to translate or explain them in Christian terms. In one sense this is understandable, given the penetration of Christianity into cultures of African and indigenous origin. In the face of the religious and cultural extermination that has taken place on this continent, many theologians and pastoral workers have felt called to make efforts to retrieve elements from these traditions. They have raised a prophetic voice against the process of dismantling these cultures, a process that continues right up to our own day. It could be worthwhile in light of this discussion for readers to refer to *O rostro indio de Deus,* a book by several Latin American authors that addresses these issues of cultural survival.[4]

However, I think we still need to grow in respect for, dialogue about, and instil a profound receptiveness to the autonomy that ought to be enjoyed by all these religious articulations of the mystery of life. In other words, every cultural group needs to be free to speak its own word in its own way, and to develop its own religious expressions, using whatever approaches it chooses; it should not be expected to interpret its heritage in the light of the Western Christian tradition or through the use of the kinds of academic tools we tend to impose on it with virtually no reflection.

I would now like to offer a brief overview of ecofeminism in Latin America, and especially of theological writings on the subject.

First of all, I should say that ecofeminism has not yet gained public recognition in Latin America, either as a theoretical construct or as a social movement that deals with the relationship between the exploitation of nature and that of women. Its influence has been relatively small, both in intellectual and in church circles. When we analyze the limited work that has been done on the subject in Latin America, however, we can see that even here the ties between feminism and ecological concerns have been multiple and varied. In fact, we can already speak of Latin American "ecofeminisms." And not only is there a variety of ecofeminisms, responses to these ecofeminisms also vary.

Some Latin American ecofeminist circles are developing critiques similar to those that have appeared in the European countries and in North America. We could speak here of an "essentialist" position: an ecofeminism that would postulate a kind of shared identity that brings together women and nature; one that would not deal with the great social issues of our day and would not see women as actors in the public arena.

In the global ecological summit in 1992, sponsored by the United Nations in Rio de Janeiro, some of these issues were debated—especially in certain feminist groups that gathered after the assembly's closing. However, the issues never came to the attention of public opinion; Brazil's major media gave them no significant coverage. In Brazil, ecofeminist debate has developed most among feminist groups in the southeastern part of the country, especially in response to Rosiska Darcy de Oliveira's book *Elogio da Diferença: o feminino emergente*. Darcy de Oliveira argued that, in entering the social arena, women should start from their own situation and from the ways in which they are different from men:

> Women are different from men because in the center of their being there are different values. They emphasize personal relationships, caring about and for others, the defense of life, the private and affective sphere, and gratuity in relationships. In other words, their identity is formed in their interaction with others. For this reason, women are more intuitive, more sensitive, and more empathetic.[5]

Probably without realizing it, Darcy de Oliveira upholds distinctions that patriarchal categories have imposed on us all—even if she does so with the intention of underlining the importance of differences.

Although she seems to insist on the revolutionary potential of these "differences," she fails to realize that it is no longer possible to assign some rigidly stylized attributes to women and others to men. In the first place, gender—the distinction between the masculine and the feminine—is like "nature," "culture," and "tradition," in the sense that it is a historical and social construct. There is no way we can work with these distinctions as if they were ahistorical concepts that could identify certain essential qualities of either men or women.

When it comes to gender, sex, and race, there are no immutable essences. What do exist are different human groups, each of which constructs its own meanings. There are no pure biological "givens": everything is involved in that evolving and constitutive reality we call culture.

However, differences based on gender have become more and more rigidly defined, both in the domestic sphere and in political and economic life. This is especially true in the urban world. Subjective values, feelings, and ambitions, including competition, are present both in the public realm and in domestic life. For this reason, to defend rigidly defined roles for women and men is to fail to perceive the current situation of women in Latin America and throughout the world.

Another reality that needs to be underlined and clarified has to do with our understanding of "nature." It is not always clear, when she speaks of nature, whether Darcy de Oliveira is referring to a nontemporal essence or whether she means the physical world—the earth, other living things, and the cosmos. In a very helpful article on the feminine as a metaphor for nature, feminist scholar Bila Sorj supports some ecofeminist positions:

> There is a tendency to appreciate the role of women to the degree that it resembles that of the feminine in nature. In other words, are women more capable of critical ecological thought in virtue of their domestic experience, especially that of maternity? Here once again, we confront an emphasis on the "singularity" of women's experience; and this ends up leading us into essentialist discourse. More attentive reflection should lead us to realize that while women do play social roles, they have a human subjectivity that always exceeds and overflows the confines of their gender identity. The involvement of women and of feminists in the ecological struggle is due less to their feminine roles in family life—although

we admit that "ecofeminism" raises some echoes in this sphere—than to access to the public realm, where they gain political experience, a wider and more diversified vision of human problems, and the confidence to criticize the existing culture and propose changes.[6]

Along with the French anthropologist Nicole Claude Mathieu, we could ask why women are more affected than men by inadequate environmental and development policies. The answer has nothing to do with women's alleged affinity with nature or with some special "sense" for the bounties of nature that they are alleged to possess. Rather, it is because "on a planetary level, in rich and poor countries alike, in the North and in the South, and in every ethnic group and social class, there are policies that give men power over women. These policies define women as a social group whose necessary role is to assure continuity (and frequently survival) in daily, material life."[7]

Although I don't rule out plausible objections to the types of thinking and action put forward by Bila Sorj and Nicole Claude Mathieu, I think much of the criticism directed at their approach remains on a very general and academic level. It almost never confronts the concrete daily problems we face in poor neighborhoods: the work women of the popular sectors do in order to survive and the destruction of the environment in which they live. Theoretical critiques often fail to show any awareness of the extreme inadequacy of the food the poor eat, of their unhealthy housing situations, and of the very bad water and air, especially in the outlying areas of large cities. These critiques don't always keep in mind that it is women first of all who have to take responsibility for daily life, for family survival, for child care, and for health and nutritional needs. It is women who often walk miles to get semisafe drinking water or to find some trough where they can hold off the animals and wash their clothes.

Beyond all this, theoretical approaches run the risk of remaining isolated in a world of privilege that has the luxury to discuss ideas and in which the exchange of ideas takes place among groups that have a very weak commitment to dealing with the real situation of the great masses of the dispossessed. Maria Mies puts it well:

The problem with "essentialism" vs. "historical materialist" discourse, as discussed by Mary Mellor, is also that it remains within the constraints of an academic, and that means idealistic, discourse only; it seems to distance itself from the fact that women and men are confronted by urgent problems which need solutions. In view of the ongoing destruction of our ecological life-base, of increasing male violence against women, and of increasing aimless civil wars and Ramboism around the world, the constructivist "essentialism" vs. "materialism" discourse seems out of place.[8]

For this reason, I don't want to spend much time on this style of debate. Instead I will attempt, as much as possible, to focus on concrete issues, issues that affect our daily lives—such as the survival of the earth and the meaning of our existence.

I have never gotten involved in theoretical debates between feminists and ecofeminists. The ecofeminist perspective within which I work in philosophy and theology allies itself neither with the essentialist point of view nor with the supremacy of the "difference"; rather, it seeks to do Christian theology in the light of a wider perspective that is very different from the one that characterizes the patriarchal world.

It will become clear throughout this book that I believe the basic issue has nothing to do with sacralizing either the world of nature or the world of women. In my view, to do either would be to succumb to an outdated, romantic vision that would be of very little practical use. Human beings, animals, and nature in general can be a source of either destruction or creation; in all of them, death and life are intertwined in a way that attests to the inseparability of these two poles. Similarly, the idea of nature can for women have either a positive or a negative meaning, as Carolyn Merchant has pointed out:

> Central to the organic theory was the identification of nature, especially the earth, with a nurturing mother: a kindly, beneficent female who provided for the needs of mankind in an ordered, planned universe. But another opposing image of nature as female was also prevalent: wild and uncontrollable nature could render violence, storms, droughts, and general chaos. Both were identified

with female sex and were projections of human perceptions onto the external world.[9]

The ambivalence of the human world, the animal world, and the physical world can be noted in every dimension of life.

If our thought and practice are to be inclusive, they need to be debated by a great variety of different groups; they can never be set up as new dogmas. This is a continuing challenge for us, because the temptation to be "in the right" is a danger that can be found in all of us.

Theological attention to ecofeminist issues in Latin America is still quite limited. The ways in which theological formulations support the ongoing domination of women and the unlimited exploitation of natural resources have still not been clearly and critically understood. We have not yet become aware of the magnitude of the complicity of Christian religious discourse in the momentous crisis faced by the planet and the human community that inhabits it.

Meanwhile, there are small, organized ecofeminist groups in countries such as Argentina, Chile, Peru, Venezuela, Bolivia, Uruguay, and Brazil. They still have little influence on feminist theological reflection in Latin America, especially in academic institutions and religious seminaries, but despite their limited institutional presence, there is already an effort to create a Latin American ecofeminist network. It seeks a broad base, and does not intend to limit itself to theological issues; rather, it hopes to take up a variety of topics that are relevant to our lives. An awareness of the need to develop a feminism that is within the Latin American liberation tradition and to relate it to the ecological perspective in the hope of building interdependent, noncompetitive relationships seems to be slowly growing. Undoubtedly, it is only the beginning of a process, but still a significant beginning.

At the moment, in my view, the liveliest ecofeminist group in Latin America is the Con-spirando Collective in Santiago, Chile. With great effort and courage, the collective has been publishing the ecofeminist journal *Con-spirando* since 1992. In the first issue, dated March 1992, they say:

In this initial issue we invite you to participate in convoking a network of Latin American women who seek to develop their own
spirituality and theology in order to better reflect our experiences
of the sacred. The very name of this journal—*Con-spirando*—is
an attempt to picture some of these experiences: the image of
"breathing together," which in itself evokes images of the planet
as a great lung of life.[10]

In the fourth issue (June 1993), the journal reproduces texts by
a number of ecofeminists, especially North American authors. In
the introductory editorial, we read, "It seems we need new ways of
understanding our place in the world. We need to re-situate ourselves, and from there to re-weave our daily lives, the web of relationships that gives form to our societies and our style of producing
the culture in which we live."[11]

In ecofeminism—ecofeminisms, if you like—we envision an energy flow that brings about political and cultural change and gets us
moving, excites our minds, revives our imaginations, and unleashes
our questions. As Latin Americans, how do we interpret this body of
visions and proposals? How do these ideas resonate in us? What gestures and actions give birth to these perspectives? What theologies
can be born of these new worldviews? How do we express the spirituality that grows out of a new anthropology? And what new
visions of political-cultural action flow out of ecofeminism?

These questions continue to be both significant and challenging
for groups that seek to reformulate the Christian faith in the light of
the challenges of our times. They continue to be reflected on and
debated in a variety of women's groups, each one using its own
methodology.

What seems significant is that ecofeminist theology in Latin
America has developed among intellectuals who are committed to
the struggles of poor women. The theoretical material we study is
often informed by the work of colleagues from the North: They
help us to raise questions about our personal and social situations,
and we do the same for them. We begin to perceive the links among
all forms of oppression and violence and, based on our analysis of
the world situation, to agree on the political-ideological links
between the domination of women and the domination of nature.

This domination manifests itself on the ideological-cultural level in our worldviews and within the whole patriarchal historical process in the midst of which we live out our lives. This means that not only women are victims of the process: So are men, and to exactly the same degree. The problem is that the type of oppression and exclusion suffered by women seems to be more openly legitimized by the current hierarchicalized system, which pushes people aside on the basis of gender, race, and class.

This is Latin America. The indigenous population, the very group that lives in closest communion with nature, is subjected to progressive extermination. The black population, which has a religious tradition that exalts the interrelatedness of all human and natural powers, is the most impoverished and excluded. Racism is on the rise, supported by several ideologies, the most virulent of which advocates "the whitening of both skin and culture." Jungles, lakes, and rivers, as objects of the greed of international capitalism, are destroyed at a frightening pace. The female population, more than any other, is deprived of civil rights. The patriarchal cross and sword have indeed been victorious, and "macho" men continue to be regarded as the most important mediators of the sacred.

Within the Latin American context, ecofeminism has been a challenging light both for feminists and for women's groups in poor neighborhoods. "I dare to think that once the links between all forms of oppression and violence became clear, from oppression in the family to the destruction of the planet, feminism had to become ecofeminism," writes Rosa Dominga Trapasso of the Talitha Cumi feminist group in Lima, Peru.[12]

Patriarchal theology, and especially creation theology, legitimized both the oppression and domination of nature and the existence of hierarchical relationships among all beings. Doubtless there were always exceptions, such as the movement founded by Saint Francis of Assisi. Even so, the Christian tradition that dominated the West held on to the idea that God stands above nature as creator and lawgiver. Nature is somehow subject to the divine will. In that sense, it is by divine command that nature gives us what we need in order to live.

Although nature contains both masculine and feminine elements, the relationship between God and nature resembles the relationship of domination between men and women. This is one of the relationships ecofeminist theology seeks to analyze. What does it mean to speak of "God the Creator"? What images and specific behaviors follow from our discourse about God the Creator? In what way have women participated in the creation and development of these theologies? I offer these questions in an overall way, as an invitation to reflection. They will not be the specific topics of this book, but these reflections may offer some elements that will help us to think them through in the light of other writings.

Some Latin American women's groups are taking ecofeminist theological and anthropological positions. Practically speaking, however, we are not certain that at the close of the twentieth century there will really be room for alternative ways of thinking to develop within religious institutions. Our church institutions have always tended to absolutize their patriarchal forms of thought and organization, as if they were "revealed by God." These institutions have failed to recognize the fact that our theologies, our attempts to make sense of things, cannot be based on dualistic or idealistic dogmas, and that they will need to open themselves to a pluralistic understanding of the world and of our Christian constructs.

Given the deplorable state of our ecclesiastical institutions, those who develop alternative styles of thinking and action will be the minorities who are capable of accepting the challenge of looking both at the world and at themselves in the light of new paradigms. The ecofeminist perspective we are building looks forward to the gradual acceptance of our need to welcome one another as members of a single Sacred Body. In other words, Latin American ecofeminism remains the "preoccupation" and the "occupation" of minorities, and especially of minorities who are women. Therefore we have neither the ability nor the temptation to introduce ourselves as the new and unique alternative to be taken up by the official theology of our religious institutions. Rather, we have growing difficulties with the term "official theology," since it reflects a history of imperialism and domination. To take a theological stance like mine requires a continual effort to remain in dialogue with others, despite the fact that this dialogue itself often hovers on the edge of conflict. Entering into dialogue doesn't mean making easy bargains; rather, it means encouraging opposed groups to open themselves on specific issues. It also means refusing to take arrogant positions that imply that we are the owners of truth and wisdom, and at the same time recognizing the fact that every group is able to make a humble but worthwhile contribution to our shared history.

Within the diversity of theologies, ecofeminist theology also demands its civil rights in social and religious institutions. It seeks to be present not only to the challenges of what philosophers and social scientists have called the postmodern world, but also to people in parts of the world that have never even had access to modernity. Our thought is linked especially to the world of the poor, of the hungry, and of the illiterate; of those who have no land on which to live and those who live on lands tainted by toxic wastes and nuclear radiation. I am talking about the growing mass of the excluded, those who are struggling for survival and dignity. I also am referring to the sacred body of the earth, which is bought and sold and prostituted for the sake of easy profit and the accumulation of wealth by a minority.

We are involved in this struggle without having any idea of its outcome. We are here because we sense that it can engage us at the gut level and nourish our hope. We are here because we realize that it can be a way toward solidarity, mercy, and reconciliation among all vitally committed groups. We are here because we love life and do not want to see it snuffed out on account of our human whims and our destructive tendencies. We are here because we can no longer put up with the system of discrimination and exclusion within which we find ourselves. We participate in this struggle because it is the very meaning of our life.

This book seeks to make its modest contribution to all those who, bringing an open heart and leaving aside prejudices, feel themselves to be part of the adventure of life and seek to make it better for all living things.

1
KNOWING OUR KNOWING: THE ISSUE OF EPISTEMOLOGY

The cultural role of philosophy is not to deliver truth but to build the spirit of truth, and this means never to let the inquisitive energy of mind go to sleep, never to stop questioning what appears to be obvious and definitive, always to defy seemingly intact resources of common sense, always to suspect that there might be "another side" in what we take for granted, and never to allow us to forget that there are questions that lie beyond the legitimate horizon of science and are nonetheless crucially important to the survival of humanity as we know it.

Lezek Kolakowski, *"The Death of Utopia Reconsidered"*

In the spirit of this reflection, the quotation above urges us to resist the temptation to allow the various dogmas we have created in the course of history to dull our cognitive faculties. It insists, rather, that we be continually alert to the flow of life. Each of the points considered in this chapter seeks to be faithful to this basic insight, while at the same time recognizing the limitations inherent in any human quest.

Epistemology in Search of Meaning

This book deals with ecofeminism from a Latin American perspective. To begin its first chapter with an epistemological reflection— that is, one based on theories of knowledge—might seem an extremely abstract approach. In some courses I have given, participants' first reaction to this topic has been alarm and skepticism. Some have even had difficulty accepting the word "epistemology," which means "knowing." For some, this term was completely unfamiliar, and for others it raised the specter of the theoretical philosophical constructs they were forced to learn in their youths, and which were far from being the object of their fondest memories. They associated the idea of epistemology with highly abstract matters that had nothing to do with concrete life issues or the everyday problems that worry us. Furthermore, it seemed to have nothing to do with the theological concerns we were interested in studying.

Often, in the early part of one course or another, I have decided to avoid using the word "epistemology" and instead simply talked about human knowing. I have tried to show how complex and beautiful it is to come to know a person or a situation. I have encouraged participants to talk about how they have come to be aware of sadness and suffering, as well as joy, in their own lives, and pointed out that their ways of sharing these are already the expression of a way of knowing. They have begun to perceive the differences among themselves in the light of their own self-expression, and to become aware of the extent to which "knowing their own knowing" is an integral feature of life. They have seen that it is possible to speak in simple terms of things that seem to be highly complex and restricted to the world of specialists.

Little by little, as their prejudices disappear, the have begun to see that the word "epistemology," which at first seemed highly abstruse, is nothing more than an invitation to think about how we know ourselves and the things that surround us in our everyday lives. Gradually this apparently arcane word has begun to be appropriated, along with other terms that have barely been part of their vocabulary. They then have begun to see that certain expressions, such as "you are what you eat" or "I love flowers," are ways of knowing or recognizing the interdependence between the life of plants or the flowers and our own lives. This is knowing; this is epistemology! Participants thus begin to describe how they tell the stories of their lives, and come to see that this too is epistemology.

It is a matter, then, of de-complicating words, of stripping them of the false outer attire that makes access to them difficult. It means giving back to ordinary people something that is part of their lives but that has, in one sense, been taken away from them by our society's scientific elitism.

Reflecting on my Latin American experience, I have come to see epistemological issues first and foremost as practical ones, directly related to our work among poor people. In other words, beginning to think in a different way requires us to take different positions on the subject of knowing: to open up spaces for new ways of thinking and to consider our own thinking in terms of how our goals affect our perceptions. This is an important task, in women's groups and in neighborhood schools, in union organizations and in biblical reflection circles. Working on epistemology is not just a matter of trying to influence the process of transmitting knowledge; it is working toward changing the hierarchical power structure itself, which continues to propagate itself in the underlying structures of our society and, in consequence, of our knowing.

Through the inspiration of Paulo Freire, many popular educators in Latin America have learned how much educational processes, and especially literacy training, can help people to commit themselves to the pursuit of greater dignity in their everyday lives. Without entering into the wider debate about differing approaches, and recognizing that it can be open to various interpretations, I would say that my proposal follows to a large extent from the same inspiration and logic that brought about the popular education movement. The ecofeminist movement does not look at the connection between the domination of women and of nature solely from the perspective of cultural ideology and social structures; it seeks to introduce new ways of thinking that are more at the service of ecojustice. It is this need that justifies my decision to make epistemology the subject of the first chapter of this book.

The first questions we need to ask ourselves are, In what ways do the feminist and ecological issues change our understanding of our own reality? Are they merely new topics to be reflected on and integrated into our traditional ways of thinking, or will dealing with them lead us to work at modifying the very models we use to think about the world?

These initial questions point to the fundamental importance of these issues in developing a new way of understanding the world—

and of the human within it—that is slowly taking collective shape among us.

When we speak of our understanding of reality (and this latter term always needs to be dealt with explicitly), we are speaking of our understanding of the phenomena that touch us—of our life experiences and our ways of knowing them. For this reason, we find ourselves in the realm of epistemology: of knowing our knowing. When I ask how ecology or feminism changes my consciousness, I am trying to introduce ecology and feminism as two issues that were not included in traditional epistemologies. We have tried to understand the many dimensions of life without recognizing, as key reference points and as realities without which knowing itself is impossible, the presence of women and of the various elements that make up the earth and the ecosystem. Women and the ecosystem were there, present but unacknowledged, but they were not regarded as constitutive elements in the process of making our knowing explicit. In other words, what we called "knowing" was in fact an awareness limited to a particular perspective on reality, itself determined by a specific group responsible for formulating this perspective. We could say, then, that these conditions were profoundly androcentric—centered on male interests and points of view—and anthropocentric—centered on human values and experiences alone.

Today we want to broaden this perspective and leave it open for new learnings. We want to bring in the issues of gender and ecology as a constitutive part of our human way of knowing.

We could ask ourselves whether this is just a matter of introducing some new epistemological content, or whether we will actually need to build a new epistemology. It seems to me that there are two things to consider. On one hand, to bring in new content is neither difficult nor problematic: Human beings are always bringing new items into their field of knowledge. On the other, the construction of a new epistemology seems like an immeasurably large task. But a large task is exactly what we are talking about. We need, little by little, to construct new styles of knowing that are intimately related to our new cosmologies—our new assumptions about the universe and its form—and to our new and more unified visions of reality and anthropologies. We need to overcome dualistic and hierarchical divisions among our ways of knowing and to underline the connections and the interdependencies among them. Similarly, we need to break out of the Eurocentrism of our knowing and of the various forms of imperialist, "corner-on-the-truth" attitudes upheld by the western world.

We are talking, then, about the immense task of reconstructing our cultural, cosmic, and vital reference points—a reconstruction that becomes more necessary every day.

Our task in this reflection will be to point to a few clues that could lead to a gradual change in our perceptions and our understanding of ourselves and of the world in which we live.

Ecofeminist epistemology is not, then, a fashionable mode of thought that can be put on like a new hat; neither is it knowledge that can be acquired like a new book. It is a stance, an attitude, a search for wisdom, a conviction that unfolds in close association with the community of all living beings. The ecofeminist perspective I develop is a kind of action and thought that, like other kinds of action and thought, opens the way to seeking a new relationship with all beings.

I will not spend time here on what could be called "mechanistic" theories of knowing—which hold that, like other natural processes, human ways of thought can be explained by the laws of physics and chemistry—or even on the different ways of knowing described in psychology and the history of philosophy. Nor will I refer to the specific method used for investigation in every field of human knowing. I want to underline the epistemological issues related to Christian theological knowledge, and especially that which has developed in the Roman Catholic context. And in the last analysis, of course, this essay offers ideas and intuitions that will need to be further developed.

Knowledge and Ethics

We know that all epistemologies lead us to ethical issues. This is so because knowing is itself an act that has consequences, both for the knowing subject and for the community. So even if they are not always evident, ethical judgments are always implicit when we deal with epistemological issues.

I want to underline the fact that every act of knowing involves an attitude toward life, both at the moment of knowing and in its relationship with the predictable or unpredictable situations that mark our everyday lives. Neutrality is not possible, even if we fail to take cognizance of the situation in which we live or of the systems of influence that affect us.

In every act of knowing there is a vision and an understanding of the world and of human beings, a vision and an understanding that can be observed in the act itself, as well as in its consequences. To know is to take a stand, even if we do so without reflecting. To know is to affirm oneself as a human being in a given relationship with a world of values. To know is to take a position in relation to other living beings, other human beings, and oneself.

Our everyday lives are full of examples of how our knowing has ethical implications; in other words, of how it affects the quality of our actions. For instance, all we have to do is get to know our own neighborhood better in order to understand how to behave in it. And when I speak of a neighborhood, I mean not only the geographical space in which a large group of houses are built, but also the persons who live in them: their difficulties, their means of subsistence, their hopes and their dreams. I think also of the local vegetation, of whether it is scanty or abundant, of the quality of the air and the color of the sky—all are part of the neighborhood I know.

My actions and my relationships with people change depending on my style of knowing. Therefore, the relationship between ethics and epistemology has nothing abstract about it: It is rooted in the concreteness of our lives.

I remember a conversation I had with two women, both Argentine university professors, who told me how much their relationship with the whole university changed once they agreed between themselves to deal with gender issues, to insist on inclusive language and greater respect for women on campus. Before that decision, they had never had problems: Their style of knowing was part and parcel of the system's approved ways of knowing. After their "feminist pact," there was conflict, but that conflict led to many positive developments.

The ethics of knowing is an increasingly significant issue; it is of extraordinary relevance. Today we can no longer speak of unlimited human knowing, and we cannot propose unrestricted scientific research without asking what interests lie behind it. Ethical issues force us to inquire into the limits we place on ourselves, for the sake both of individuals and of the ecosystem. Within this perspective, ecofeminism insists that there is an ethical dimension to all human knowing.

The Hierarchical, Anthropocentric, and Androcentric Bias of Patriarchal Epistemology

Philosophical theories of knowing created within the western tradition have always had an anthropocentric, or human-centered, and androcentric, or male-centered, bias. This does not mean they are false, or that they have deliberately pushed women aside. It does mean, however, that their treatment of human knowing has been limited: They refer to the experience of a part of humanity as though it were the experience of all. At first glance, we might think that this is perfectly just and in fact inevitable, and that it could not really be otherwise. After all, it is human beings who know, and rational knowing is the prerogative of the "anthropos," of humanity. Furthermore, defining the function or task of knowing in a "scientific" way and performing that task was accomplished most often by male human beings, by those who were called "andros," by those who universalized knowing in the light of their own experience of knowing and of power. This meant that when we spoke of scientific knowledge, of philosophical knowledge, of theological knowledge, or even of "true" knowledge, we were always referring to knowledge gained and disseminated by men. What was left to women and to the poor was so-called experiential knowledge, knowledge based on everyday experience; but this was not automatically recognized as real knowing.

In earlier times, we spoke of degrees of knowledge, of depth of knowledge, of breadth of knowledge, and of specialists in this or that kind of knowledge. And very clearly, the poor and women were always associated with the lowest levels of abstraction—of knowledge, of science, and of wisdom. The hierarchizing of knowing runs parallel to the hierarchizing of society itself that is characteristic of the patriarchal world. It is a hierarchizing based on the increasing exclusion of the majority of people for the sake of a male elite that monopolizes both power and knowledge. The hierarchizing of knowing is related to social class, but also to gender. The male gender has a monopoly on the knowledge that is recognized and socially accepted. It is also true that racial issues (some scholars prefer to call them ethnic issues) influence our knowing. In general, blacks and indigenous groups are presented as those who know the least. The history of domination has so deeply marked the foundations of our culture that we end up claiming, as if it were our own, the type of knowledge put out by those who hold political and economic power. We fail to see the degree to which this attitude limits us and raises between peoples barriers that restrict the true sharing of knowledge.

We can also see the processes of domination and exclusion in our own knowing—in the mass media, for example. The media always present the news and other types of programs in ways that link the hierarchical society in which we live with their own scale of values. More and more, they dictate the knowledge and attitudes that most of the population should accept. They ignore the life of the outcast and excluded, indifferent both to their point of view and to their sense of life. They regard them as "nobodies." In the words of Eduardo Galeano:

> The nobodies: nobody's children, owners of nothing. The nobod-
> ies: the no ones, the nobodied, running like rabbits, dying
> through life, screwed every which way.
> Who are not, but could be.
> Who don't speak languages, but dialects.
> Who don't have religions, but superstitions.
> Who don't create art, but handicrafts.
> Who don't have culture, but folklore.
> Who are not human beings, but human resources.
> Who do not have faces, but arms.
> Who do not have names, but numbers.
> Who do not appear in the history of the world, but in the police
> blotter of the local paper.
> The nobodies, who are not worth the bullet that kills them.[1]

The very same social hierarchizing is expressed, then, in the hier-archy of knowledge and in ethnic and sexual hierarchies. This hierarchizing affects our understanding of the social system in which we live and the ways in which we know our neighbors and ourselves. This is the model we accept and reproduce on all levels of our lives; it is our patriarchal heritage.

Above all when it is found in the social and historical sciences, knowing based on androcentrism attributes special importance to the actions of male figures: to thought produced by men and to their glorious feats. Other actors are always secondary. In other words, patriarchal ideology is a part of our way of knowing: It conditions our thinking without our clearly realizing it. In Latin America, for example, we often ask how things are going in the church in a given city, and the answer almost always describes what bishops and priests are doing. The same thing is true when people ask about Brazil's social situation. The answer always tends to refer first and foremost to the role of the government, which by definition is composed mainly of economically elite males. In concrete terms, this means that our knowing is marked by androcentric, hierarchical patterns. And these patterns are recognized as the official ones: They are the kind of knowing we publicly espouse, however often our everyday experience tells us otherwise.

The act of knowing, then, is contextual: It is influenced by sex, place, time, and date, and is also marked by ideological assumptions and sexist leanings. Androcentric knowing also leads to anthropocentric knowing, in which only human actions and reactions are taken seriously. If a war kills hundreds of people, for example, but at the same time destroys the rice fields serving dozens of villages, an anthropocentric narrator will regard the destruction of the rice fields as absolutely secondary and virtually without importance. Although the rice fields are the population's survival base, they will not be seen as relevant either to victory or to defeat. To realize this we need only look back at the two world wars, the Vietnam War, the Rwandan war, or any of many others.

In any act of aggression against nature, the real target is the local human inhabitants. So there is no direct intention to destroy the fauna, flora, or fish in the rivers. Despite this, however, aggression against human beings also becomes aggression against all of nature, and the latter aggression is used as a weapon against human beings. We poison nature in order to destroy all of life because in that way we destroy human life. We conquer nature in order to make it an ally of the victors against the vanquished. We manipulate it, using the same destructive technologies we use against human beings, and force it into subordination via the victors' terror tactics. We use nature as a victim and also as a weapon.

The same thing happens with women. They too are a war target, and their bodies are used as a means of sowing terror in the civilian population. They are raped and brutally beaten, and thus used as pawns in the process of provoking ever greater hatred among resistance groups, which thus become more vulnerable to the enemy's trickery. All this has been pointed up, once again, within the last few years, in military and paramilitary actions in Haiti, Rwanda, and Serbia.

We do not often carry out this sort of historical analysis. The use of nature, of the fauna and flora, and of women as weapons in war and conquest gets little attention in our analyses. It is barely noted in our body of so-called historical knowledge, and almost never is it treated as an important ethical consideration.

We usually count the dead in war, but we almost never mention the destruction of the environment, the death of animals, the poisoning of natural springs, and the destruction of the present and future means of survival of those who have not died. We do not mention the deaths of birds and other animals, the forests that were burned, or the flowering fields that were trampled. We do not speak of the filthy and poisoned water where once there was a beautiful lake or river.

The starry sky, obscured by poisonous clouds of war, is forgotten. The air, which has been made almost unbreathable by gases used in chemical warfare, is rarely mentioned. Women who have been raped and killed, or who have cared for the wounded, go unremembered. We do not mention the interdependence of all life systems, even though it is present everywhere.

Many would argue that to speak of nature in wartime conditions is to turn our backs on human beings, to show concern instead for less important beings such as birds and flowers. In fact this argument is often made, understandably so despite its anthropocentrism. But it fails to fathom the depth of the connection among all the beings and energies in the universe. It fails to clearly grasp either

the interconnecting web that is inherent in life itself or its significance in assuring life's continuity.

For us human beings, clearly, it is our own species that matters
the most. We do not hesitate in choosing whether to save a nest of
baby birds or a human child: Human beings automatically move to
save the child, as the bird struggles to save her offspring. This is a
biological matter: It is instinctive in all animals. However, we need
to go beyond this immediate reaction of self-defense, of our biased
attempt to save only what is left of our own species.

We are aware that, despite progress in human knowing, both
nature and human beings are systematically used to serve the political and economic interests of a minority of the population. Furthermore, nature and human beings both are co-opted in "war
games" bent on destructive purposes, and then are largely forgotten
when it comes time to write the official histories.

It seems ever more important to ask ourselves how we understand history. What position do we take when confronted by the
facts, and what are the values upon which we act? What kind of
knowledge do we develop, with what objectives, and using what
means? Once again, the issue of epistemology becomes an ethical
one—for both the present and the future. What we know, how we
know it, and how we make it known are all related to the way in
which we lead our lives and how we value our own lives and all lives.

We know we do not constantly reflect on our consciousness. In
fact, most people rarely think about it. They simply know, without
realizing that the way they know is the fruit of the environments in
which they live, their educations, and their social positions. It is
also a product of the prevailing ideology, which they may have
adopted more or less consciously, or simply accepted without even
thinking about it or choosing it. Most people fail to realize that
they could change their ways of knowing or that those ways are in
fact continually modified by the marketing and consumer society in
which we live.

Thus we are not constantly questioning our ways of knowing or
the conditions that affect them. Knowing is something quite spontaneous for us. The task of thinkers, however, and especially of
philosophers, is to stop and think about these issues and then to
help people who are interested by making it possible for them to

understand the personal and collective consequences of their styles of knowing. Our duty is to raise the level of our awareness, opening it to broader perspectives in which tenderness and sharing in solidarity can be recovered as highly important elements in the processes of knowing and educating. This should be a consideration not just in our wider societal relationships but also in everyday domestic life.

In order to make the work of philosophers more accessible, we will look at the patriarchal epistemology that informs our theology and go beyond this to an ecofeminist epistemological perspective. I am not proposing the simplistic idea of substituting one for the other, nor am I interested in destructive criticism of the epistemology on which our western Christian tradition is grounded. Rather, I want to open the problem up and consider it as a challenge to be dealt with. The idea is to loosen the soil of our certainties and to ask to what degree these certainties rest on foundations that might be more valid at one time and less so at another. It is to think of life as a process in which change is sometimes gradual and sometimes sudden, and in which both the present and the future are significantly influenced by our cognitive choices. This chapter on epistemology aims to focus on precisely this objective.

Patriarchal Epistemology in Theology

I would like to underline some features that I think are characteristic of patriarchal epistemology. My purpose is to use critical analysis to understand some of its repercussions in our lives as Christians. Despite the fact that it has allowed innumerable persons to express their deepest convictions, patriarchal epistemology undoubtedly reflects an understanding of the world and of human life that is beginning to be a problem for us today. It is, then, with the deepest respect for all human achievements that I take the liberty of opening up this domain of critical reflection.

ESSENTIALIST EPISTEMOLOGY

One of the most important features of the patriarchal epistemology that continues to influence Christian theology is its essentialist character. Even when it tries to be realistic and starts off by examining the material reality in which we all live, this epistemology always looks to a reference point that underlies this reality and seems even more important than the reality itself. For Christian theology, human beings have an essence, that which makes them "this" and not "that," and it is their essence that defines them as specific beings. We always look for the constitutive essence of each thing, for the way God wills each thing to be. It is as if all our knowing were more than mere knowing, and all our so-called ethical actions ought to adhere to the will of a superior reality or match a natural constitutive reality that is prior to ourselves. It seems we are not what we appear to be in our everyday lives. We are in a sense pre-defined, and this prior definition is to some extent inaccessible to our knowing, while at the same time it constitutes the governing principle of that knowing.

Everything operates as if, throughout the course of our history, for a thousand and one reasons, we had obscured this sort of ideal or essence, and our whole task were now to restore it to clarity in the midst of life's ups and downs. This restoration process is nevertheless understood as one that cannot be totally accomplished within history. Thus human beings are able—despite innumerable obstacles and as part of a process that is never completed—to seek to recover some of their true likeness and to restore the ideal on the basis of which they were once created. The movement is always a turning back, even if life moves forward: an endless turning back to a prior state, as if that state were the fundamental basis upon which to judge the present. Each new generation has to begin the process anew in an endless historical dynamic, until we arrive at the "end times."

Throughout the history of Catholic theology, this understanding of human nature has been taken to be grounded in Scripture and was affirmed as part of God's revelation. This predetermined human essence was understood as the equivalent of the human situation before the "fall," before humanity's sin. And it is to this that we almost always return in order to discover our forfeited wholeness.

How could this ideal essence have become established in the human imagination? How did it develop to the point of becoming the model we seek to emulate? How did it become so universal, to the point of our attempting to eliminate the differences that arise from the fact that we are cultural beings? These are some of the questions that haunt us when we take on the philosophical task of reflecting on our theological frame of reference.

To speak of essentialist epistemology is not to deny our human fragility or our lack of inner consistency. In other words, it does not mean denying that we have the paradoxical feeling of being both more and less than ourselves. Neither does it mean denying our difficulties in loving and doing good. We do what we would not and we fail to do what we would, as Saint Paul says. Our dreams are always larger than ourselves, and frustration is a frequent experience in our lives. This is not essentialism; it is our concrete, lived experience—at least during recent millennia. We know that well before the Greek tragedies were written, a sense of the drama of human existence had developed, caused by our paradoxical acquisition of the ability to be both builders and destroyers of life, to be either greater or lesser than ourselves.

We sometimes fail immediately to recognize essentialist epistemology, especially when it begins by describing human activity and the difficulties we have on various levels of our relationships. It is also hard to recognize when it refers to problems of injustice and social inequality. However, if we look closely, we will see that in the very act of theological knowing we have a way of denying the phenomena we are observing; instead of acknowledging these phenomena, we speak of the need to model ourselves on a given ideal of what a human being is, of what human society should be, and of obedience to God. And these preset ideals are always rooted in the past—in times of yore, in some earlier moment of ahistorical purity, or in a given divine revelation—or else they are imagined in some blissful future, a final parousia.

The most striking thing is that these ideals are often sought in the biblical tradition, as revealed data above and beyond empirical reality. It is as if these ideals could offer us certitudes that legitimize our perceptions and our actions. Once again, this is what we call an essentialist-oriented epistemology.

Essentialist epistemology is somewhat fundamentalistic in dealing with the Bible. This does not mean it necessarily interprets the texts "literally" or insists that they are factual in the way religious fundamentalisms do. But it does mean that it takes the Scriptures or the Bible as essential and irrefutable, as texts that ground our being in the past or in some ideal state or ideal essence willed by God. Essentialist epistemology recognizes that what is written in the Bible is expressed within a specific cultural context, but it assumes that it offers "something" that is above and beyond all cultures. And when we ask what that "something" above and beyond all cultures is, or how it can be apprehended by other cultures, or even how we can identify it as a divine reality, the answers we get no longer manifest logic or reason.

Thus the biblical fundamentalism to which I refer can even take on progressive and revolutionary colors, but it still reflects a strain of epistemological and anthropological essentialism.

Another form of this essentialist epistemology sets up future models for knowing and behaving, as well as models for human society, as if we were journeying toward a specific, predesigned, preestablished objective. Writers have taken biblical images that appear to have been present in the beginning of history, or appear to be concrete aspirations for a better world, and transported them to the end of history. So, for example, they speak of a terrestrial paradise not in terms of origins but in terms of a future hope, of desire, of the collective dream of the Christian community. My friend Carlos Mesters's book, *Paraiso, saudade ou esperança?* is a good example of this. Commenting on the first chapters of Genesis, he writes:

> The ideal God has willed for humankind is set down in the first part [of the book]. It is Paradise. Within this narrative, the ideal of Paradise acts as a contrasting image that stands in opposition, element by element, to the present world, which is itself described in the third part. If it is not God, then who is it that is responsible for this overall malaise in the world and in life. . . ? ADAM, humankind itself, is responsible: humankind and no one else. In humankind we find the source of evil, although—and here is the narrative's other objective—humankind itself, by its own conversion and initiative, is able to bring about the elimination of evil and to attain the ideal of Paradise. All efforts in this direction will be successful, because God's will does not change.[2]

This rather dated text could be questioned in many ways, but the first thing I want to point out is that it nourished the hope of many Latin American groups in the 1970s. Today, this very idealistic and anthropocentric formulation of that hope seems flimsy; we would have to question many aspects of this understanding of the human reality and of the "ultimate reality" that sustains all, and which for better or for worse we call God.

Some might object that what I call the essentialist perspective is really the expression of human hope, of a hope that could be called the affirmation of the fundamental goodness of human persons and of the possibility that they can be happy. In other words, it is saying that good and not evil will have the last word in human history. I can see a certain value in this objection, but I think it still remains within the essentialist perspective, which attempts to describe what human beings are and affirms that they are essentially good. This sort of predetermined definition of humanity as being on the side of the good seems ever more questionable in our day and age. My questions to the essentialists would be, What does our personal experience teach us? What does our experience of living with human joys and sufferings reveal? What, concretely, do we perceive in the growing violence in our countries? Has the time not come to try and rethink our human experience—not in terms of worthy ideals and essences, but based on the perplexing cosmic reality of which we are a part?

MONOTHEISTIC EPISTEMOLOGY

Monotheistic epistemology teaches that there is a divine, centralizing model that makes human knowing possible. Although this monotheism has specific cultural roots, it attempts to impose itself on all cultures as the expression of the will and the truth of the one Creator God. In concrete terms, this epistemological monotheism is expressed in different ways. It is no novelty, for example, to hear that God is the "object" of theological knowledge. Thus theology attempts to grasp God's way of acting, God's desires or projects, God's will, and, to a certain extent, God's being. Thus God becomes an "object" of knowing—but a far from objective one. For the philosopher Immanuel Kant, for example, God is a postulate of practical reason and therefore cannot be grasped by pure reason. God is an object with no objectivity, without a socially identifiable personality. Nevertheless, it is about this present-and-absent object that theology speaks. Theology does not speak of God's way of existing; it takes this existence as a given. It speaks of this existence as an incontestable "given."

The issue I raise with patriarchal theology is not its effort to speak of God, of the Mystery that envelops us, but the pretentiously "objective" way in which it speaks, and the historical consequences of this way of speaking and its influence on the lives of specific social groups.

Theological discourse about God gives God a historical substance, an image, and a role. But who are the people who give God a role? Human beings, undoubtedly; and, within a patriarchal structure, especially male human beings, who are most responsible for the conventional image of God in our societies and who enjoy the largest allotment of power.

When we examine the image of the One God offered us by men of a specific social rank, in a sense what we are seeing is the men in whose image God is depicted. We recognize their values, their hierarchies, their countries, and their dreams. We know those who speak of God, then, and we virtually ignore those who are silent, those who do not speak publicly of God. This is the main thing I want to underscore in this section. I want to show how much traditional theology's discourse on God reveals the actions of men as expressions of the divine, and how much it veils and obscures all that falls outside patriarchal criteria. This, of course, is a fundamental epistemological issue. Through examining traditional theology's discourse, we can once again observe how the male gender becomes the primary criterion of knowing, and how this discourse devalues other perceptions.

It is interesting to examine a few biblical examples. These examples may help us to get a concrete sense of what we call epistemological monotheism, or monotheistic epistemology. Genesis, for example, features a hidden narrator who relates God's great feats. God said, "Let there be light," and there was light. God said, "Let the earth put forth vegetation: plants yielding seed, and fruit trees of every kind . . ." and the earth brought forth vegetation. God said,

"Let us make humankind in our image, according to our likeness; and let them have dominion over the fish of the sea, and over the birds of the air, and over the cattle, and over all the wild animals of the earth, and over every creeping thing that creeps upon the earth" (Gen. 1:3, 11, 26).

The transcendent and mysterious character of that creative breath has not always been respected. It is worthwhile to remember, therefore, that in the text it is human beings who not only named creation as the work of God's word, but also named themselves as the work of the same word. And this word is absolutely transcendent, beyond all words. If we were to examine the text from an epistemological point of view, we would realize that a *discontinuity* can be noted in the text itself.

The Transcendent, who creates and justifies all, is of a different order; this is another being, one that is absolutely different. Transcendence, as a superior reality, is absolutely "other," and thus becomes the underlying ground of all that exists.

But since humanity is the only creature that can name its own origins—name God, that is—it has, in a way, received the power to refashion God in its own image and to thus make itself the center of creation. At the same time that humanity names God as its own center, it names itself as the center of history. Anthropocentrism and monotheocentrism—the assumption that worship of the one God is the only legitimate form of religion—are identified with each other and distinguished from each other in the same process. The one depends on the other for its existence. So, because western monotheism named itself as the center of creation, it was able to take an imperialistic stance and destroy expressions of the divine it regarded as inferior, while at the same time progressively excluding women from so-called sacred power.

In not a few historical episodes, individuals and cultures were treated with contempt, destroyed, and conquered, and empires were set up, all in the name of our supposed knowledge of the true God. In the name of God, women were silenced, burned, and subjugated at the hands of a power that proclaimed itself the one true way.

Another example drawn from the Bible may help even more in understanding the issue of monotheistic epistemology. In chapter 3 of Exodus, in which the call of Moses is related, the hero of the story is Moses but the principal actor is God. "I have observed the misery of my people who are in Egypt; I have heard their cry on account of their taskmasters. Indeed, I know their sufferings, and I have come down to deliver them from the Egyptians, and to bring them up out of that land to a good and broad land, a land flowing with milk and honey . . ." (Exod. 3:7-8).

Once again, the "person" of God understands the people's need for freedom and appears to take the initiative in their exodus from Egypt. We could go so far as to say that the people make their experience into a "word of God." Still, it is not transmitted as "our word" or "our experience," but as a word and a decision that come from above and beyond us, rather than what it is: a clearly masculine historical experience.

The episode of Moses' being called reflects the basic structure that governs discourse on God's liberating actions. One can always tell when absolute transcendence intervenes in the world of immanence, that is, of experiences lived out by human beings. The justice human beings need seems not to come from themselves, but from God. The condemnation of evils that cause death and destruction also seems to comes through divine action. The logical conclusion is that, in the final analysis, only God knows what human beings need. This basic structure of reality leads us to posit a sociopolitical order grounded in the absolute transcendence of a God who appears to have a direct influence on the course of history, even though God's action is not always victorious. This seems to apply also to the sociopolitical structures currently in place. These basic structures appear to justify the authority of those who have the power to liberate the people, and so seem to favor the continuation of the hierarchical structure in order preserve the social order itself.

Contemporary biblical studies show beyond any doubt that women participated in the liberation process described in Exodus. Looking at our knowledge of the event, however, we see that our perception was limited to actions by men and by divine transcendence, which was alluded to in primarily masculine images. Our knowing is conditioned by those who "hold the cards," that is, by those who possess the power both to know and to decide within a given social order.

ANDROCENTRICALLY BIASED EPISTEMOLOGY

The center of all theological knowing is located in masculine experience. For example, the great leader in the struggle for freedom in Exodus is, as we know, Moses. Feminine figures virtually disappear from the reader's view. We almost never notice that it was three women who prepared Moses' journey: his mother, his sister Miriam, and the daughter of Pharaoh who raised him. Our reading and interpretation of the text obscure these women's presence; if the women are not hidden totally, then they are mentioned very discreetly.

Phyllis Trible, Professor of Sacred Literature at Union Theological Seminary in New York, has shown in various writings just how often records of women's actions in the Bible were literally erased by patriarchal domination. Just as physical creation (light, water, and vegetation) appears to be the work of a "voice" or a word that is masculine in its historical expression, so also the liberation process—the struggle for social justice—appears to have been reduced to a strictly male initiative. Reading the narrative without perceiving these reductions was typical of all patriarchal teaching. And we are aware of how much this reading influences our perceptions, our actions, and our religious, cultural, social, and personal identities.

Human history is understood as absolutely dependent on the will of a Supreme Being whose historical image is masculine. This Supreme Being appears to take part in history, and although we cannot always say which side this Supreme Being is on, the biblical world seems often to have placed this Supreme Being on the side of those who love justice and mercy. And this side is presented as more masculine than feminine. This seems to imply that all the great social and political decisions in history, as well as the great works of justice and mercy, come from the male sex. The domestic world, the world of women, does not seem to be part of the great adventure of bringing about justice and peace; rather, this is the world on which God's punishments most often fall. The story of Miriam, the sister of Moses and Aaron, is a typical example.

In a recent issue of the *Atlantic Monthly*, the journalist Cullen Murphy relates a conversation he had with Phyllis Trible that makes this situation clear:

Miriam moves with the people of Israel into the desert, where-upon she disappears from the Book of Exodus. But she reappears later in the Bible, in connection with what seems to be a severe clash with the leadership, one from which Miriam emerges the loser—accounting, perhaps, for her diminished prominence. The reappearance occurs amid the jumble of the Book of Numbers, wherein Miriam and Aaron are heard to question the authority of their brother, asking the question Trible and others ask more broadly: "Has the Lord spoken only through Moses?" The Lord does not punish Aaron, but Miriam is struck down with a skin affliction, possibly leprosy, for her rebelliousness, and later dies in the wilderness of Zin.[3]

It is interesting to recall that similar behaviors are reproduced today in our patriarchal culture. Women are always blamed, and regard themselves as guilty, when their families do not grow harmoniously or when children have problems in school and elsewhere. Officially, history is always made by men, but its negative consequences frequently fall upon women's shoulders.

The same thing happens in the churches. Women always are held more responsible and receive greater blame than men. Look, for example, at all the issues surrounding birth control and family planning. Male leaders are always easier on those whom they perceive to be in their own image and likeness!

Finally, let us not overlook an issue that, as this century draws to a close, seems to me important. All the theological, christological, and mariological dogmas that have been proclaimed, especially in the Roman Catholic Church, have been the result of controversies among the various male theological schools of thought and their alliances with the holders of secular power. Women have barely even given their consent to these discussions. Today, however, the situation seems to be changing. We are seeking to express our faith and our convictions in our own way, and this behavior will undoubtedly raise serious questions for traditional dogmatics. "Has the Lord spoken only through Moses?"

THE EPISTEMOLOGY OF ETERNAL TRUTHS

Especially in theology, patriarchal epistemology bases itself on so-called eternal truths. What are these truths? They are the unquestionable truths, those that always were so and always will be so. More than that, they are the ground on which our true knowledge rests, because they are in some way expressions of the divine light within us.

Within a theological perspective, the affirmation that God is Absolute Being and creator of the world belongs to what are called the eternal truths. Added to this are the so-called revealed truths: those that cannot, according to Christian tradition, be changed by different sociocultural contexts, even though they emerge from within one such context. It is as if they appeared in concrete history but were born of a reality that is beyond or prior to that reality. This perspective opens us to the world of natural human experience and at the same time to supernatural revelation, which is a gratuitous gift of the goodness and mercy of God.

In this perspective, supernatural revelation is not to be questioned. It should always be taken into account in any theological work, as well as in the everyday faith life of believers. Epistemologically speaking, it amounts to the juxtaposing, in our own cognitive experience, of two types of phenomena: one that comes from divine revelation and another that has to do with human faith and experience. Within this perspective we also situate ourselves on two distinct cognitive levels: that of natural knowing and that of supernatural knowing. The one is not necessarily opposed to the other, but the supernatural has undoubtedly predominated over the natural, just as the spirit has predominated over matter.

To make this epistemological structure more understandable, I will cite a passage from a book by Ronaldo Muñoz:

> We, who believe in Jesus Christ, believe that through his resurrection from the dead his GOD was confirmed as the true God and the "god" of his judges was condemned as false. We believe that in this "crisis," in this sentence handed down by God in the conflict between Jesus and his attackers, we received the definitive key for recognizing the image of the living God in any time and any social or ecclesiastical situation, and for recognizing the image of the living God and distinguishing it from all caricatures and counterfeits.[4]

The level of certitude that can be inferred from these affirmations appears to come from the Platonic-Aristotelian metaphysical structure, which was used in traditional theology to interpret the tragic experience of Jesus in his struggle to defend the life of the outcast. The resurrection is affirmed as an event that took place after Jesus' death and as the victory of "his God." We are not talking about symbols here: if we were, it would always be possible to open up new interpretations. Rather, this is an "eternal truth," a "revealed truth," a constitutive and immutable truth of our faith. There is a sense in which any lived experience that could relate directly to our own seems to have dropped out of sight. This opens the way to formulating statements of principle that tend to make us uncomfortable within the tragic reality of our concrete lives.

In the above text, the true God, the Father of Jesus Christ, is affirmed as the true God and thus as the unquestionable truth. The proofs for this affirmation have a certain historical character, despite the fact that they are interpreted in the light of a dualistic— that is, involving both natural and supernatural ways of knowing— and an ahistorical metaphysics.

In contrast, in a nonmetaphysical structure, the resurrection would be affirmed first and foremost as Jesus' own historical practice, a historical practice that led to his death. This practice is continued by his disciples and is constantly itself resurrected. In a different theological structure, the metaphysical dimension of the resurrection—so necessary in the patriarchal scheme of things, because of the affirmation that Jesus is truly God and truly human—is not mentioned. Instead, there is an acceptance of the mystery of the life process. There is silence in the face of his silence, and the mystery of life and death is embraced as a reality that always goes beyond all human understanding.

There is silence, too, in the face of the highly subtle distinctions between false gods and the true God. I believe these distinctions are responsible for injecting elements such as value judgments, a certain moralism, and a reduction of transcendence to the level of historical conflicts into the Platonic-Aristotelian metaphysical structure of this style of thought. Theoretically, too, this way of thinking leads to flagrant contradictions. Who has the authority to affirm such eternal verities? How do we establish their eternal nature, and in what exactly do these eternal attributes consist? What would these truths be like if they were not upheld by their supposed eternity? To what historical model do they correspond?

If we detach our thought from the dogmatic framework and examine Jesus' teachings in the light of the suspicions I am raising, we find nothing in the teachings that refers to a body of eternal truths. His proposal for universal brotherhood/sisterhood is neither a political program nor a metaphysical affirmation. Rather, it is an orientation toward life itself, a road that needs to be continually built, to be laid out in the light of the unexpected and expected events of every day, in the light of encounters with the outcast. Comparisons of the reign of God to the yeast a woman works into the flour, or a great banquet in which all are satisfied, or the multiplied loaves that ease the multitude's hunger: None of these is metaphysics. These are wisdom lessons drawn from everyday life, from the realities that touch our bodies and weave the texture our relationships. We will take these questions up again in greater detail in the chapter devoted to Jesus.

ARISTOTELIAN-THOMISTIC EPISTEMOLOGY

The epistemology that is most widespread in the Roman Catholic Church continues to reflect the Aristotelian-Thomistic structure that prevailed in the Middle Ages. In other words, the way in which Aristotle—and later Saint Thomas Aquinas—understood and organized their knowing became, so to speak, the glasses through which we saw and understood our life and our Christian faith. Aristotle, who lived in the fourth century B.C.E., and Aquinas, who lived in the thirteenth century, even today to a great extent provide the frame of reference within which we understand what we call the "truths of the faith."

In very general terms, this way of understanding the world distinguishes between truths obtained by way of natural reason and truths of the faith. There is no contradiction between the two, Aristotle and Aquinas taught, but there is a difference. Natural reason can prove the existence of God, but not of the Trinity, the incarnation, or the resurrection. These latter truths of faith are known through the revelation given in sacred Scripture. Reason can never refute the truths of faith, and it should in a certain sense submit to them.

Concretely, then, this perspective maintains that the whole range of things we know naturally can be changed, but not the truths of faith, the order of things revealed by God. There is a sort of basic, unchanging structure that is understood to be above and beyond the contingencies of space and time. Nevertheless, this "immutable" structure, which came directly from God, was explicitly revealed at a certain time and in a certain place and is accepted by believers as the road to salvation.

Divine revelation occurs in a given historical moment and is experienced as a free gift bestowed on us for the sake of humanity's salvation. According to this traditional theological perspective, it cannot be changed, for to do so would be to run the risk of altering the very "deposit of faith" that was given to us by God.

From an epistemological point of view, this means that theological knowing always has to take place within this structure of immutable truths. So the questions we can raise about our faith, and above all about the formulas in which our faith is couched, are allowed to go only so far. They cannot question affirmations regarded as "truths of the faith" or as revealed data. We can say many things about God, about Jesus Christ, and about the virgin Mary, but anything creative we might offer must necessarily continue to affirm the so-called revealed truths that have been confirmed by ecumenical councils in their dogmatic declarations. These "revealed truths" come almost to have a life of their own: They end up becoming truths that cannot be questioned in light of Christian communities' history and lived experience. This situation also leads to teachings that sanction the power invested in male church authorities to act as the guardians of fidelity to these doctrines. These authorities exercise control over what the faithful can and should believe, claiming that their power comes from Jesus Christ, the founder of the church, in compliance with the absolute will of God. And although there is much talk of faith communities and of the need for consensus among the various members, in reality there has been very little room for such democratic endeavors in the history of the Christian churches.

For these reasons, and undoubtedly for others as well, the church has opposed modernity and refused to engage in a more open dialogue about the world's problems. Its foundations and its truth were "not of this world," although its power made itself clearly felt in this world. The Roman Catholic Church in particular held to an epistemology that ran parallel to the rationalistic and mechanistic epistemology that developed in the modern world. As we all know, it refused to accept the autonomy of the scientific enterprise. It condemned, persecuted, and in some cases even killed those who dared to dissent from its teachings, above all when the teachings were presented as eternal verities.

Christian epistemology, and especially the version that developed in the Catholic church, affirms some formulations of the faith as immutable truths that subsist within the very process of history. It is as if everything were changeable, but, in order guarantee the immutability of God, some realities have always remained the same.

This framework, which has concealed the fundamentally dualistic structure of Christian theology, does not permit descriptions of the human values inherent in the experience of Jesus' followers in any way but that coded in dogma and regarded as unquestionable truth. We could go as far as to say that the experience of Jesus, his struggle against antihuman forces, has been reduced to an intellectual framework that often insults our reason, does violence to our perceptions, and assails our hearts. And this dogmatic, dualistic framework does not, in my view, allow the flexibility necessary for understanding the values that gave meaning and substance to the life of Jesus—values that could do the same for our lives today.

We can certainly speak of the historical universality of values. Love, sharing, mercy, and the practice of justice are values without which shared human life would be impossible. In this sense, these values would be universal even if their interpretation might sometimes be specific to a given situation, or rife with ambiguities. To keep these ambiguities in mind is important in order not to fall into new forms of idealism.

Some readers might object that after the Second Vatican Council, or with the advent of liberation theology in Latin America, a new epistemology has appeared. I believe Vatican II heralded a new willingness to deal with major world issues, especially those facing the so-called First World. The council brought with it a greater effort to dialogue with other churches and religious bodies; it also opened a wider dialogue on social issues throughout the world. It created a more open space for debate on the questions and challenges raised in the world of science. Strictly speaking, however, there was no change in epistemology. Christian cosmology and anthropology also remained the same, even though among so-called progressives its dualistic language was softened.

Liberation theology's great contribution was its refocusing of attention on the plight of the poor as a fundamental theological issue, and its encouragement of a spirituality centered on the struggle for liberation from the various oppressions, especially from so-called social sin. It pointed up the intimate relationship between adhesion to Jesus and the struggle against social injustice and its daily assault on life in Latin America.

Liberation theology opened the door to the writings of modern Enlightenment thinkers such as Karl Marx. Despite the unquestionable value of their work, however, these authors understood history in terms of the mechanistic structure that prevailed in the science of their day. So although liberation theology did move beyond classical and medieval epistemology, it ended up using a modern epistemology that is still somewhat mechanistic and in which the notions of class struggle, the classless society, and the reign of God appear, on first examination, to be in harmony with one another.

In fact, liberation theology did not in reality propose a new epistemology. All it did was to bring some aspects of the epistemology that characterizes the modern era into a theological perspective that sought the integral liberation of the Latin American poor. For example, liberation theology's reinterpretation of the life of Jesus of Nazareth does not question traditional doctrine or deconstruct christological dogma, but instead recasts it in the light of the option for the poor and of the struggle for justice.[5]

Therefore we can say that in liberation theology there is an attempt to reconcile two different epistemological systems without eliminating either of them. The task, then, is to discern which of the two is more actively present in liberation theology's theological discourse itself. The answer is not easy to come by: The issue itself is complex, and many theologians of liberation deal with it in their writings. Besides, the limits of the present reflection are such that we can offer no exhaustive analysis of this subject. Meanwhile, however, a few examples might help us better understand the insights I am attempting to offer here. Let me begin with a quote from another friend, Gustavo Gutiérrez:

> The God made flesh, the God present in each and every human person, is not more "spiritual" than the God that is present on the mountain or in the temple. That God is in fact more "material." That God is not less committed to human history but is, on the contrary, more deeply committed to bringing about peace and justice among humans. That God is not more "spiritual," but is certainly closer, more visible, and at the same time more interior.
>
> Ever since God made us humanity, every human person, and history itself are all the living temple of the living God. There is no longer anything that is "pro-fane," that lies outside the temple.[6]

First of all, I want to make it clear that I am not criticizing the author's thought or questioning its undeniable value; rather, I seek to offer a theoretical-practical treatment of it, looking for arrows that can point to new directions for us today. Nor is this an attempt to get Gutiérrez to say things he could not have said, given his own formation and the social and ecclesial context in which he acted. Rather, it is an effort to examine how certain lines of thinking and action become part of social movements, and how we need to follow the various threads that make them up in an attempt to understand their structure.

The fundamentally anthropocentric and androcentric character of liberation theology appears unquestionable. It speaks of God in human history, a God who in the end remains the Creator and Lord. It thereby reaffirms the entire Thomistic tradition on God and on the incarnation. It senses no need to reexamine the cosmological and anthropological foundations of the Christian faith. It reaffirms the goodness and justice of God's being without raising questions about the repercussions, throughout human history, of traditional or historically conditioned images of God.

I am not making a value judgment. Rather, I have cited just one example from a pioneering work of liberation theology in order to show how the "event" that was Jesus of Nazareth is understood within a dualistic epistemological perspective. The theology's structure continues to work on two levels, even when there is an attempt, as in the case of the author just cited, to get beyond the distinction between the sacred and the profane. The judgment on history is still of a transcendent nature, and is defined by the fact that Christian revelation precedes it. It is as if Christian revelation were able to stand in judgment on history and possessed all the elements necessary to make that judgment.

This style of thought, which first appeared in the 1970s, seems to continue unchanged in the 1990s. One text reads as follows:

> The ultimate motive for our commitment to the poor and oppressed is not to be found in the social analysis we use, or in our human compassion, or in any direct experience of poverty we might have. These are all valid motives, and they undoubtedly play an important role in our lives; but for Christians, this commitment is grounded fundamentally in the God of our faith. It is a theocentric and prophetic option that is deeply rooted in the gratuity of God's love and is demanded by it.[7]

It is worth stressing that although we can be in agreement with all aspects of Gutiérrez's ethical position regarding the challenge of the poor to the Christian community, we still discover in his work a type of thought structure and an epistemology that leave us within the Aristotelian-Thomistic epistemological frame of reference. The "distance" or "discontinuity" between God's life and human life continues to be underlined. I am not saying this frame of reference is wrong, but it does seem unable to deal with the reality in which we find ourselves. Furthermore, it no longer responds to the challenges we confront now, at the end of the millennium.

A major question, then, faces those of us who are seeking new directions. Is Christianity conceivable apart from the traditional philosophical framework? Are we able to think about it from within other frames of reference that might demand changes in its traditional formulations? Can we reflect on these apart from the dogmatic formulas that have set their stamp on so many centuries? These questions haunt us, and we have not yet found really satisfactory answers.

My personal answer, a provisional one at this point in my own quest, is that although we continue to swim in a sea of uncertainties and doctrinal debates, it is still possible to find a way that differs from that of classical Greek or Thomistic philosophies. And because I believe in a new epistemological framework in which the experience of the "Jesus movement" can be expressed, I think there is room for the epistemological approaches developed in the next section.

Ecofeminist Epistemology

Because of its rather different perception of human beings and their relationship to the earth and all of the cosmos, the ecofeminist perspective endeavors to propose a somewhat different epistemology. I say "somewhat different" because no one can claim to be starting from zero. We are one body in process, a living body that is growing; we cannot deny all our earlier moments and former phases, as if we could learn to know again from zero, or as if we could begin a new history that is out of continuity with the past. Besides, we know very well that to know, organize, and reorganize the meaning of all that surrounds us is always a relative task, and is never fully completed.

What we call "knowing" is the most plausible way we have found to say something to one another about the mystery that we are and in which we have our being. It is one manifestation of our reflexive way of existing and articulating for ourselves our images of the universe, of human relationships, of our perceptions, and of our desires and dreams.

Certain affirmations, themselves drawn from lived experience, form an integral part of ecofeminist epistemology. These affirmations are sketches whose ill-defined outlines express aspects of the quest we begin ever anew in the world of knowing. We move within a horizon in which we can always add new perceptions and include different approaches, recognizing the constant challenge and mystery present in the term "to know."

Knowing is not primarily a rational discourse on what we know. To know is first of all to *experience*, and what we experience cannot always be expressed in words. What we say we know is a pale reflection of what we experience. What we say about what we experience is no more than a limited "translation" of that experience. Therefore, what we experience can neither be fully thought through by reason nor exhaustively expressed in words. Because of this, within the perspective I am developing, it is fundamental to ask, To what human experience does this affirmation correspond?

To attempt to express in tentative and limited words what our experience is vis-à-vis this or that is to struggle to translate into words not only the vibrations that go through our bodies but also our meditative silence on things and facts in life. This could be called the second step in what we call "knowing." The first step is ours alone: it is what we feel happening on the periphery of our body-person, of our intimate personal being. The second step is the expression of what we know, and this expression takes a variety of forms in the light of the different situations to which we are exposed.

In the last analysis, what we call theological truths are experiences some people have had and have tried to express within their own cultural settings. We repeat them as if they were ours, but often we do so without making them our own. Sometimes we repeat them as if we had learned them by rote.

If we do not make these experiences our own, we run the risk of losing contact with the vital meanings they bear, meanings we receive and also to which we add. Our religious affirmations must necessarily be related to meaningful experiences in our lives. Often we turn traditional religious statements into "truths" that are somehow above and beyond our bodies and our personal histories. We give them something resembling an existence of their own, and make them to some extent independent of the limited experience that brought them forth and the limited words in which they are expressed.

To the degree to which we distance these truths from their origins and from ourselves, we act as if they had some hidden power over us. This is not just a personal process but a collective one as well. Most of us accept these religious truths as higher experiences that occurred in other times and that have perhaps come from other worlds: experiences that are handed down to us in order to be accepted, confirmed, and contemplated. This attitude partially justifies the development within religions of so-called sacred powers; it also justifies religions' authority over persons, the manipulation they countenance, and the fears they provoke. It is as if "the wise and the powerful" in the religious hierarchy somehow knew the secrets of religion and had a profound understanding of its mysteries. To insist on raising questions on the basis of experience is, among other things, to democratize these powers to some extent, making it clear that they exist in a variety of forms in various human beings and groups.

It follows that when we ask the question, To what human experience do we refer when we speak of God, of the incarnation, of the Trinity, of the resurrection, and of the Eucharist? we are filled with alarm. Sometimes we believe we are on the brink of atheism or heresy. We believe we have lost our faith, because these questions are appropriate only for those who are suffering from doubt or who have lost respect for the church's authority. We are seized by fear for having dared to raise such questions.

Nevertheless, these are the key questions that give meaning to the ecofeminist perspective I am describing. To recover our *human experience*—to permit the meaning of our deepest beliefs to develop in our minds and bodies—is the guiding principle of this epistemology. And to recover our human experience is, in a certain sense, to accord it the value it really has, above and beyond the multiplicity of words and expressions we use to describe it. To recover our human experience is, in fact, to place ourselves within the tradition of our ancestors, of those whose bodies vibrated as ours do when they experienced the attractions and repulsions we ourselves undergo as we relate to so many different situations in our everyday lives.

All this also opens us up a critically important dimension of recovering our human experience: struggling against certain alienations that hold us captive to an authoritarian system that limits our ability to drink deeply of our own experience. To recover our own experience does not mean affirming some isolated, individual, closed-off-within-itself reality. Nor can it be done within an anthropocentric perspective. The anthropocentrism that certainly remains a part of each of us needs to be complemented by a wider biocentrism, an acknowledgment of the central importance of all lifeforms. Our reflexive human experience does not exist in isolation from the whole of our Sacred Body. We cannot detach our knowing from our human reality, but neither can we detach it from our wider cosmic identity.

Beyond any doubt, it is on the basis of our own personal experience that we ground ourselves experientially as being on the earth and in the cosmos, part of the earth and part of the cosmos, and having within us both the earth and the cosmos. It is because of my own breathing that I perceive the air and sense its presence and its importance as it permeates all living things. But since the air is larger than my breathing, I can speak of it with some degree of authority only to the extent that I experience it as vital for myself. And it is because of the attraction I feel for other bodies that I can faintly discern the earth's enormous attractive power. As Rosemary Radford Ruether writes, "The capacity to be conscious is itself the experience of the interiority of our organism, made possible by the highly organized living cells of our brains and nervous systems that constitute the material 'base' of our experience of awareness." A few lines later, she continues, "Human consciousness, then, should not be what utterly separates us from the rest of 'nature.' Rather, consciousness is where this dance of energy organizes itself in increasingly unified ways, until it reflects back on itself in self-awareness. Consciousness is and must be where we recognize our kinship with all other beings."[8]

On this basis, we are justified in speaking about a few characteristics of feminist epistemology, an epistemology that is in the process of developing and is, for that reason, seeking its own frame of reference.

INTERDEPENDENCE IN KNOWING

The central assumption of ecofeminist epistemology is the interdependence among all the elements that are related to the human world. This affirmation comes from our own experience. We need only pay attention to what is going on with our own bodies. When we feel intense pain, for example, even the most habitual acts become difficult. When we are breathing with difficulty, even our thinking and our ability to express tenderness are affected.

Interdependence means accepting the basic fact that any life situation, behavior, or even belief is always the fruit of all the interactions that make up our lives, our histories, and our wider earthly and cosmic realities. Our interdependence and relatedness do not stop with other human beings: They encompass nature, the powers of the earth and of the cosmos itself. In this sense, knowing is a human act insofar as it refers to the particular types of conscious processes and awarenesses that characterize the human being as a form of living organization. However, the animal, vegetable, and cosmic forms of consciousness are also a part of our makeup. This other kind of interdependence does not come to full, conscious awareness, and so it is rarely considered. We do not recognize its importance because it seems obvious that we live in a given place and that in that place we breathe, eat, walk, and sit. Furthermore, our senses are seldom educated to perceive this interdependence's great importance. Once we do recognize its importance, however, we will be able to care for the earth and all its inhabitants as if they were close relatives, as parts of our greater body, without which individual life and consciousness are impossible.

The ecofeminist perspective seeks to open us to the importance of this greater body, which is far larger than our individual egos, in order to enhance our ability to respect and care for it. It is not a matter of denying my individuality, my subjectivity, and all the joyful and sorrowful experiences that are a parts of my personal being. Rather, it is an invitation to a deeper perception that includes our greater self, and thus an openness to recognize other resources that are available to us in life and that are not exclusively limited to what falls within the anthropocentric horizon.

A new understanding of human knowing also becomes possible on the basis of this interdependence. We need to open ourselves to experiences that are wider than the ones we have grown accustomed to for centuries. Within our educational processes, we need to introduce the notion of communion with, rather than conquest of, the earth and space. This could diminish competitiveness in our schools and in the economy, and could open us up to the possibility of cultivating qualities that, owing to the exclusive and hierarchical character of our current system, have been forgotten.

The history of western philosophy has revealed various facets of our human nature, from our attributes as rational animals to our existential loneliness and our identity as beings destined to die. Although all these philosophies have their own particular values and can also express much of what we experience, ecofeminism invites us to step somewhat outside the closed subjectivity that sees the world and other humans as objects subservient to our will.

It is not just a matter of describing the relationship between human subjects and the objects of our knowing. Ecofeminism affirms that, strictly speaking, all objects are contained in the subject. And the subject itself is both subject and object: It is not separate and independent, but rather is interdependent—interrelated and interconnected with all it proposes to know. Personal knowing is only one aspect of that relationship.

The thing to do, then, is to relate subjectivity to objectivity, individuality to collectivity, transcendence to immanence, tenderness to compassion and solidarity, plants to humanity, and animals to humanity, based on a perspective that is all-encompassing and intimately interwoven. This perspective allows us to broaden our understanding of human life, and especially of human suffering. The existential drama of the individual human being can no longer be blown out of proportion, as if it were an isolated situation; instead, we know from experience that the pain of the whole is mysteriously felt in every being. To be aware that our tragic existential situation of tribulation, violence, and destruction, as well as of joy, tenderness, and hope, is lived out in an intimate relationship with the whole of our Cosmic Body opens us gradually to a new understanding of our human condition. In this epistemology, what we call the human is probed in its astonishing association with and dependency on what we call the nonhuman. Therefore, as we will see later on, it is not enough to interpret our human experiences in one or another existential, modern sense. We need to seek a new understanding of our personal existence within the larger self that is the Sacred Body of the cosmos.

Many people would argue that recognizing the interdependence among all things is pointing out the obvious, and that the fact of recognizing it does nothing to change our consciousness. But I think the thing we often acknowledge is a mechanical or purely formal interdependence, like that of a car motor with the fuel it needs in order to run. What I am proposing is not a mechanical interdependence but a living one: a sacred interdependence that is vibrant and visceral. It is not like the relationship between a motor and its fuel; rather, it speaks of the relationship between *life* and its multiple interconnections—a relationship which, at this juncture, would certainly invite us to produce fewer cars and less polluting fuel.

This sacred interdependence would, for example, require a radical modification of the transnational market economies, which fail to respect regional cultures and almost always abuse both the land and the populations that inhabit it. It would call for a new understanding of the makeup of nations, one that would recognize ethnic groups along with their customs and cultural expressions. It would also require the construction of a new network of relationships among peoples. Furthermore, it would require that we rethink Christian theology not on the basis of preset dogmas but of the concrete lived experience of groups that find their inspiration in the very same fountainhead of wisdom that inspired Jesus of Nazareth. In fact, we need to welcome this source of wisdom, recognizing it as both multiple and diverse, at times emphasizing one facet of this life-giving wisdom and at times another. In this sense, we are talking about opening a new dialogue among religions, one that is based on respect for the variety of religious expressions and above all on the desire to labor together in exploring new ways of sharing life among humans in the context of our earth-systems. In this sense, instead of referring to non-Christian religions, we would better speak of dialogue among different religions; this would help us drop the insulting attitude of imperialist superiority that has characterized the Christian world.

Reflection on the interdependence of knowing should open a new page in the history of Christian theology, encouraging us to use a language that is humbler, more existential, more tentative, and more open to dialogue.

KNOWING AS PROCESS

Patriarchal epistemology emphasizes a particular quality of knowing: its linearity, or the idea that progress always moves in a straight line. Linear thinking evokes a path of rectitude, a path that clearly manifests positive moral connotations. It is far removed from circuitous thought patterns, which imply twisting, morally devious ways. Along the straight but rocky path of linearity, the purpose of theological knowing always stands out clearly. It can best be described as "true knowledge of God" or "true knowledge of Jesus Christ." But if we speak of knowing in linear terms, then we also need to speak of linear causality. This means that we always have to go back to the beginning of the chain to look for causes, and in the end we will find the first cause. This is a kind of circular linearity: the beginning always appears as special, enlightening, and regenerative. To some extent, of course, this view remains meaningful in terms of seeking alternate perspectives. At the same time, however, we need to go beyond this linear model and be open to the complexity of the reality-in-process we really are.

Despite the difficulties inherent in the term "process," then, the ecofeminist perspective prefers it over linearity. To speak of knowing as a process means that the process by which new elements are constantly being added to overall human knowledge does not necessarily follow a predictable causal path. To know is to perceive, to understand, and to rearrange the universe of which we are a part and in which we have our being so as to transform it into "meaning." And this is an ongoing process, one that is in constant flux, like the bits of colored glass in a kaleidoscope, in which the bits continually form new patterns and all the pieces are in constant motion. It takes only a slight tilt to make the whole thing change shape. In the same way, we do not hold up any single moment in the past or the future as a paradigm for all time. Rather, we affirm the extraordinarily dynamic nature of the knowing process, adapting it to the vital needs of the great variety of human groups.

Some people might argue that there are human populations that have not changed some of their cultural habits and that these remain the same even in our own day, at the same time that other groups are trying to move beyond the atomic age. But this can in no way be taken to mean that our knowing is unchanging; rather, it shows that it varies according to the changing circumstances we all experience. It is especially important to remember that knowing is always carried out within a given cultural context. We cannot estab-

lish one type of culturally conditioned knowing as a paradigm on
the basis of which all the others must be judged. This is why we say
that every act of knowing is relative to the world in which it is carried out and to the persons who carry it out. So, once again, the
term "process," in all its many and varied forms, seems to better
describe not only everyday human experience but also the experience of Christian communities, especially in Latin America.

THE NECESSARY BOND BETWEEN
SPIRIT AND MATTER, MIND AND BODY

A great deal has already been said and written about the unity of
body and spirit. A lot also has been written about the integral
nature of the human. It is not enough, however, to formally affirm
this unity. We need to specify its implications in order to create a
new theological anthropology. Affirmations of the inseparability of
body and spirit have often been put forth in opposition to traditional dualism, only to end up disguising that very dualism. As
Rosemary Radford Ruether says:

> This concept of two kinds of body allowed theology to explain the
> immortality of the "risen body," as the doffing of the mortal body
> for the immortal, "spiritual" body. If all matter is equally "mate-
> rial" and mortal, and there is no longer a heavenly realm spatial-
> ly located at the top of the cosmic system, then this world picture
> of where God dwells and the soul, with its transfigured body,
> "goes" at death disappears.[9]

Traditional Christian anthropology was based on a dualistic distinction between the things of the body and those of the mind. As
we know, this distinction was brought into the theological world in
order to emphasize godly matters over worldly and human ones. It
also favored a somewhat vulgarized theology of the resurrection,
especially for popular consumption, thus preserving a dualism we
would prefer to avoid.

Within the traditional philosophical perspective of our theology,
the discourse on body and spirit is more than just using dualistic
language in order to look at our human reality from two different
perspectives. In fact, it refers to two different "substances" simulta-

neously present in that reality. What we have here are a clearly defined metaphysics, cosmology, and anthropology that focus on and grant superiority to one world to the detriment of another; to some parts of the body to the detriment of others; to one sex to the determint of the other; and to the will of the Creator as opposed to that of creatures. This means we think, work, and act not only as if our universe contained these divisions, but as if God had willed it to be that way. God is imaged as the One who imparts grounding and legitimacy to these divisions—or, more accurately, to these imaginary constructions of reality.

Within an ecofeminist perspective, these separations or divisions disappear, and so we are invited to live the oneness of the matter and energy that are our very makeup without knowing what that oneness really is. No longer can we have the spirit struggle against the body, angels against devils, and God against humanity. Rather, we need to begin again at all levels of our activity and reconstruct the unity that we really are, as well as the unity of our being in all the evolutionary processes that have taken place in space as well as in time. At the same time we will welcome our own mortality along with that of the birds and flowers, of our dreams and our gods. We will welcome the transformation of our individual bodies into the mystery of our Sacred Body. And we will do this precisely because life rushed into this universe and became vibrantly mortal. Similarly, the love of this instant must be intense, respect for all beings is a duty, the struggle for justice is a light for us all, and happiness is possible and is the right of all beings.

There is a beauty in this indissoluble unity and in the intercommunion that invites us to develop life options that refuse to put off justice and tenderness until tomorrow, or happiness until some imagined eternity; life options that take a new look at what seems ephemeral and accidental—at the passing moment, a sunset, a flower . . . even at death itself.

GENDER-BASED EPISTEMOLOGY
AND ECOLOGICAL EPISTEMOLOGY

Ecofeminist epistemology introduces the issues of gender and ecology as *mediations*, or ways of understanding both the world and human beings. These mediations are not tools, mechanisms, or contrivances for knowing, in the sense that we would use them simply as ways of knowing reality. Within this perspective, "mediation" has a wider definition: a reality that is a means of knowing, but at the same time a part of and a constitutive purpose of the knowing subject. A means is not a tool I use and then cast aside when I no longer need it. In this sense, a means is present in the beginning, the middle, and the end of every aspect of the knowing process itself. In other words, the feminine dimension is constitutive of the human reality, just as the ecological dimension is, despite the fact that both these emerged only recently into the light of historical consciousness.

To speak of gender in epistemology is to affirm that in the social construction of human knowing, the masculine and the feminine need to express their particular ways of being in the world. Today, what we women are arguing against is the practice of assigning an a priori masculine character to social knowing. In bringing up the gender issue, what we are contending is that we should abandon the universalization and the overgeneralization of the masculine at the expense of the feminine. Universalization means that masculine knowing is taken to be paradigmatic, or as constituting a framework for all meaning. Overgeneralization means that we don't know when a given statement refers to the masculine or to the feminine. We often speak of "human rights," for example, but we know that in practice only men enjoy these rights. Within this generalization, there is in all probability not even an awareness of specific situations in which women could have a real chance of gaining access to this or that right.

The gender issue, then, when introduced by feminists, will break down the myth of masculine universality in the various fields of knowledge. It has in a certain sense proclaimed the need to have another look at human knowing, revealing this knowing's limitations and showing the extent to which official history has failed to include women and oppressed peoples. "We need only remember Hegel's belief that Africa has no history," writes Seyla Benhabib. "Until very recently neither did women have their own history, their own narrative with different categories of periodization and with different structural regularities."[10]

The masculine can no longer simply be the synonym of the human, and the earth's ecology can no longer be regarded as a natural object to be studied and dominated by humankind. Opening up epistemology to gender and ecological issues brings in new frames of reference for our knowing, broader ones than those established by patriarchal epistemology.

Some people fear that ecofeminism might want to introduce a new essentialist perspective by seeking to affirm the difference between specifically masculine and feminine epistemological perspectives. However, we are not dealing with biological or philosophical essentialism but with the contextualizing of our knowing on the basis of men's and women's own everyday experience. We know how vigorously patriarchal society has insisted on the separation between the public and private domains. The public domain has been eminently masculine, while the private or domestic domain has been eminently feminine. This society has also attributed strength and courage to men and fragility and fear to women. This is not essentialism, however; rather, it is a culture built on the ideologizing of certain biological and cultural perceptions. And this in turn depends on our styles of approaching the world, of acting and of living out our social roles, and on our way of understanding all of these. We are not trying to promote some predetermined feminine essence, nor are we attempting to tame some irrational aspect of nature. Rather, we are dealing with concrete relationships in the de facto situation in which our understanding of women developed and remained reduced to the domestic sphere.

To introduce feminism into epistemology or to create a feminist epistemology is to affirm the reality of gender as something that not only should increase our knowledge but should alter the underlying principles—the foundations—and the concrete expression of our knowing.

At this point, we can say that traditional cognitive processes are being challenged, and that feminism is one of the social movements that has contributed most to this challenge. Introducing the feminist perspective into epistemological reflection has not brought about a radical change in the act of knowing; but it has led to a change in its perspective, in its conclusions, and in its content, and in the organization of knowing, of society, and of power. It has also led to the relativizing of certain affirmations traditionally regarded to be cultural or even scientific "truths": the intellectual inferiority of women, for example, or even their supposed intuitive ability.

Feminism raises suspicion regarding the easy assumptions of the patriarchal tradition and questions the objectivity and apparently asexual character of science. It does so in order to reiterate the affirmation that human knowing is situated knowing: that it is based on our social, cultural, and sexual reality. The path of knowing is recognized as a groping path, along which every hypothesis and every perception is corrected, refined, modified, and complemented through generations of incessant searching.

Gender and ecology also modify theological knowing. The affirmation of an absolute divinity whose image reflects that of his human and historical male "double" can no longer stand up to the insistent criticism of feminist movements in Latin America and throughout the world. Nor is it possible, in the face of the complexity of history and of the unfolding universe as described by contemporary science, to uphold a masculine-imaged divinity that dominates and presides over all natural phenomena, altering them according to his will.

In various parts of the world, ecologists are recognizing the importance of appreciating so-called native cultures. In Latin America, as we know, these cultures are found not only in the indigenous world, but also among many living African traditions. A world in which ancestors and the powers of nature enjoy privilege of place is once again being appreciated as a cultural value: No longer are these cultures accused of being, as some missionaries used to say, "of the devil."

"Ecofeminism lets me talk about my beliefs the way my own culture does, without feeling embarrassed," an Aymara Indian from Bolivia told me after a course I held last year. "I don't have to make them acceptable by arguing that they contain Christian elements; they simply are what they are, and they're not what they're not." This process of revaluing indigenous cultures is not being carried out by "repentant whites," but rather by the sons and daughters of those who were the victims of colonial processes in which racism was used as a weapon to impose "white," masculine values.

We are unquestionably involved in a process that will have major repercussions throughout the world. For this reason, it becomes an inescapable duty for the entire human community to take care to respect our personal histories and the histories of the great variety of peoples and ethnic groups; and also to raise our voices in protest against the violence we discover in any of them.

A vibrant solidarity begins to make itself felt: a solidarity among the multiplicity of human groups with an eye to their own survival and the survival of our planet's biodiversity. This survival is one of the ethical challenges that lies at the very heart of ecofeminist epistemology.

CONTEXTUAL EPISTEMOLOGY

Ecofeminist epistemology is contextual epistemology. In other words, it is a demand of the historical moment in which we live, and develops out of local contexts long before it opens up to a global perspective.

To say, then, that this epistemology is contextual means that we cannot absolutize our present way of knowing; rather, we need to admit its historical and provisional character and the importance of always being open to the new referents that history—and life in general—will propose. In concrete terms, a contextual epistemology seeks to take the lived context of every human group as its primary and most basic reference point. Thus we cannot judge feminist groups in northeastern Brazil with criteria applicable to such groups in São Paulo or New York. Neither can we take models of base community life developed in some Latin American countries and simply apply them to African countries, and vice versa. Contextual epistemology presupposes that an appreciation of the immediate context in which our knowing evolves needs to be fully developed before we open it out to wider horizons and articulations.

This contextual epistemology requires a cosmology/anthropology that is equally contextual, while at the same time it needs to be open to dialogue in order to appreciate the fact that there are universal elements present in every context. And these common elements are undoubtedly an expression of the fact that we are all part of that extraordinary expression of *life* that we call humanity.

The interconnection that unites all aspects of human life, including our beliefs, constitutes the groundwork on which this new web of relationships, behaviors, and meanings must be built.

Contextual epistemology upholds the tension between the local aspect of human knowing and its universal character. Knowing anything is knowing it from within some concrete context. And it is precisely this local character, this quality of being spatiotemporally limited, that opens out into universality. Universality does not mean that a concrete knowing is valid for all human groups, but rather that all knowing has a universal localness about it. What is most universal about knowing is not the type of content that is learned, but the "located" way in which we learn the universality that marks us all. In the final analysis, it is on this basis that the human world discovers its universal diversity.

In this sense, to speak of feminist and ecological epistemology is already to envision, perhaps in embryonic form, an understanding of the world that stands somewhat apart from our traditional notions. And this is what we will attempt to develop in later chapters.

HOLISTIC EPISTEMOLOGY

Cartesian epistemologies are based on the famous phrase *Cogito, ergo sum:* I think, therefore I am. These epistemologies have conditioned us to understand human knowing as limited to certain mechanical processes that take place in our inner or subjective realm and expand outward into the so-called objective world. And it is on the basis of this subjectivity that they affirm the rationality and the scientific character—the objectivity—of their knowing.

Holistic epistemology attempts to underline the fact that we are not just parts of a greater whole: The greater whole is also part of ourselves. Furthermore, we know in the particular way we know because the evolution of the greater whole paved the way for this to be the case. Our present style of approaching reality, and of being aware that we know it, is rooted in this evolutionary process, which went on before us and goes on within us.

Holistic epistemology opens us up to the possibility of multiple ways of knowing what is to be known, of appealing to the diversity of cognitive capacities we have within us. These different capacities cannot be reduced to a single, rationalistic mode of discourse. The holistic perspective also affects theology, inviting it to broaden its horizons beyond monotheistic discourse about God, beyond catechetical learning, beyond a dogma that can become authoritarian and punitive and can even exhibit fascist characteristics. A holistic approach to theology opens the doors to the many-sided human experience of relating to the values that give meaning to our existence—values that could, in that sense, be called "sacred."

AFFECTIVE EPISTEMOLOGY

Bringing the affective dimension into the realm of knowing appears likely to frighten even the most coolheaded philosophers. Affection is related to seduction; it involves a passionate approach to other people and to the things we want to know. Affection is related to eroticism, to the senses, and to emotions that respond to gut feelings. Emotion and passionate involvement lead us to discover things that would normally pass unobserved in the act of knowing.

Bringing in affectivity points to the impossibility of drawing a sharp line between objectivity and subjectivity. It also opens us up to the world of emotion as a source of knowing rather than as the dark side of reason. When it is cut off from the passion, allurement, yearning, charm, and wonder that the universe's innumerable inhabitants inspire in us, human reason loses its vigor. What, after all, exactly is this reality we call reason? Is it possible to separate it out and make it something apart from our being, something superior, better, nobler? How would it survive all alone in its rational purity?

Making reason into a rigid, cold inner figure bound by strict rules of behavior has led to the imprisonment of creativity. It has exiled reason from itself and alienated it from the totality of our being on which it depends and from which it nourishes itself.

Reason does not exist "in itself"; it is not something that has an independent or autonomous existence within us. We are reason, emotion, sentiment, passion, and allurement all wrapped up in one. We are the extraordinary blend that is able to emphasize one aspect of itself at one time and another aspect at another time.

This is why we can no longer accept the traditional distinctions that say men, masculine beings, are more rational, whereas women, feminine beings, are more emotional. We can no longer divide human beings up on the basis of divisions imposed by patriarchal structures and set forth as though they were something natural.

An epistemology that is characterized by affectivity will recognize that the immense spectrum of emotions and feelings is manifested in all men and women according to their individual characters, their life situations, and their cultures. Nature and culture are not two separate realities in the human world; they are interconnected components that allow us to be what we are and allow the earth to be what it is today.

INCLUSIVE EPISTEMOLOGY

Ecofeminist epistemology tries to be inclusive. In other words, it does not impose rigid limits on knowing. It is inclusive, first of all, in recognizing the diversity of our experiences. This inclusiveness has not only cognitive but also ethical consequences. This means that we are not guided by a single, normative model or paradigm, whether it be in culture, in our way of living out our Christianity, or in our sexual orientation. According to this perspective, there is no one model or criterion for determining what is authentic knowing.

This inclusive character also influences the various fields of knowledge. For example, a sociological study opens out into other fields and in a certain sense depends on them. It undoubtedly has a certain autonomy and makes its own specific contribution, but it is not independent of other fields of knowledge.

We try, then, to overcome all mechanistic theories of knowing, those in which the whole is seen as merely the sum of its parts and each part can be regarded as a mechanical entity or a relatively independent component. Inclusive epistemology speaks of the reciprocal interdependence in which we live and have our being. If at some point we emphasize one aspect of knowing, we should be aware that this emphasis is methodological and arose due to the impossibility of devising an all-embracing discourse. Despite this, what we know is related to other knowledge, and especially to all those things none of us knows.

Our knowing is at the same time a not-knowing, and what we do not know is surely greater than what we do know. Knowing is not that which opens us up to knowing; rather, it is what we do *not* know that whets our curiosity and our desire to "see what we still don't see."

Once again, this epistemology relativizes our ambition to dominate the world through the development of the sciences and of the various kinds of imperialism they bring with them.

This inclusive aspect is just as essential in theological knowing. What we call "the experience of God" or "the experience of the divine" is always an inclusive experience: our perceptions, our intuitions, and our ecstasy are aptitudes that express themselves in a thousand and one ways without any one of them exhausting any other.

Religious experience is polyphonic and multicolored, despite the fact that in the depth of each of us we hear something of the same note or perceive something of the same choir. It is a search for the meaning of our existence, a groping for that "mysterious something" that is within us and at the same time surpasses us.

For this reason, an inclusive epistemology welcomes the great multiplicity of all religious experiences as different expressions of a single breath, a single pursuit of oneness.

This is not some new idealism. Neither is it a cheap, uncritical inclusivism. What I am trying to propose is the rearticulation of our lives' deepest values in the very heart of our cognitive processes.

2
THE HUMAN PERSON
FROM AN ECOFEMINIST
PERSPECTIVE
≈

After laying the foundations for an ecofeminist epistemology, our next step will be to consider the human "person," the subject/object that is able to reflect on itself and to be the thinking dimension of the universe. Reflecting on the human person may seem at first glance to be of little interest—especially since we imagine that everyone already knows what a person is. We might have the feeling we are wasting our time on notions that are already familiar, and that we ought to be moving forward in seeking solutions to the urgent problems that face us in the final years of this century.

This is not the case, however. We human beings are, again, in some sense the thinking dimension of the universe: We have the ability—however limited—to reflect on the universe, and we have an important task to carry out. This is especially true of those of us who seek the path of justice and mercy, and are unable to be content with the patterns imposed by our current cultural systems. We are daily challenged to rethink our understanding of who we are as human beings.

To reflect on the meaning of the human person is to accept the challenge of becoming creators of ourselves and of the entire living world, and to be capable of overcoming the growing isolation imposed on us by economic liberalism and the transnational capitalist system.

According to this system, in its various manifestations, there is no need for us to think: All we need to do is let powerful technocrats think for us. But to break the system's hegemony and accept the challenges of this historical moment, we have every reason to rethink our understanding of the human person.

The notion of "person" is one of the most central in both social life and theology. It is on our understanding of "person" that we base our notions of humanity and of God. It also constitutes the basis on which we build our understanding of social action, political and economic theories, and religious practices.

The concept of "person" has a historical development that began before Christianity, continues within Christianity itself, and will continue after the Christian dispensation has come to an end. Because of my own Christian background, my reflections will begin from there—above all, from elements present in the heritage of many Latin American Christian groups.

In many parts of the world, and especially in Latin America, there are groups that tend to identify the notion of person with that of citizen. The purpose of this identification is to be able to rank us all on the basis of social class, gender, and ethnic identity. The struggle for full citizenship is not a new one, but in every historical period it has taken on different features in the light of the problems faced by this or that group. Sometimes it has appeared in struggles for women's and illiterates' right to vote; at others it has sought recognition of the equality among the various ethnic groups inhabiting the same country; and at still others it has surfaced in the demands of indigenous groups that their land rights be respected.

My task in this chapter will be to look at the overall notion of citizenship and then add a more philosophical reflection on the human person. Although in practice these two levels of reflection are not always found together, I do not think it is possible to separate them.

My own reflection is drawn from many persons' experiences and enhanced by the contribution Christianity has made to Latin American culture. Thus, for example, a group of poor women in my region of Brazil was unable to accept the fact that within the regime of economic liberalism the poor are not regarded as persons—and among the poor, women even less so. The group argued that dictators, generals, torturers, and those who rob the people should not be regarded as persons. The poor do have dignity, however, and for this reason they are persons. Despite their poverty, these women considered themselves to be more truly persons than men: It was they who always took responsibility for family life and for their children when the men abandoned them.

This conversation helped me to grasp the different levels on which we understand personhood, and to see how these understandings vary depending on the situation in which the questioners find themselves and the types of questions they ask. In that particular group, the women were reflecting within the world of morality and values; they were not involved in an analysis of the system of exclusion per se. Neither was it a philosophical discussion; rather, it was a reflection on everyday life, and it drew its categories from the women's own experience. For them, personhood was a quality of humanity, a value to be esteemed rather than a concept to be discussed. For many of them, to be persons was to be different from animals; it was to be respected as "people" and to be the subjects of rights and duties. This, to some extent, reveals the complexity of reflecting on the human person, while at the same time it shows the urgency of doing so. Thus it is of fundamental importance that we understand what kind of discourse we are involved in, and who is speaking of whom.

Beginning to Talk about the Human Person

To speak of "persons" in terms that are somewhat different from those used in recent Christian tradition is not to deny what has been said or discovered in the past. We human beings constantly need to correct our understandings of ourselves, our affirmations, and the certainties we have acquired. If we fail to do the work of rethinking both our thought and our image of ourselves, we can bring about disastrously unbalanced situations in our personal and social lives.

Often we discover something very good and place the greatest possible emphasis on it, but eventually this exaggerated emphasis prompts us to lose our sense of proportion or even behave destructively. We create a kind of disproportionality at the very heart of the good things we think about or create. Sometimes we go far beyond what we wanted to, while at other times we don't go far enough. It seems we are marked by extremes: Exaggeration is a part of us, a characteristic peculiar to the beings that we are. We often drift toward one extreme or the other, urged by our passions and by the pursuit of security that is also characteristic of our species.

My basic thesis in this chapter is that human beings are prone to radicalizing certain behaviors, to the extent that we turn initially positive learnings into negative values. In other words, we are prone to tampering with the positive meaning of some value or learning and making it destructive and exclusive. Similarly, we can make good things emerge from disastrous predicaments, and create gestures of mercy in the midst of clearly acknowledged situations of oppression. This peculiarity appears to have surfaced again and again in the course of human history.

Beyond this, I am personally committed to affirming our need to develop a more open-ended attitude toward all our established concepts. This means accepting the fact that none of these concepts is more than a perspective, a tentative point of view adopted in order to deal with everyday life and with the broader sweep of history. So everything we say about human beings describes some limited aspect of their reality that we have been able to grasp, and is almost always based on our own limited experience. I would underline this difficulty by recalling, for example, our inability to fully understand the relationships established by an autistic child or a mentally disabled person. We struggle to discover "something." We speak of the child's personal world without being part of that world, and we always speak of it in terms of our own situation, as if we were some absolute criterion of reality or normality.

My own position in the face of life is by no means a skeptical one; rather, it is an attitude of profound respect for that which is different from myself. I am aware of our theoretical and practical inability to grasp the multiplicity of worlds that make up our universe, the multiplicity of humanities that are found within what we call the human, and the multiplicity of persons who are present in what we call a person. Our reference points are always limited and relative, but we often forget these limits and treat them as absolutes.

We are tempted to absolutize our knowledge. This is especially true for groups of specialists: scientists, politicians, and theologians. Today we realize that these positions are just one more expression of a pretentious reductionism from which we need to liberate ourselves. At the same time, in order to be able to respect the great variety of approaches to reality, we need to be ever more clear in acknowledging how partial our own knowledge is. It is with this in mind that I turn to the next section of this reflection.

Questioning the Autonomy of the Human Person

When Christianity began to affirm the autonomy of every person, this seemed to be an unusual way of countering an exaggerated emphasis on the idea that our lives are directed by a destiny we are powerless to change. This destiny was given different names, including that of "God," and it was invoked in order to justify social inequalities and the wide spectrum of injustices we come across in everyday life. It manifested itself in a variety of forms and took on diverse cultural trappings. For example, the religious approach of some Old Testament traditions was to understand every individual human life as destined to follow certain preestablished paths. If a child was born with a physical defect, for example, the most likely question would be, Who sinned and caused it to be born this way? It was customary to regard a handicapped person as a sinner, someone who was expiating a fault committed by some ancestor. For the world of ancient Greek culture, there was a kind of inexorable destiny against which human beings had to struggle to attain their freedom, but the final victory seemed almost always to belong to destiny itself.

Considering the many extreme attitudes that have arisen in the course of history, Christianity's defense of the importance and autonomy of every person became urgently necessary in order to allow for some balance in people's lives. We began the process of defending the autonomy of the human person in order to underline the value of every human being, of his or her freedom, and of the great respect owed to every person. Especially the early centuries of our era, this was a just and necessary response to a society that lived according to a hierarchical, exclusive scale of values strongly rein-

forced by various cultural traditions, and in which religious principles were invoked to justify ostracizing many human groups.

Disdain for outcasts, invalids, the sick, foreigners, women, and
children was very common, and was brought about largely by the
chasms among different social strata. It was necessary to correct
this imbalance in order that life in all its forms could continue to
prosper and individuals could live with more dignity and respect for
one another. Following this line of reasoning, we went so far as to
speak of the person of God, and of God taking on our own personhood. God was present and recognizable in everyone, especially the
"little ones," slaves, the sick, prostitutes, the outcast, and public
sinners—that is, in those who were not ordinarily recognized as persons. This was an amazing achievement, not only for Christianity
but for all of humanity, because every step that improves relationships among human beings is surely a step in the right direction for
all of humanity.

Meanwhile, today, human life and history continue on their evolutionary course, and the poles that attract us push us toward
extreme positions. They radicalize a belief, a behavior, or a value to
such an extent that it ends by doing destructive things to us. This
pattern is very common. An example of it is the good food that we
enjoy, but that does us harm if we eat too much of it. The same
thing happens in social, cultural, and religious processes. If we place
exaggerated emphasis on one kind of solution to a problem, we will
certainly risk creating another problem.

The respect Christianity showed for every person led to the
development of autonomy and self-determination among individuals and peoples. This appears to be an extremely positive development, as long as we look at these values without regard for their
concrete historical consequences. Nevertheless, after two thousand
years of effort in favor of the autonomy and self-determination of
every person, we begin to see some appalling behaviors. Because it
was promoted in a dogmatic, absolute, univocal, and unlimited
way, what was originally affirmed as a value seems to have turned
into an antivalue.

We have gone from promoting the autonomy of individual persons to the unrestrained exercise of our passion for possessing, for
self-assertion, and for power. French scholar Paul Ricoeur called it

"the decadence of possession, dominance, and prestige." Regarding possession, Ricoeur shows that in the early stages, there is nothing wrong with having things. We need to "have" in order to be who we are, to cultivate the earth, and to build relationships with family and friends. But having is also a trap, and here Ricoeur reminds us of Marx's teaching in *Das Kapital*: "Capital is abolished by humans: It is reified and made into a thing. This is the great fetish by which humanity is dehumanized. Based on this, Marxism speaks the truth: In a world dominated by the emblem of money, thought and words are only varieties of the great fetish."[1]

From the autonomy of countries and social institutions, we have arrived at that of transnational corporations, which exercise their supposed autonomy by an expansion that respects neither persons nor local societies. Acting as a law unto themselves has become an entrenched practice, especially by groups that have comparatively great political and economic power as well as technological know-how. Acting as a law unto themselves and attributing to themselves the law of God has also become the habit of those who hold religious power, especially fundamentalist groups of all creeds.

From this deceptive autonomy, the step to claiming the right of intervention was an easy one—especially as it was taken up as a habitual behavior by the great western powers. Economic and/or military intervention has been permitted and even justified in the name of the self-determination and development of peoples. This justification, which was partially inspired in religious traditions based on the Judeo-Christian heritage, grounded itself on the claim that it was necessary to help backward, enslaved, and underdeveloped peoples to arrive at a level of evolution more in accord with the progress of all of humanity and with the "will of God." In order to "help," it became legitimate to use intervention, interference, coercion, and murder. In order to foster "development" or "freedom," it became acceptable to displace customs, beliefs, and divinities. In the name of "progress," we could destroy the earth and its inhabitants, because the most important thing was that the "word" of those who possessed the truth be preached and become victorious.

Invoking autonomy as the "children of (the western) God," conquerors attempted to abolish all traditional understandings of the human person encountered in vanquished lands. The Christian notion of the human person introduced by the West imposes an exclusive model of autonomy, an exclusive model of being children of God, and an exclusive model of economic and cultural dependency.

But today, in many different settings, questions arise. Who defines freedom and autonomy? Do we think our understanding of freedom and autonomy has no need to shift with changing times and places? Are our notions of freedom and autonomy valid for all social groups and cultures, and for both sexes? Are we not involved in an imperialistic absolutizing of certain concepts? Are we not insisting that "the others" follow a path to autonomy prescribed by a minority, despite the fact that this minority dominates the others because it has more power and knowledge?

Religions have not always been faithful to their own ideals, and often they have become accomplices in spreading a notion of "person" that excludes the majority of people and favors the culture and interests of dominant minorities. These processes undoubtedly have both conscious and unconscious levels; they cannot be judged simplistically. But the question always returns: Who are we as human persons? From what point do we start in describing our attributes? What are our constitutive values? What are our criteria for saying a given man or woman is a person? Is it enough to be alive and to have human features in order for someone to regard himself or herself as a person? Or is being a person "something more" than the biological makeup of human individuals?

The issue becomes extraordinarily complex—and extraordinarily relevant, above all when we look at the number of marginal people regarded as nonpersons who inhabit every country of the world, and the number of skilled torturers who define themselves, de jure, as persons.

There are de jure and de facto persons, and there are illegal persons who, as a result of their pitiable histories of struggle for survival, are barely even de facto human beings. The issue of personhood goes beyond rationalistic, phenomenological, or existentialist philosophical descriptions. It goes beyond the statements of religious principle that continually repeat the phrase, "God loves all persons." To speak of the human person requires that we go beyond theorizing, beyond prescribed sequences of words, and beyond some ideal to be upheld. It means recovering the concreteness of our being: its social, ethnic, sexual, earthly, and cosmic condition.

At first glance, Latin America appears to have a definite model of what a person is: the white, westernized, wealthy man, the possessor of economic and political power. He is regarded as a person on account of his relationships of superiority. He defines himself by his power to subjugate and dominate "others," most especially women. He defines himself as "Number One," the one who has power over others. His is the number one sex, the number one king, and the number one God; and he is the number one individual, destined to be served and obeyed.

Despite all the social changes that are taking place in the world, these anthropological foundations continue to govern most of our behaviors. Once again, then, the question: To whom do we apply the "definition" of a human person found among Christian churches, or in the communications media, or among far-flung groups throughout the Latin American continent?

This question challenges the traditional reflections of personalist philosophers. These philosophers offered absolutely extraordinary descriptions of the value of every human person, of our inviolable mystery and our inviolable right to life and dignity. They described the reality of the person in a world of values in which human greatness balanced off the fragility and the concrete evil observed in our actions. Today, however, our traditional reference points have been challenged by ubiquitous violence and by the individualism and exclusivity that prevail in our globalized society. It seems the ideals that acted as blueprints or guidelines and instructed us on how to be human are betrayed on a daily basis. We no longer know how to find the human within ourselves.

More than in the past, we behave destructively and in ways that exclude others. We are nature's greatest predators and humanity's greatest murderers. In the name of progress and our personal security, we justify all kinds of violence. We compete ferociously to affirm our autonomous individuality and to aggressively conquer the earth, showing no respect for its integrity.

The notion of a free and autonomous person has been co-opted by the ruling classes, by colonialism, and by neocolonialism, by the capitalist free market, by contemporary wars, by advanced technology, by ideologies, and by religions utilized in promoting rivalries and eliminating poor peoples, especially blacks and native peoples, in order to uphold a power elite as it takes advantage of all the good things of the earth.

The aggrandizement and radicalization of this kind of individualism and autonomy demand various corrective measures that we, men and women of today, are responsible for carrying out. Our generation agrees that even our finest discoveries and acquisitions could lead us to destruction if we place too much emphasis on them or fail to recognize the utterly extraordinary integrity and interdependence of life in all its dimensions.

Ancient wisdom taught that virtue lies in moderation. To return to the way of moderation, to a new equilibrium, is not a denial of the achievements of the past and the present, of our history and tradition; rather, it affirms them in a different way. It also involves readapting these achievements to meet today's needs. Within this perspective, the ecofeminist understanding of person does not annul earlier perceptions; instead, it helps rebuild a new balance that supports respect for all of life. It helps in its own way to restore justice in the midst of the calamitous injustice in which we live.

This new approach makes no pretense of being the final word on the human person. Naturally, it is only one contribution among many, and in the course of the life process it is bound to be reworked, rephrased, reconsidered, corrected, and improved upon, just as all others have been. Its originality is not that it is an absolutely unique word in the western world's great marketplace of ideas. It recognizes its own fragility, as well as its debt to patriarchal traditions. Even so, it seeks to present itself as an alternative word on the world of the human.

Once again, we find it appropriate to seek a notion of "person" that responds to the great challenges of our age, and to the tradition of love and mercy that has always marked our kind of humanism.

The Patriarchal Perspective:
Its Value and Limitations

Let us begin by recalling a few things about the word "person." The Latin "persona" is a translation of the Greek word "prosopon," which means mask. The persona was the mask used by actors in the Greek and Roman theater. It not only allowed actors to hide their faces; it also helped them reveal the individual personality of the character being played. The mask, then, has a profound meaning that deserves to be underlined. Masks indicate the variety of roles every person can play in the complex network of human relationships. Classical theater masks showed that each person is really a multitude of persons that correspond to the life situations in which he or she is involved. The "person," the mask that is worn, invites spectators to ponder what lies behind it. So each of us comprises a variety of masks, but we are far more than the sum of those masks.

But what is this reality, a reality that is displayed in a thousand masks but still seeks to be more than the masks themselves? Is there a fundamental, elementary face that lies behind the social images through which it expresses itself?

The changeability of the masks we use—the masks we are—has been a puzzle for thinkers from Greek antiquity down to modern times. In order to set up a kind of counterpoint to the astonishing diversity of roles that make up our characters, philosophers and religious figures spoke of an essence within each human being, a fundamental nucleus that makes a human being absolutely unique. They accepted the likelihood that we can at least speak of this essence's existence, in spite of the disparities that mark the life of each human being. They tried to define or explain this essential nucleus by making it something godlike, spiritual, composed of divine "stuff." In this way they offered a counterbalance for and a secure foundation to undergird the changeability that seemed to characterize us. There was something essential, unchanging, and eternal underlying this visible sequence of changeabilities.

Thus the patriarchal world shows us the masks and speaks of something behind them, a kind of atemporal "essence," a reality that is above and beyond history, culture, and individualities. It is precisely this reality behind the mask, this "true person," this human ideal, that has become a problem today, when we are confronted with the multiplicity of masks we use. Is it really true that we can speak of a human ideal beyond the mask? Can idealistic descriptions of the perfect man or woman still hold together today?

Can we know in advance what we ought to be? Can we still speak of finding a common human essence in which we can all acknowledge one another above and beyond our personal and cultural diversity? Or should we merely embrace the shifting reality of our makeup and stop asking questions about the "essence" that marks us all?

In the course of this reflection, I certainly cannot offer any convincing answer or totally novel solution. We are slowly and collectively seeking a new way of articulating our human and cosmic situation. So I will keep these issues in mind throughout the chapter, recognizing that I am addressing delicate and critical matters.

To begin with, I would like to offer a quick overview of the notion of "person" within the patriarchal perspective in which we find ourselves immersed. Then I will go on to develop this notion within an ecofeminist perspective.

In this first sketch, as I attempt to explain some aspects of the richness of, as well as the limitations we are beginning to distinguish in, the traditional notion of "person," I will use two texts. The first is *Personalism*, a book written by Emmanuel Mounier in 1952;[2] the second is the recently published catechism of the Roman Catholic Church. They may seem to be at opposite ends of the spectrum, but my aim is to show the complex and multiple range of views we find in examining reflections on the subject of the human person.

In the opening pages of *Personalism*, Mounier offers a brief history of the notion of "person." He emphasizes in a special way the contribution of Christianity to the broadening of this notion. If we were to look into Greek antiquity, we would notice great diversity in the way this idea was understood and lived out. The human person was subject to the will of the gods and bound to a preestablished destiny. The individual person found its highest expression in the collective idea—or rather ideal—of "person," an idea that, as we have seen, has its own inherent meaning.

Mounier underlines the fact that, under Christian influence, a significant novelty appeared: the idea of personal autonomy. It is rather easy to demonstrate the reasons for this novelty. According to Christian teaching, the person created by God is a unique and indissoluble whole whose unity precedes its multiplicity. Therefore, we can speak of the uniqueness of the person and of the person's freedom and autonomy. The person has an eternal destiny foreordained by the Person of God, and therefore the human person is intimately linked to the Person of God, who through the incarnation took on the human condition. God becomes a historical person by means of our humanity. Within this perspective it becomes clearer why, in the Christian view, human beings are the only beings made in the image and likeness of God. Mounier saw Christianity as bringing about a qualitative historical leap in the evolution of our understanding of the human person and in the attainment of our humanity.

And since we human persons are also rational, we are a source of freedom. Freedom is intimately linked to rationality. In fact, Mounier saw freedom as the unique prerogative of rational beings; it stood in opposition to what he called the "irrational" natures of other beings, which are essentially subordinate to ourselves.

This understanding of the person places human beings at the center of all creation and makes us the beings closest to God in the hierarchy of creation. It underlines the transcendent destiny of human persons, which is made manifest in our penchant for endlessly surpassing ourselves and in our unceasing tendency to become more than we are.

This view of the human person fails to acknowledge our intimate and articulated bond with the earth and with the entire cosmos. Essential to Mounier's viewpoint is the belief that human beings are the center of creation. This view is strongly supported by the notion of two orders of being, one natural and the other supernatural. Human persons live in a constant tension between historical values and those that go beyond history, those represented by Christianity. Our lives unfold in the interplay between two poles: contingent history, on the one hand, and eternity on the other.

Mounier's reexamination of the notion of person contributed to the formation, especially in Europe, of a generation of intellectuals and activists that made a great contribution to many social movements, especially in the early part of the second half of our century. Today, however, we have to acknowledge that this notion of person is being called into question. As the turn of the century approaches, it is no longer adequate in dealing with the complexity of the human person. The idea of a natural and a supernatural order, of transcendence within history and beyond history, and of existence and essence is no longer adequate to explain the human and ecological catastrophe we are experiencing—or to offer viable alternatives for our time.

Turning to the *Catechism of the Catholic Church* published in 1994, we can see that its notion of "person" is based on the idea of a breakdown of the original innocence in which God created humankind: The sin of Adam and Eve led to a distancing between creature and Creator.[3] Despite this, however, according to paragraph 356, "Of all visible creatures only man is able to know and love his creator. He is the only creature on earth that God has willed for its own sake, and he alone is called to share, by knowledge and love, in God's own life. It was for this end that he was created, and this is the fundamental reason for his dignity."

Paragraph 366 adds, "The Church teaches that every spiritual soul is created immediately by God—it is not 'produced' by the parents—and also that it is immortal: it does not perish when it separates from the body at death, and it will be reunited with the body at the final resurrection."

Paragraph 374 continues, "The first man was not only created good, but was also established in friendship with his Creator and in harmony with himself and with the creation around him, in a state that would be surpassed only by the glory of the new creation in Christ."

These texts illustrate the perpetuation of a tradition that has been handed down from the first centuries of Christianity and continues into our own day. We have undoubtedly inherited more elegant and precise doctrinal formulations, but it is significant that at the end of the twentieth century we still witness an "official" return to the same mythical-religious theme, which is taken to be divine revelation. The catechism makes no reference to critical studies on this topic—not even those carried out in recent years.

Although for many centuries this understanding of humanity was helpful in affirming the value of the human person, today we sense its limitations. The contemporary world's complexity and cultural diversity, the progress of science, the questioning of traditional myths, and all the consequences of our past decisions: All this creates in us the need to understand ourselves in a new way.

The catechism's understanding of humanity is marked by an absolute *discontinuity* between the Creator God and all of creation. One senses a radical divide that separates the greatness of God, the smallness of humanity, and the "irrationality" of the "rest" of creation. The mythical underpinnings of this theological language cannot hold up in the face of the challenging questions we are asking ourselves today. The text reveals an understanding of humanity based on a specific image of God and of divine authority. It takes for granted a world order established by God, and this order appears to be understood in a static way. It stands in contradiction to our experience of reality as fluid and changing, and places us in the context of a language that is no longer our own and that no longer touches our heartstrings. It does not move us to let ourselves be charmed by the beauty and goodness that surround us. It does not open us to tenderness, compassion, and solidarity toward our fellows and toward the whole cosmos.

What we note in these catechism texts is a hierarchical understanding of the world, one that is not necessarily Christian. This is the worldview that has helped legitimate a long train of oppressive situations and abuses of power throughout our history. Within this hierarchy, male human beings enjoy special privileges and are called to dominate the earth, or at least that is what they have done during many long centuries of our history. Women are second-rate: they are called to be submissive, and their life purpose is to satisfy the desires of their husbands.

This hierarchical worldview justifies not only the ascendancy of male human beings, but also the power of one ethnic group over another, of one religion over another, of one social group over another, and of one sex over another. It is, in a certain sense, an accomplice to the present situation of destruction that affects many peoples as well as the planet earth itself.

To raise our voices against this dramatic situation is not, as I said earlier, to deny the benefits that have also derived from the notion of a free and autonomous person. Rather, it points to the need for a broadening of our perspective. The recent discovery of the interdependent linkages among all things invites us to reflect on and articulate the notion of person in a different way. We wish to overcome exclusivist dualisms, not only on the theological level, but also in our social, economic, political, and cultural relationships.

"Person" in an Ecofeminist Perspective: A Tentative Construction

Speaking of "person" in an ecofeminist perspective obliges us, first of all, to offer a number of affirmations that have grown out of the current historical context. The excesses of the traditional understanding of "person" have produced many casualties. Women, the marginal poor, and the ecosystem are among the victims that cry out today, vigorously demanding relationships that embody greater justice. It is the poor and outcast who make known the consequences of the unlimited economic development project to which we are being subjected.

We now have a new contextual, circumstantial, and collective perspective that seems to be a helpful starting point for a fresh articulation of the notion of "person." When we speak of a context, we are referring to the various concrete situations within which our lives unfold. The destruction of which we are victims—and for which we are responsible—is going on here in my neighborhood, in my city, in my country, and in other countries. It is not a distant war about which we hear talk, but a suicidal and murderous conflict in which we are directly involved. We begin, then, with the global phenomenon of regionalized destruction and oppression that we encounter in relationships among human beings. But we also need to go beyond regionalism. I offer the present study as a new anthropological and cosmological vision for the next millennium, a vision that is the fruit of a national and international collective and creative effort. The term "ecofeminism" may not survive for long, but that is of no importance whatsoever. The important thing is that the values embodied in this vision be respected, along with their local articulations. The important thing is that the affirmation that we are all one and the same Sacred Body in multiple and diverse expressions, an affirmation that arises from our own experience, be allowed to stand and to serve as the basis for the diversity of our reflections.

RELATEDNESS AS A CONSTITUTIVE
DIMENSION OF "PERSON"

The first thing to be affirmed in an ecofeminist perspective is the collective dimension of "person." This collective dimension is not only anthropological but also cosmic. And in this collective dimension the most important thing is neither autonomy nor individuality, but relatedness.

What does this "relatedness" mean? In the first place, let me point out that the word "relatedness" is not taken from any particular philosophy, thought system, or school of spirituality. It has been adopted because of the need to speak of a reality that seems so fundamental that it is shared by all living beings. Instead, many of us who were working in an ecofeminist perspective suddenly found ourselves using a shared language that reflected our perceptions regarding the complex and extraordinary web of relationships that is called *life*. The term "relatedness" has slowly begun to enter our everyday, oral language; it has the advantage of not needing much explanation, because it is explained by everyday life itself and its innumerable circumstances.

Within the perspective I seek to develop, relatedness is the primary reality: It is constitutive of all beings. It is more elementary than awareness of differences or than autonomy, individuality, or freedom. It is the foundational reality of all that is or can exist. It is the underlying fabric that is continually brought forth within the vital process in which we are immersed. Its interwoven fibers do not exist separately, but only in perfect reciprocity with one another—in space, in time; in origin and into the future.

If we understand relatedness first of all as the constitutive relationship of communion we have with all beings, then we will have to acknowledge that the person is much more than the individuality recognized by my consciousness. Furthermore, my individuality does not end with my human characteristics and my network of human relationships. These no doubt have to do with my individuality as well, but it is much more than this, even if I am not aware of the fullness of being that brought me forth. My personal memory is very limited.

The education we give and receive limits our perception too much. I remember very little about my less immediate ancestors. I know next to nothing about their personal stories or the histories of their cultures or home countries. I know nothing about the natural environment in which they lived, the vegetation or the birds and animals that were part of their daily experience. It never occurs to us that the birds and the climate, the trees and waters, are part of their personal histories and their personal realities. And if I don't think of this with regard to my most immediate ancestors, what can I say about the process in which life and the first human beings were formed? I never even think of the eons-long learning process that allows me to stand upright or to choose and eat the foods that keep me alive.

Our reduction of the description of a person to the individual and anthropological sphere and to the few years in which an individual lives begins to seem very limited and incomplete. We consider ourselves to have scant connection with the earth, with the physical, chemical, biological, and cosmic powers that allow us to be who we are and to seek what we seek.

The person we are within the patriarchal perspective is a very limited, individual, and anthropocentric being. Yet despite this, we consider ourselves to be the only beings who are able to think and therefore to be entitled to dominate nature.

An ecofeminist treatment of humanity seeks to introduce a perspective that is limited and unlimited, finite and infinite, dependent and independent, voluntary and involuntary, transcendent and immanent, constructive and destructive, exclusive and inclusive. This means that what we call a voluntary process fully retains its involuntary character, that what we call infinite retains its finite character, and so on. Relatedness is not a synonym for moral goodness; rather, it points to the vital power of the interconnection among all things, independent of any anthropological ethical judgment we might make about them.

We are, fundamentally, relatedness. But how can we better understand this primordial relatedness, which seems to be our constitutive grounding—to be prior to ourselves and to go beyond our individuality? I would like to deal with this in a series of steps: relatedness as a *human condition*; relatedness as an *earthly condition*;

relatedness as an *ethical reality*; relatedness as a *religious experience*; and relatedness as a *cosmic condition*.

Relatedness as a Human Condition

To begin our reflection on relatedness with humanity is in no way a return to the anthropocentric mentality that has long characterized us. Rather, it reflects a dynamic that is a component of our very humanness. We enjoy a growing awareness of our identity in relation to the cosmic whole to which we belong. To begin with the human is merely to select a starting point that is limited to our own condition and to the intellectual path we are following. We can begin only from the limited point that is ourselves. So it is our own situation that prompts us to build a discourse that begins with our world and with ourselves.

Relatedness: A Reality That Goes beyond Consciousness. To speak of relatedness as a human condition is first of all to reaffirm our connection with all that lies beyond the realm of our personal consciousness. Our cultural tradition has overvalued "consciousness," made it more or less coterminous with our definition of the human and regarded it as the source of all social and political transformations. Not long ago, we in Latin America talked a great deal about consciousness-raising: becoming aware of the roots of oppression. We assumed that if we became "conscious," we would already be on the road to the solutions we needed. This behavior was urged especially upon the poor. The poor should become conscious of the oppression and exploitation in which they live as a step toward achieving liberation. In this process, popular educators were to be responsible for bringing about a new collective consciousness and for channeling this into a more or less preset political project aimed at liberation.

One thing we did was to limit this consciousness to the realm of a social, political, and religious project. At the same time, we saw it as a psychological project aimed at bringing into the light of consciousness the frustrations and difficulties that were holding back our personal and social growth. Once they became conscious, these difficulties could be dealt with and, to some extent, overcome. In religious terms, for example, we spoke of our "conscience," which is aware of things we have done, and of our "examination of conscience."[4] "Conscience" was more or less the criterion for determining the degree of someone's guilt.

Consciousness was linked to a specific kind of rationality, a specific understanding of our psychic and social processes. Already embedded within this notion of consciousness were individual and collective proposals for the solutions to our problems. In other words, "consciousness" was already oriented toward a given objective.

This notion of consciousness, which is quite well developed in modern times, had the advantage of making us feel personally responsible for various problems that flowed from our actions. It also had the advantage of pointing up the connections among social, psychological, and religious processes that lay at the very heart of what was called consciousness. At the same time, this concept also set its own limits. Our consciousness was to some extent confined to a single model of awareness: one that was western, rationalistic, male, and white. This model was regarded to be consciousness as such. Anything that fell outside of it was not part of the consciousness-raising project, because it did not square with the project's model of rationality. Socially aware people, then, were those who followed a more or less preset path to arrive at the sought-after "consciousness." And it was intellectuals committed to consciousness raising—and religious leaders, in the case of religious processes—who to a great extent defined the acceptable parameters of the consciousness-raising process.

This was already an undoubtedly selective process, one limited to those who had the ability to participate in it; further, this "ability" was determined on the basis not only of individuals' personal capacities but also their ideological choices.

The idea of relatedness does not deny this type of consciousness, but it affirms consciousness as a prior and infinitely more comprehensive reality. Human consciousness is one among many kinds of conscious relationships, and is conditioned by a variety of personal and cultural dimensions of the overall relational process within which all things live, are born, die, and are transformed. What we call "consciousness," in its various aspects and usages, is inherently dependent on our basic and fundamental relatedness.

We could ask what difference relatedness could make in human behavior when it is marked by so many conditioning factors. In the first place, I think that, although it affirms the value of conscious processes, it also relativizes their value; it gives them a place as constituting an important form of perception, but also as one that is limited to a certain context and is related to a given historical process. Beyond this, it helps us to see that consciousness is one form of human presence in the world; but that, within the complexity of our vital processes, other forms exist as well. Consciousness does not necessarily bring about the needed or desired transformations. It is not only blocked by the thousand and one limitations inherent in my "consciousness" and that of others or of other historical projects; it also is unable, in itself, to move people to action. We are more complex than our consciousness, more unpredictable than our plans, more unreliable than our decisions, and more heavily influenced by our fears and laziness than we realize. We fail to follow through on our own decisions and convictions, and we do what we feel like doing instead of what is important. At one moment we get excited about something, and the next moment we are excited about something else. Examining relatedness will point up the complexity of our relationships and the need for candor in recognizing them as important variables in carrying out any collective activities, especially those that have the "common good" as their aim.

Finally, relatedness can open us up to a dimension of ecojustice in which the life of other beings is essential to the living out of human justice. Ecojustice is the kind of justice we seek and live out when we affirm our bodies as part of the Sacred Body of the universe.

A Relatedness That Goes beyond Western Rationality. The relatedness that has developed among us is characterized by an emphasis on "objective" laws and on the laws of so-called scientific knowledge, which at first glance seem clear enough. We have expected that, just as we can understand certain objective laws in the physical world, we can also uncover objective laws in personal and social behavior. Persons, groups, and events that fall outside the rules of scientific objectivity have been regarded as nonscientific or as exceptions. And the exceptions themselves have always been seen as anomalies, abnormalities, oddities, and so on.

Compared to scientific objectivity, all other forms of knowing seemed to be of scant significance. Intuitions, attractions, bodily memories, forebodings, and common sense were regarded as hardly even worthy of consideration. In practice, we created a kind of "split" between what we called reason and our other faculties, as if reason could somehow subsist without the rest of the complex whole that we are. And as we very well know, this split has been expressed in a gender division within the very act of knowing. Men have had the superior faculty, rationality; women have had intuition, emotions, and feelings. This dualism has estranged us at the very heart of our being.

To affirm relatedness as a primordial and foundational reality requires us to eliminate dualisms and other forms of separation. It also requires us to affirm human rationality, but a rationality that is connected, integrated, independent, creative, open, and willing to engage in dialogue. Emotions are as much rationality as analytical rationality is emotion. They are different expressions of relatedness, manifestations of dimensions of ourselves that are differentiated but still united within the totality of our being. And on the basis of the totality that makes up our being, we could say that intuition is also rationality, but a rationality that brings together a larger body of personal feelings, perceptions, convictions, and apprehensions. We need to defend the unity of our being and refuse to acknowledge, as we have been accustomed to in the patriarchal system, a hierarchical order among "parts."

This more unitary perspective leads us to a more holistic understanding of the reality that makes us up, and does not exclude from rationality other dimensions that are just as much a part of our being. Thus we may be able to overcome the divisions within ourselves, as well as the attitude that, on account of our reasoning powers, we are superior to other beings and are entitled to stand in judgment on them all. This latter notion reflects the hierarchical dualism of the traditional rationalist philosophies on which patriarchal theology has built its discourse.

Relatedness as an Earthly Condition

We are earthly beings. Not only are we of the planet Earth, we are also of earth, in the sense of the soil that makes it possible for seeds, plants, and trees to grow: the earth that feeds us and allows us to live and share in life. There is no opposition between planet Earth and earth as soil, but I am speaking first and foremost of the soil on which I live, of the geographic area in which my life develops, and of my personal experience as an earthy being. My initial relationship with the earth is not with Earth as a planet that is part of the solar system, but with the earth on which I took my first steps; on which I smelled my first smells, both pleasant and unpleasant; on which, in time, I took firmer steps; and on which I jumped, rolled, and shed tears.

My initial relatedness with the earth is with the soil upon which I was born and through which all my other relationships have been mediated. This earthy relatedness is spatial and temporal. It is the reason we always long to return to the land of our respective births and seek our ancestral homes. The earth, to each of us, is that specific piece of earth. And that piece of earth is also the planet earth on which we dwell as one body.

The Christian tradition in which we have been educated has always insisted on opposing earth to heaven. In the context of this opposition, it taught us to wish for heaven—to dream of it and to think of ourselves first and foremost as citizens of heaven. The earth is just one planet among many, a place we are merely passing through. We are all destined for heaven—the place in which God dwells, the place of all that is good, eternal, and beautiful. In that place, there will be neither pain nor loneliness, neither cares nor blemishes.

The story of our denial of Earth in favor of heaven is very old. I will not go into it; all of us are at least somewhat familiar with it. It is worthwhile, however, at least to remember that this denial was part of us; that it was embedded in our flesh, in our ways of knowing, and in our dreams of freedom. Only now are we attempting to leave this attitude behind, because we no longer feel inclined to seek heaven.

Heaven is not our mother, and our earliest bond is not with an ideal heaven but with our mother's body, the earth's body, the body of a woman or a man. It is with this material reality that surrounds us that we feel a connection: for better or worse, but in relationship. Christian tradition often cut us off from our bodies, from our earthly dreams, and from our love of the earth. Today we are recovering our earthly citizenship. We are creatures of the earth, of the soil—and we live out of this terrestrial relatedness and feel an urgent need to rebuild it, to stop harming our own body, to stop exploiting and destroying it.

Relatedness as an Ethical Reality

We all know that social life makes ethical demands. In this context, ethics is a network of relationships designed to respect the integrity of all beings, both individually and collectively. In all ethical conduct, there is a certain collective consensus about what should be regarded as the "common good." Thus we say a behavior is "unethical" when it fails to honor certain basic rules of social living, of respect for the various social groups and the communities of living things that share the same planet.

The issue that interests us here is to know how relatedness changes the ethical relationships among humans and with other beings. To speak of relatedness is not to appeal to a transcendent principle or a higher divinity that should act as a sort of rationale or moral grounding for our actions. Relatedness, or the interdependence among all beings, is a constitutive experience of the very universe in which we live. It is a constitutive reality for the universe and for life, and in human beings it takes on special configurations that we call ethics. We appeal to ethics not in the name of any religious creed, but rather because we see it as the vital foundation of our personal and collective lives. In this sense, the ethical dimension, which implies respect for all kinds of living beings, can be apprehended by human beings in the very act of welcoming the extraordinary relatedness that animates all living things. Meanwhile, after thousands of years of patriarchal formation of our perceptions, to grasp this as a constitutive dimension of our reality is not an easy task. Thus ethical relatedness requires a whole educational process aimed at rebuilding our self-understanding. This educational process is slow and continual, and will be necessary in all social institutions and religious creeds. We could compare ethical relatedness to our own Judeo-Christian wisdom tradition, which has shown itself able to renew and re-create the lives and relationships of individuals and groups.

"Wisdom was created before all other things, and prudent understanding from eternity. The root of wisdom—to whom has it been revealed? Her subtleties—who knows them?" (Sir. 1:4-5). It is in the spirit of wisdom that humanity seeks and hopes for redemption, and it is in the spirit of wisdom that all creation, as Saint Paul says, "groans in labor pains" (Rom. 8:22) in order to be freed from the multitude of slaveries that holds us in subjection. There is, then, a wisdom that is understood in different ways by the different human groups; there is a wisdom that can be read in the very history of the universe and of the earth, one that makes us all able to understand the presence of this power, which "helps us in our weakness" (Rom. 8:26). There is a wisdom that can be learned, cultivated, and loved. As Ecclesiasticus says, "Come to her like one who plows and sows" (Sir. 6:19) in order to taste her fruits.

It is this wisdom that teaches peoples to seek justice and freedom and to call them by many names; it is this wisdom that teaches long-sufferingness and patience, mercy and prophecy; it is this relational wisdom that awakens us today to the ecological crisis and prompts us to seek ecojustice in the name of our entire Sacred Body. And this wisdom is not the privilege of just one group or of any one religious creed; it is here, a part of life, present in our collective breathing and in our ability to feel in ourselves the groans of the outcast of the earth.

Relatedness as a Religious Experience

What is this "thing" we call religious experience? It has become more and more difficult to answer this question. What seems certain is that what we call religious experience is a manifold experience, one that can be expressed in many different ways. One of the most common expressions in religious language is discourse about the experience of "union" with the divine, or with the whole; the overcoming of the fragmentation caused by the masks and divisions with which we have to deal in our everyday lives. I will deal with this issue in more detail in chapter 4.

The experience of being one with the whole, of not being opposed to the whole, of feeling "in communion with," has been sought in many different ways ever since the time of the earliest human groups. The experience of being "one" is not necessarily harmonious, peaceful, and serene. On the contrary, the very search for this "unity" is often marked by conflict, sometimes violent conflict. It is enough to consider struggles for national unity, or even the search for oneself, to understand the conflict-ridden character of the struggle for unity.

This points up the paradoxical nature of our search for unity, as well as the paradoxical nature of what we call "religion." The ecofeminist perspective seeks precisely to underline the paradoxes and the plurality of the paths that are part of this search, and the need for dialogue among the different paths. It insists that speaking in religious terms does not mean limiting ourselves to any recognized institutional religion; rather, it is opening ourselves to a more or less conscious dimension of the relatedness that is part of our constitutive makeup.

Relatedness as a Cosmic Condition

To speak of relatedness as a cosmic condition does not, at first glance, seem difficult for us, as contemporary people, to understand. But to speak of ourselves as human beings in the midst of the same cosmic relatedness requires us to give up some of our anthropocentrism and some of our imperialism vis-à-vis the rest of the cosmos. This means, once again, to welcome the cosmos as our body, and thus to recognize it as a "subject" and not merely as an object subordinate to our will to conquer.

If today, as Brian Swimme and Thomas Berry say, we are able to tell the story of the universe, it is because we include ourselves in that story and are expressions of universal relatedness.[5] Within this perspective, we open ourselves up to a humbler dialogue among peoples. All are an expression of the selfsame universe story that generated us. We will survive only insofar as we all recognize our personal responsibility to the whole.

Part of welcoming our relatedness as a cosmic condition is making the effort to educate ourselves experientially in order to feel ourselves to be a reflection on, and an expression of, the universe story.

OPENNESS AND EVOLUTION AS INHERENT
COMPONENTS OF OUR BEING

I identify with the position already developed by other authors, such as Rosemary Radford Ruether, that we human beings are in the midst of an ongoing evolutionary process.[6] This means that we can no longer call ourselves beings who are mostly good but who have been corrupted by society or by sin. Nor can we define ourselves as evil beings saved only by the grace of God. These kinds of statements, which are typical of our tradition, continue to feed our theology, but with every passing day they seem to become less adequate in answering some of our most critically important questions.

Although it is possible to distinguish philosophical from theological discourse, in practice many philosophical and theological conceptions end up converging and intermingling in the very heart of our culture. So when we criticize the Christian notion of person, we are criticizing not only its theological formulation but also the philosophical underpinnings upon which it is built. What we can affirm regarding these philosophical underpinnings is that, traditionally, the human person is always referred to in substantialist categories. This means that the human is understood as a determinate "substance," and that any conceivable change in the human would have to preserve the same substance or the same structure of understanding. Human beings would then be defined in such a way that they would be prevented, in a certain sense, from any novel form of participation in the dynamics of life or any attempt to "utter themselves" in a different way.

The classic notion of the human person in Christianity, as I explained earlier, distinguishes between two kinds of discourse on human beings. The first is drawn from common sense and from our self-awareness. The second comes from revelation, and is more or less immutable in theological terms.

The Belgian philosopher Jean Ladrière gives a good summary of what we are according to revelation:

Human life is ordered to an eternal destiny. The present life is no more than a preparatory phase, although it is the decisive one in the sense that humans are responsible for their future destinies. By their actions they become, in this life, worthy or unworthy of eternal happiness, and it is their entire being that is included in this destiny. The dissolution of the body is just a transitory episode . . .

But death does exist. It is regarded as a consequence of original sin, and thus as a newcomer in human history and the result of a spiritual event in which humanity's relationship with God was placed in jeopardy.[7]

In Ladrière's view, Christian revelation would usher us into an order of being different from that of ordinary experience. In our ordinary experience, we live with the concrete realities of evil, death, suffering, and an unknown future. Revelation raises us to the level of the so-called certitudes of the faith and opens the door to a hope that exists on the theological-anthropological level. In my view, however, these certitudes seem to uphold the same dualistic viewpoint found in the Greek tradition within which Christian theology was inspired and built. There is still a supernatural order that is superimposed on a natural order regarded as purely anthropological. The former order, which showed the imprint of Platonic metaphysics, was called the divine order: It remained above and beyond the empirical world, even when it exhibited the limitations characteristic of that world. No one ever asked, for example, what reasoning led us to conceive of this supernatural order or what human experiences prompted us to affirm its existence.

To speak of openness and evolution is, first of all, to recognize the order of historical experience as the primary and most important source of our knowledge about ourselves and about the world, which is our body and our source of life. Although this order of knowing far from exhausts our reality, it is the only one that is accessible to us. And it is on the basis of the experiential order that we discover ourselves as being in evolution not only in our bodily state but also in the accumulation of knowledge that characterizes us. It is on the basis of this evolutionary openness, of this growth process, that we open ourselves to the mystery that envelops us and within which we have our being. And it is this process that leaves us dumbfounded in the face of the immense greatness of which we see only the smallest glimmer. We are in awe when we contemplate the starry sky or even widely reproduced photos of the earth, the blue planet of the astronauts. We feel swept up by the beauty of the trees in autumn and the promise of life in early spring. We are caught up in feeling during lovemaking and in moments of suffering and tears. It is in our body and through our flesh that our knowing takes place.

What we call Christian revelation cannot be reduced to a kind of static metaphysics that assumes we already know what human beings are and who God is. The ecofeminist perspective assumes that, despite the fact that we are human beings, we can know neither God nor human beings by a priori deduction. We will never know human beings any more than partially, and it will always be from clues left behind, from their dreams and from their relationships with all the beings that make up the universe. We know only a particular story of humanity, the one that is told and interpreted by ourselves.

We are no longer interested in saying that human beings are good or bad by nature. We are no longer interested in giving human beings a sort of preexistent essence that is prior to concrete, living human beings. We do not speak of human beings before the fall, any more than we speak of Rousseau's noble savage being corrupted by society. Nor do we speak of "original sin" as a sign of a break with God, an expression of a kind of "defect" that came upon us. In the worldview we are fashioning, in fact, that break does not exist. What does undoubtedly exist is the destruction of life processes, of human groups, and of persons as a result of the "barbarity" we have developed within ourselves. What does exist is the profit we are able to extract even at the price of ostracizing others. What does exist is hatred, the brother of love, which comes to take on murderous qualities within us. We no longer ask where the evil in us comes from; rather, we ask how to escape the destructive process in which we are all involved with different degrees of guilt. We ask how to "negotiate" escapes from the sort of evil we produce, endure, and teach. Even though we struggle against evil, we know it is part of us: it is our body, just as good, love, and mercy are.

In this situation of evil and destruction, the divine milieu itself is affected; our Sacred Body is bruised and mortally wounded. In traditional terminology, "original sin" would be the development within us and outside us of a capacity for destruction and exclusion in which all human beings are at once victims and culprits. This destructive capacity takes on a particularly dramatic form when it becomes violence against the "innocent," against those who are victimized without having been directly involved in the evil that occurs, who are immolated on the stage of history without ever having a choice.

Within this perspective, we can no longer speak of either an original or a final paradise, but only of the process in which we have been involved—and in which we remain involved. By analogy, we might say that doing evil or good, even without knowing what we are doing, is like eating and drinking: It is a vital and necessary part of our lives and of human history.

Ecofeminism has not turned back to a naive naturalism or to some earlier innocence that would try to speak of humanity "before the fall." On the contrary: We would question the kind of naive naturalism we have become aware of in some ecological organizations and in movements that seek to revive primitive cultures, whether they be indigenous or black in origin. In many forms of Latin American "culturalist" discourse, there is a clear tendency to see these cultures as if they were free of any violence or evil. (When I say this, however, I am in no way refusing to recognize and vehemently protest the colonialism, economic liberalism, and racism that even today continue to victimize these groups.) At the same time, there is a naive attitude that believes in Rousseau's "noble savage," even though this notion has no verifiable historical grounding. We ought to ask ourselves whether these movements do in fact retrieve values that could undoubtedly be retrieved, or whether they are still another way of manipulating the oppressed cultures that are so often utilized by minority interests.

Opening and evolution are two processes in which all beings, including human beings, are involved. They encompass all institutions and theologies, even Christian ones, despite Christian claims to "eternal truth." It is on the basis of this process-oriented openness that our one Sacred Body stays alive in its great and extraordinary diversity. And it is on this basis that we maintain and joyfully celebrate the indivisible mystery of our being.

MYSTERY AS THE ORIGIN OF ALL BEINGS

I would like to be quite explicit in affirming the mysterious origin of the cosmos, of all beings, and of humanity itself. This affirmation means refusing to place what we call ethical perfection at the beginning of all, as if everything had started out as good and then evil had raised its head somewhere along the way. To speak of initial ontological and ethical perfection requires us to present imperfection, sin, and our ability to be selfish and destructive as realities that arose from a quasi-deliberate historical break or rupture. Also, it is to posit an imaginary construction of our original state as one of idyllic perfection. This perfection would be identified with the all-powerful Being, with being in itself: with the Creator, who is above all other beings. In reality, however, perfection is a powerful guiding idea that arises out of a particular understanding of humanity and the universe. This perfection is not found in any concrete material situation or in any specific historical time and place, although with Jesus we have moved toward making it a concrete reality within the human sphere. The notion of ontological perfection led to the appearance of a series of theoretical paradoxes that survived by virtue of dogmatic proclamations of the essentialist variety.

On the basis of this dualistic vision, the idea of the origin of evil as an "event" that arose within human life and had consequences for all of nature would be explained in various ways. One would be human beings' freedom to compete with a divine and absolute being, and thus to choose their own impulses over obedience to a supreme will that had the goodness to create us. This would mean that God created human beings with the freedom to accept or reject God.

The ecofeminist perspective does not spend time reflecting on this freedom to accept or reject God as supreme being, because it no longer speaks of the supreme being as an autonomous, separate person; neither does it mention this being's qualities or prerogatives. Since we are a single Sacred Body, we are within the divine, and in a certain sense we are this divinity. The individual is not annihilated, but is instead related to a wider whole without which life would be impossible.

I begin, then, with a specific point of view, which is that we should not affirm any traditional ethical-anthropological or metaphysical system as necessarily being the right one for human beings. For example, we should not assume we can say that the good existed in the beginning and that evil was introduced as an accident along the way, as if it were something from which we could later be freed in order to affirm the absolute triumph of the good.

The ecofeminist position affirms not only the mystery of our origins but the effort to bring about ethical improvement in the future of humanity and of the cosmos. Ethical perfectibility would be more in the line of the challenges we human beings set for ourselves when we think about our future. We begin by refusing to affirm that human beings are constitutionally good and that we were corrupted by our situation. Rather, we can more or less affirm the origin of ethics as a fruit of our humanization process, of our collective growth, and we can bank on the improvement of this ability within us and the gradual construction of a world in which shared life, within a context of respect for differences, can become more and more a reality.

Perfection, then, would no longer be an ideal we seek as we would a preestablished formula that is already known or revealed. Rather, what we would call the road to perfection would be a gradual, dialogical, spatiotemporal process that would allow beings to go on living, to avoid voluntarily hampering their own development, and to seek balance and a shared existence—one based on a community of differentiated beings that vitally need one another in order to continue to live.

Perfection is not a preestablished state, and neither is it a state at which we necessarily have to arrive. It is not a model to be learned or copied. It is not a person we should imitate as if that person had attained the required human qualities in an unlimited quantity for all times and all places. I do not mean we should not be inspired by the multitude of people who pass through our lives, or that we should refuse to be nourished by their lives or to allow them to be reference points for us.

Each new generation must rediscover, through mutual aid and surely also by learning from its past, new forms of shared living that will permit, to the greatest possible extent, the flourishing of the life of all beings and the development of each individual. This presents to us the challenge of thinking through an ethic with new foundations and new reference points that are most adequate for each human group and context. Beyond this, it opens us to new forms of dialogue and shared living.

To affirm the mysterious origin of all beings allows for ecstasy, admiration, surprise, and wonder, as Brian Swimme says.[8] Far from falling into a mechanistic materialism, we open ourselves to praise, to the canticle of the universe, to the ecstasy that makes us feel at the same time our grandeur and our smallness, our one body and our individuality, our tentativeness and, in a way, our eternity.

Christian tradition is imbued with these mystical intuitions, and the ecofeminist perspective seeks to recover them as our tradition, our collective inheritance, our humanization and "cosmification," all of which have been in a process of development for thousands of centuries.

To acknowledge the mysterious origin of all beings is to affirm their freedom in the vital process of evolution itself. It is to affirm the contexts of their lives—their adaptations to life in accord with needs that have arisen, and the direction taken by the life within them—in order to be able to affirm the unique sacredness of each one's life. To affirm the origin in mystery of all things is to affirm, as well, their reabsorption in the life process, their mysterious transformation beyond all our individual dreams and accomplishments.

The remaining evidence of these mysterious origins does not give us the key to their secrets. They persist as a kind of challenge to us, and prompt us to assume a respectful and reverent attitude that welcomes the greater mystery that envelops us.

The philosophical references we consult are no longer Platonic, Aristotelian, and Thomistic, and the intuitions and experiences of Jesus of Nazareth have been opened up to a whole new world of understanding and meaning. Consequently, the various religious traditions are part of this greater movement we call the evolution of life. They constitute different poetic "variations," musical chords with different tonalities, separate roads that lead to a shared wisdom. In this sense, the human person is a kind of "word" capable of allowing other words to resonate within it, as if it could hear in itself the voices that draw it forth and remain in silence in the presence of its own mystery.

3
GOD: AN ECOFEMINIST APPROACH TO THE GREATEST OF MYSTERIES
≋

The search for God is a path we never succeed in leaving behind. All generations walk it in their own ways, often without so much as pronouncing its name. It accompanies us throughout our lives. It is part of our questioning the meaning of life, a questioning that is phrased in a thousand and one ways and that appears and reappears in all cultures and challenges all individuals. In the last analysis, questions about God are questions about ourselves: about the fact of being alive, of being here, of being confronted by countless situations and questions.

We are always returning to this "something more" that is both here and there; before us, within us, and outside us; first and last; transcendent and immanent; good and perfect; existent and nonexistent; spiritual and bodily—and enveloped in *mystery*.

To seek God is to seek our own humanity, in an attempt to speak of ourselves beyond our own limitations and contingencies and to heal a kind of wound that we feel within us always. To seek God is to seek meaning, a meaning that is expressed in a thousand different ways and always demands to be expressed anew, because no language is able to exhaust this meaning.

Relatedness as a Language and an Experience of the Divine

To speak of the search for meaning is to go beyond our religious traditions' habitual distinctions between theists and atheists. "Atheism" is a word that always refers to one or another way of giving meaning to our lives, and it always stands in opposition to certain specific interpretations, expressions, beliefs, creeds, theologies, and powers. In the perspective I am developing, in this sense, atheism in its various forms could be regarded as an expression of the human search for the meaning of life. Atheists usually say, "I don't believe in God." Many are speaking about God as a being-in-itself, a separate being with its own will. They are not referring to the meaning of life. In the interest of broadening our understanding of God, and in light of the inherent problems that plague our traditional images of the divine, I would dare to avoid using the word "God" so as to be able to stammer out something about the ground of our being. However, because of my spiritual formation and the Latin American culture in which I live, I am unable to avoid the word. So I am attempting to speak of it, but in the light of a different understanding.

In the preceding chapter, I offered a novel understanding of "person." Now I will try to offer a different notion of God, fully aware that I will have to face some problems about which we have little clarity and regarding which silence might be the best answer. Sketching out this different notion is not an individual effort but rather a collective one, a task of the contemporary culture in which we live—and especially of women, with their countless questions about life.

In many parts of the world, in East and West and in North and South, a new understanding of humanity is being worked out as the current millennium draws to a close. We feel the urgent need to refashion ourselves as a human species, to re-create the fundamental values out of which we live. We feel the urgent need to reinvent our dreams of love and justice and our capacity for communion, mercy, and solidarity. We have a growing sense of weariness in the face of the endless violence that assaults us and the absence of respectful ways of struggling for a world that embodies justice and solidarity.

Thus the collective search for God becomes the task not just of so-called theologians but of all those who share a passion for life.

As we have seen, the first and most basic characteristic of the human person is relatedness. As I see it, relatedness is the primary and the ultimate ground of all that exists. Relatedness, as expressed in human language, means "experience" as a condition and a value. However, it goes beyond the human world and beyond all we can articulate. Both the world we see around us and humanity within it are expressions of the relatedness that characterizes all things. It is on the basis of this experience, and on going beyond it, that we can thus affirm that God is relatedness.

To call God "relatedness" is to use a word to express something that goes beyond all words; it describes an experience, but goes beyond all experiences. It speaks of God as possibility, as opening, as the unexpected, the unknown; as physical and metaphysical. This is a relatedness that has no exact definition: it cannot be reduced to a given being, a given species, or a given system. It is not relatedness in itself, or separate from the fullness of all that exists; rather, it is relatedness as a continual presence that is made explicit in different ways in different beings. It is, then, the relatedness in all beings; it is not in itself and for itself. In describing relatedness in this way, we are trying to say that this seems to be the only way, limited as it surely is, to grasp this reality, to express it and to live it out. It is a multiple relatedness, encountered in its variety of expressions.

Relatedness is not an entity apart from other beings; rather, it is a mystery that is associated with all that exists. Relatedness is *utterance, word, attraction, flux, energy,* and *passion,* insofar as it is the materiality and spirituality of all that is. It is this, but it is also that; and it cannot be fully represented by anything that is. We are all both created within and creators of this relatedness. We are of its substance and it is of our substance, independent of the precise space and time in which our concrete lives are lived out. We cannot explain it; we can only consent to its unutterable mystery as the ultimate ground of all that is. Today many authors say we are "a single sacred body." But "body" is not just the materiality we perceive with our senses: It is not limited to our immediate perception. Our "body" has dimensions we do not know, although we often think that it is only what we know.

Within this perspective I especially want to cite Sallie McFague: "The model of the Universe as God's Body unites immanence and transcendence. At once a powerful image of the divine immanence, for everyone and everything becomes potentially a sacrament of God, it is also, though perhaps not as obviously, an image of divine transcendence."[1]

This perspective leads us in some sense to overcome the dualisms that have marked our Christian tradition when it has spoken of God. In this tradition we have spoken of God as pure spirit, above and beyond all beings, at the same time that we spoke of God's incarnation. At one moment, we underlined the spirit dimension as a need to go beyond historical contingencies, while at another we emphasized the divine presence in human flesh in order to point to the concrete need for love and mercy.

The schools of thought that accentuated mistrust of matter underlined the spiritual transcendence of God. Those who were concerned with social problems and the acute pain of humanity emphasized the God who takes on human flesh and redeems it. This oscillation, which was sometimes paradoxical, seemed to "balance out" the two great tendencies mentioned above, both of which were present in the life of Christian communities.

Today we seem to feel differently. Dualism is felt to be inadequate in explaining the complexity of reality. Opposing the material and the spiritual as if they were separate substances is turning out to be obsolete and inconsistent in the face of our world's violence, our progress in scientific knowledge, and our contemporary understanding of the universe. For these reasons, we open our hearts to speak of another aspect of the ecstatic and terrifying experience of being a part of life, a life that is far greater than our individuality and is barely perceptible on the basis of that individuality. At the same time, we have the poignant experience, despite our limitations, of discovering our ability to intuit the greatness of the mystery that we are and within which we have our being. As Emmanuel Levinas says, we are able to start from ourselves in order to live and acknowledge the greater Being.[2]

To speak of relatedness as the mysterious reality of God is, in the final analysis, to affirm that God is not a pure essence existing in itself; rather, God is *relationship*. And it is by means of relationships

and of relational behaviors that we speak of God. It is through relational behaviors that we affirm, "This is divine!" And we say this on
the basis of our fragile, limited, contingent, and ephemeral experience. Long ago Saint John said that those who do not love their
brothers and sisters do not love God! And on the basis of what can
be experienced, of a limitedness that blossoms forth, we welcome
the experience of the unlimited. Within this perspective, the word
"God" is the name we give to the extraordinary relationship that
evokes ecstasy and leads us to see flashes of the greatness of the
mystery of the Divine Body. To speak of God is to speak of that
which is beyond us. To speak of God is to affirm the "something"
that we are and that goes beyond us, based on human experience
and moving beyond it.

For us human beings, this relationship is personal: We speak of
it out of our personal experience. We only delight in love when it
refers to concrete persons, we only struggle for justice when there
are individuals who suffer injustice. We only seek the beauty of living beings and of all things because their beauty is a part of us; this
beauty attracts us, dwells in our flesh, and is part of our living tissue. Therefore God is and is not a person. This relatedness is
expressed personally, humanly—and is at the same time far more
than human and far more than simply personal.

For this reason, we no longer speak of God as existing before
creation, but, in a way, as concomitant with it. We no longer think
of God first and creation later, because this sort of gap between
atemporality in God and temporality in creation does not make
sense to us. We no longer speak of the presence or absence of God,
but, basically, of *presence*. It is a presence that is hard to speak of in
traditional terms. Traditional discourse on God referred to a separate, preexistent being who could be invoked in all life's joyful and
difficult circumstances. God was spoken of as the first cause of all
that is, as the beginning or starting point of all that exists. All the
questions that have later assailed our minds and hearts need to be
dealt with anew in the light of this new moment in our understanding of the universe.

Relatedness is not a discourse about the person or the being of
God, but about what we perceive of the mysterious Body of the
universe to which we belong. And, unquestionably, we are moving

into a different cosmology, a different anthropology, and a different theology. This new theology needs to make its way humbly and without pretenses, recognizing that it can only dimly and gropingly make out the ever-present clues that point to the greatest of mysteries.

In this perspective, what we traditionally called the "absence of God" continues to be an expression of a dualistic approach that leads us to place God always on the side of the good. We thought of God as absent from the hell of warfare and from the hell of betrayal and destruction. We thought of God as absent from the most serious situations of social injustice and exclusion. We though of God as absent from what we call "evil." We thought of God as far above filth, ostracism, and destruction.

But why should we speak of the presence or the absence of God? Why should we always open an escape hatch that enables us to justify the goodness or evil of human actions on the basis of something that lies beyond the human? Why explain natural catastrophes and their consequences as somehow linked to the designs of a Supreme Being above and beyond creation? Why do we have so much trouble accepting what Edgar Morin calls the gospel of perdition? Here is the bad news, he says: "we are lost, irremediably lost. If there is a Gospel of the Good News, it should grow out of the Bad News that we're lost. But still we have a roof over our heads, a home, and a country: the small planet on which life grew its garden, where humans make their home—where, despite everything, humanity ought to recognize it possesses its shared dwelling."[3]

As long as we are unable to accept the reality of our "perdition," we will go on talking of the presence and absence of God. If the good is absent or is not winning the day, then we speak of the absence of God. Theories about the absence or the silence of God have marked a good part of the theology produced in this century. But it appears that this absent being is still imagined as a concrete and living reality that's here or there. Furthermore, this is a different and perfect being, and thus one for whom it would be unworthy to get mixed up in the squalor of our lives. In fact, this is a being on whom I can call for help and before whom I feel unique, whether or not my request is granted.

This God evokes profound anxiety and a multitude of unanswered questions, despite the fact that all the anguish and unanswered questions are inside ourselves. Despite its goodness, this is a tragic divinity. It is a divinity that is limited to my existential situation; reduced to it, made in its image and likeness. It is a barely anthropocentric God.

It could be argued that we can call upon God only from within our concrete situation. And although I fully agree that we are conditioned by our life situations and by the persons we are, I think we can gradually prepare ourselves to consider other images of ourselves and of the mysterious reality we call God. In fact, this is one of the tasks theological ecofeminism has set for itself. We will not solve the critical problem of human anguish and suffering, but we will get in the habit of understanding ourselves not on the basis of a tragic and dualistic worldview but rather out of a unitary and very realistic perspective. This does not mean we will be able to leave anguish and suffering aside, but we may be able to face them in a different way. This in turn means opening ourselves to other points of view and in some sense moving beyond mere human suffering. We will be able to understand the suffering of the earth, of animals, and of the cosmos in addition to human suffering, but we will see human suffering as neither superior nor inferior to other kinds of suffering. This taking on of our collective pain is characteristic of the great religious traditions of history, and especially of the Jesus movement. However, this tradition has been obscured by individualistic attitudes of all kinds.

In the perspective we are developing, God is in all and all is in God—including suffering, dirt, and destruction. I do not affirm the individuality of God, as the traditional perspective does, but rather God's relatedness, the understanding of which surpasses us. If I affirm the individuality of God, this is really a projection of my own individuality, of my ability to feel that I am I, that I live and breathe, and that I am tied to all that is, while at the same time I am distinct, different, and unique. I speak of the mystery that surpasses me in terms of my own life, my own existence; and so I almost spontaneously tend to "reduce" God to an individual or a person, in order to make God in my own image and likeness.

The term "to be" is a linking term, one that points to existence. This is also what a relational presence is: It links everything with everything, and everything with all. Relatedness is existence in conscious processes and also beyond humanly conscious processes.

To speak of relatedness leads us to a somewhat imprecise discourse, one that seems relative—and to some, perhaps, universalist and abstract. The effort to understand this relatedness sometimes makes us uncomfortable. Although we live out relatedness in our daily lives, we have trouble accepting it as the "divine milieu" in which we have our being. Discourse on this ultimate, mediating, and primary *reality*, in which we have our being and about which we babble words and express intuitions or to which we address complaints and petitions for comfort, can only be approximate, poetic, and intuitive. But the patriarchal world never taught us to recognize the poetry in our lives; neither did it teach us to deal with approximations and intuitions. It always oriented us toward certitudes, especially when it dealt with religious discourse. The patriarchal world always made distinctions between the good and the bad, the just and the unjust, and the masculine and the feminine; it always erected clear boundaries around what it pompously judged to be good, just, pure, and perfect. The closing of this century offers us the great challenge of learning to think of ourselves in categories that are no longer oppositional, but rather inclusive.

One critique aimed at the ecofeminist perspective is that it is associated with a kind of "imprecision," almost a "vacuum," regarding the notion of God. This seems to disconcert people who are used to having a clear picture of the unlimited being of God. They like a God who is a perfect "substance," an independent being—a God who, in the last analysis, is not limited by mere human fragility.

We often hear people say, "I can't accept the idea of God not being an individual person," or, "I can't pray to someone if I don't know who it is." Or they say, "How can I tell my children about God? I can't ask them to pray to and obey a *whole* with no visible face."

"It makes no sense to pray to an energy or to a relatedness." "You can't identify God with the world, or the creator with the creature, or you'll lose the sense of transcendence that's the foundation of our morality!"

"You give the people no definite face of God," they go on. "The people need spiritual materialism in order to live—in order to be consoled, controlled, and helped." "You're destroying the Christian tradition and changing the very content of the faith." "How far do you intend to go?"

There are many questions of this kind, and the answers are not always easy—mostly because people do not have the kind of attitude that would open them to answers that differ from those they are used to. Even if they see problems with their own answers, they often resist novel attempts to answer these questions: They prefer to go on with the same habitual answers to avoid modifying their security systems in any way.

Most people cannot even perceive the intimate relationship between our beliefs and the understandings of the world and of humanity that we take for granted. They are unable to grasp the contextuality and provisionality of our discourses on the so-called eternal truths of religion. Furthermore, they do not accept the fact that our discourse on God is always relative to our experience and to our place in society. If our experience changed, our discourse on our beliefs would probably change as well. Even if we continued to use the same words, they would not have the same meaning.

Despite the difficulties involved in giving answers, I have always taken people's questions seriously and tried to offer them at least some clues that can help them find their own answers. And just as I do this in my work with groups, I will try to do the same in this chapter. I will try to begin with the specific questions people ask me about God and use those questions to open the way for new answers. All my attempts at answers will be from an ecofeminist perspective. This will undoubtedly constitute a new style and a new model for "speaking of God," one that flows out of the lived experience of various groups scattered throughout several countries.

I will begin by setting out some of the questions that are most often raised in the various courses, forums, and meetings at which at I have spoken, and the kinds of reflections I have offered in response. I am aware that my answers are incomplete, but they have been useful in sparking conversation about the eternal issue of the search for meaning or, in traditional theological terms, the search for God.

Issues Raised about
Ecofeminist Discourse on God

- I can't accept the idea that God is not a *person*.
- I can't pray to an energy flow.
- We must not fall into pantheism.
- The poor need concrete images of God.
- The ecofeminist perspective fails to stress the image of a God of Life committed to the poor.
- What do we do with biblical images of God?

I CAN'T ACCEPT THE IDEA
THAT GOD IS NOT A PERSON

In Latin America, this has almost always been the first objection raised when the ecofeminist perspective is broached. The distinctness of God and God's radical independence in the face of all other beings have been a part of our Christian heritage, especially in the West.

One of the difficulties we have in accepting a different kind of theological reflection is that we have not yet assimilated the fact of the interconnection and interdependence among all beings, much less integrated this with the fact of our relative human autonomy. Our mindset was formed in a patriarchal tradition that posited a break or discontinuity between a Supreme Creator and all of creation. The idea of a divinity that pervades all beings, times, and places was seen in this tradition as a primitive, mythological notion that had been almost totally forgotten by Christian theology. For the superiority of this Supreme Creator over all others to be upheld, this being had to be above and beyond the general run of beings. And in order to uphold our understanding of the relative autonomy of human beings, we had to compare it to the absolute autonomy of the Divine Being. The latter had to be a being in itself, all-powerful and independent of all creatures.

Within this dualistic antithesis, we not only had to grasp the concept of God and of creation; we also needed to understand the notions of "perfection" and "imperfection," and "purity" and "impurity." We set up pure and perfect beings to contrast them with our own experiences of impurity and imperfection. We set up powerful beings to contrast them with our own fragility and weakness, which we experienced in so many situations. It was, in a certain sense, a way of denying our own relative and contingent natures. In reality, we know that we can barely imagine what a pure and perfect being far above us could be. All we can do is deduce it as a hypothesis in order to continue with the life we have received. In the discourse of the mystics, to experience God's life directly seems almost impossible; they always refer to this "absolute" in analogous and symbolic images.

Most of the time, we fail to see that we are dealing here with a mental construct, a making sense of our experience, the using of a set of cultural parameters in order to grasp at the mystery that is alive within our own being. These parameters have been regarded as eternal and proclaimed to be "truth," especially within the western Christian tradition. Institutions and powers were built on these truths; so were dogmas and liturgies, inquisitions and prejudices. On them were built missions and tasks to be carried out. Much blood has been shed for them and much destruction wrought, and many loving acts have been undertaken in their name. And all this building up and tearing down has been carried out in order to separate God radically from creatures, as if we were seeking to uphold God as an untouchable "moral reserve" that would permit human beings to draw back from their evil actions. Meanwhile, history has showed that even this point of view has its radical limitations: We continue to shed blood, mostly innocent blood, and to justify our actions in God's name.

The great limitation of our present theology is its struggle to maintain these mental paradigms and constructs without reflecting on the deep changes we are going through, especially in the light of the development of contemporary science and the often destructive consequences of our "conquest" of the planet. The old reference points were undoubtedly useful in earlier centuries, but now they show themselves to be inadequate. Now we see just how much their claimed eternity is really contingent and limited by their context. We see just how much their proclamations are fruits of a static worldview in which the so-called eternal verities are accorded more value than the flow of truths that has emerged in the course of history, truths that are really tenuous expressions of that mysterious fabric within which we have our being.

We do not even dare to reexamine the philosophy that upholds our theology. We do not dare to inquire into the meaning of the terms we use in building the many meanings of our lives. We say, for example, that God is an eternal and immutable person and at the same time the creator of all that exists. Emmanuel Levinas reminds us that "[a]n eternal subject is a 'contradictio adjecto,' because a subject is in itself a beginning. An eternal subject not only cannot begin anything outside itself: it is itself impossible, because as a subject it should be a beginning and this excludes the possibility that it could be eternal."[4]

On the basis of my work with various groups, especially women's groups, I have observed that there is enormous difficulty in encouraging people to adopt an alternative kind of philosophical approach in their everyday thinking. It is not that people are consciously Platonists, Aristotelians, Thomists, or Cartesians. They probably know nothing of these philosophies. But these philosophies move unconsciously through their veins: They are part of people's cultures, their spiritual formations, and their educations. They show up in the dualistic and mechanistic way in which they understand human beings, as well as in their relationships with other beings and with the so-called Supreme Being. At first glance, they are unable to see that the vital process of development of our One Body is sacred, and that our universe demands that we develop our ideas about it and seek ways of loving it with greater justice and tenderness.

Theologies seem not to be concerned with adjusting their formulations to the specific issues the people raise. They are more concerned about adjusting the reality of the concrete lives of men and women to their theoretical concepts, which are drawn from other times and situations. They call these formulations "God's revelation," as if all this discourse were not woven of human experience, in all its greatness and precariousness.

With some exceptions, the churches have always sought to subordinate the concrete context around them to their doctrines—and consequently to their power. They have claimed that the great issues of every culture and historical period must be clothed in the same traditional garb, the same basic meaning structure, as if this were something universal and revealed by God. Often, they have declared it possible to muffle our cries and heal our pain only by subordinating ourselves to the world of perfection proclaimed by theology. They have pronounced many discourses on the goodness of God, on spiritual joy and happiness, while our stomachs growled with hunger and tears of distress burned on our faces, and while the weapons of war killed our children and our hopes.

Traditional theology sees God as a person with a will, a purpose, a plan for salvation, and a historical project. All God's plans are good and perfect, even if we never see them realized in the concrete. This divine personality was clearly fashioned in the image and likeness of the human personality. Sometimes religious authorities agreed to speak of the Person of God in analogous terms. However, we know that all this theology is built on the fundamental idea of the uniqueness of God's being—a metaphysical notion.

The ancients discovered in this idea a principle of authority that allowed them to demand ethical behavior or to impose their worldviews. In the last analysis, the church always used God as the ultimate justification for its power and its actions. It needed God's authority in order to wield power and exact obedience. In the end, it is easier to exact obedience by appealing to God's power than by appealing to that of human beings!

In *his* name the church meted out love and punishment. In *his* name it intervened in the people's lives. In *his* name it exhorted and taught the nations. In *his* name it admonished women and slaves to obedience. The church's voice has always been considered to represent God's person and God's power. Whereas democracies tried to speak in the name of the people, the churches claimed—and still claim—to speak in the name of God, and their actions were always thought to be for the good of the people.

Politically and socially, God had to be a person with a will in order to legitimate actions imposed on persons. And sometimes God has become a rigid, intransigent, vengeful, and even bloodthirsty person.

For anthropological reasons, too, God had to be a person. "Ask and you shall receive, knock and it will be opened to you." We can only ask if there is someone there to hear, or knock if there is someone to open the door! But to whom, in fact, did the door open? Did this metaphor of need and power not end up being co-opted into history, becoming part and parcel of its struggles, reflecting its claims, its racism, its sexism, and its illusions, as well as its hopes and consolations?

A metaphysical, anthropomorphic, and anthropocentric God became a necessity within the psychological structure that evolved throughout the history of patriarchal culture. This meant that, in the traditional theology we were taught, God was regarded as another "I," an ego of infinite excellence whose designs were inaccessible to human beings. The affirmation of this other ego, which is understood in the light of my own ego, offers a sense of paternal or maternal security even if my prayers are never answered. There is always the possibility of enjoying the complicity of this other ego within the confines of my own ego. There is always the hope that this ego will recognize me, listen to me, and respond with what I hope for. And if this fails to occur, some people hope that another time their prayers may be heard with more sympathetic ears. Others despair, feel guilty or rejected, and ask why God has forgotten them and why God does not heed their petitions and supplications.

God as another "I" in the image of the human continues to be preached by religious authorities. The fear of God's dissolution into cosmic or anthropological dynamics seems always to be present. "There is none like God," the authorities say. "None has power like God's." "No one can stand up to God's sovereign will." "Only God saves." "Only God can do everything." "Only God knows all." Although we could accept the existential meaning of these affirmations, in the religious sects that are growing by leaps and bounds among the poor, these affirmations are often used to manipulate people's behavior. They are not presented as metaphors or attempts to express the greatest of mysteries that envelops us; rather, they are taken literally and thereby bring with them the danger of using people and persuading them to follow disreputable leaders.

The need to affirm a higher power—a power presented as being in *discontinuity* with all the powers of the cosmos, the earth, human beings, animals, plants, and even life itself—appears to be of fundamental importance in maintaining the hierarchical organization of the society in which we live. Within this structure, to affirm God as a person who is totally different, superior, and other is in a sense to remain within the same hierarchical logic.

Within an ecofeminist perspective, the first thing we need to admit is that the human person is *relatedness*, a special relatedness despite the fact that it participates in the relatedness of the whole universe. Because of this, we personalize all our relationships, from the simplest to the most complex. This means that in a certain sense we understand all that exists in light of ourselves, of our genetic and cultural situation and our creativity and unpredictability. This is the case not only of human beings but also in some way of animals. In a certain sense, a dog perceives the universe on its own terms, just as an ant or a bee does. Animals experience the world, respectively, as a dog does, or as an ant or a bee does. Saint Thomas Aquinas said that everything that is known is known in the manner of the being that knows it.

In our anthropocentricity, we human beings have always thought we were the center upon which all converges; thus our image of God was thought out and articulated as the center onto which all things converge. Our personal God could not avoid being the Absolute Being that dominated all that exists. We neither used nor even remembered the analogous or metaphorical perspective.

As I explained earlier, in the light of a more analogous approach to knowing, we could go so far as to say that God is a person in an analogous rather than an ontological sense—that is, in the sense that we can make an analogy between God and our idea of "person," but we cannot say that God's being is a person. For the human world, this relatedness wrapped in mystery is personal, despite the fact that we must affirm it as also more than personal.

Today, there is a growing awareness that we can no longer be the center by means of which all is dominated. Rather, we have to be the center through which all enters into fraternal communion. We are trying to decentralize our power to possess and dominate in order to build new meanings based on relatedness, independence, and universal brotherhood/sisterhood. Today we are aware of the extraordinary fact that we are all made of the same cosmic matter and energy, and that there is no single pivotal reality on which we all depend; rather, all depends on all. The center is in all and in everything. In this sense, we could even keep the word "God" as an indicator of the surpassing reality that is the sustaining source of all life and movement and about which we can only babble muddled words that somehow reflect our own experience.

We are opening ourselves to a new model for understanding humanity and the cosmos, and so we can no longer go on insisting on the traditional notion of a God/person—that is, a separate being superior to all that exists, a kind of superperson with the power to "control" the universe, human life, and the morality of our actions.

This is not first and foremost a theoretical topic. It is a practical one. We are trying to address the issue of the destruction we are doing to ourselves and to the entire cosmos, not just in terms of our devastating political and economic practices but also in the light of our theological-anthropological worldview. Today we face the issues of hunger, illiteracy, disease, and violence in the world, while at the same time we struggle to modify our centuries-old beliefs. Our beliefs are implicated in all these processes, and this means that we need to face the destruction of the economically poorest ethnic groups as a religious issue as well. It also demands that we regard the contemptuous treatment and exploitation of women as a theological issue.

This means that when we approach the situation from the perspective of universal relatedness, there is a real complicity of religious bodies and of various theological systems with the perpetuation of dependency, violence, and oppression.

The notion of God as a person who is metaphysically asexual but historically identified with the male sex, and especially with the powerful of this world, is no longer adequate in dealing with the great issues of the survival of humanity and of life itself on this planet. The original sense of God as inaccessible to human knowing has been obscured by ideologies and dogmatisms of all kinds, and it is our urgent task to seek it out anew.

In an ecofeminist sense, then, we would say that God is relatedness, and, as such, also personal—and therefore neither different from persons nor above them. By analogy, God is a human person, the sap of human life, but also the sap of the life in trees, in flowers, in animals, and in all that exists. By analogy too, God is man, woman, breeze, hurricane, tenderness, jealousy, compassion, mercy: Mystery.

The personhood of God must no longer be the object of religious manipulation. For this reason, it is better to speak less of God and from this point on to refrain from mentioning God's will or the divine plan as realities that are absolutely separate, superior, and good. It would be better to silence this latest chapter of our discourse on God. To acknowledge that the greatest of mysteries that envelops us simply "is," is to agree not to take in vain the name of that sacred energy which pervades all beings.

I CAN'T PRAY TO AN ENERGY FLOW

People who raise issues of this kind do so with a great deal of anguish. It is as if someone wanted to take away their own particular way of praying, or even their gods. I try to reassure them, and invite them to reflect more calmly on these doubts. The idea is not to introduce some new divinity or to violently tear down people's beliefs, but rather to go ever farther in accepting our human responsibility in the face of life.

The first thing we need to do is give a general answer to the question, Why do we pray?

To begin with, praying is a human need, like singing, dancing, or listening to music. But it is a human need marked by gratuity and freedom, by the desire to be at one with myself in the presence of the mystery that sustains us all. It is a human need that varies in intensity and form from one person or culture to another.

There is no one style of praying, then; there are many, just as there are many kinds of music, many poems, and many dance forms. Praying is a multiple and diverse form of contact with our deepest reality, with our "I," with our personal and cultural histories, and with our desires and fears. So praying is something more expansive than an act carried out in the context of one or another religious institutionality.

In the dualistic and exclusive patriarchal tradition in which we were brought up, praying is, in the first place, an act of praise and adoration toward God; in the second place, it is a supplication or request that God satisfy certain needs. The idea that we are fragile, evil, and sinful led us to develop an ever more acute sense of helplessness and guilt. God, who is infinite perfection, seems to be the only one capable of improving our situation or solving our problems. We need only recall the great mortifications that were practiced until very recently in various Christian communities—penances inflicted on the body in order to obtain the favors begged of God or the saints. These were very common behaviors in convents and in some lay religious groups. Whippings and mortifications were regarded as corrective and expiatory practices. To evoke the goodness and clemency of God, the faithful had to show that they recognized their sinful state and then do something to expiate their guilt. Disease, plagues, drought, storms, and death were regarded by groups in various historical periods as scourges sent by God. In a number of appearances, the Virgin Mary seemed to interpret the so-called punishments that fell upon the world as divine actions aimed at the conversion of sinners, for our sins were many.

To recall these traditions is not to deny the stubborn persistence in life of fragility, or our felt need to build security systems. It does mean attempting to unveil the structure and the experience of what we call "praying." Prayer is then shown to be a way not only of avoiding punishment by "God's strong arm," but also of expiating our faults and acknowledging that we are repentant and chastened sinners. "I have done what is evil in your eyes," says the penitent in Psalm 50; "therefore in your eyes I repent." But this repentance "in your eyes" has to be something concrete, says Jesus. It has to lead us to specific historical actions that in fact proclaim a change in our behavior. Otherwise we will go on talking of a purely idealistic reality that has no connection with our daily lives. In Jesus' perspective, words cannot be mere literary forms; they have to show a certain efficacy.

Praying has seemed to be a purer and more elevated activity than others. We have been accustomed to saying that "to pray is to raise our hearts and minds to God." Prayer has been regarded as a very special moment in life. And, in general, it was something we did after tragedies struck, as if through it we sought to appease God's anger and to receive some soothing consolation.

These actions show that when we pray, we project our personal situation. If I ask something of someone in prayer, that "someone" has to be a concrete individual with a selfhood that is different from mine and with a great deal more power than I have. Similarly, if I praise someone, my praise is aimed at "someone" who deserves it and can accept it.

God becomes this "someone" in my own image and likeness, one who listens to my entreaties and laments as if I were the only person in the world who was crying out at that moment. But God also appears in the power of the saints, who are very much present in Latin American Catholicism. With them, I can establish solid bonds and create relationships of power and submission, of tenderness and reverence. The saints in some way represent divine power, since they live life on a different level.

This has been the behavior of the great masses of believers, especially Roman Catholics, in Latin America and doubtless in other parts of the world. It has also been the doctrine imparted by those charged with catechizing the people.

Despite this, a sense of orphanhood seems very widespread among us; the need for, at least, the feeling that "somebody" is listening becomes ever more urgent. This need is what, even today, makes it so difficult to suggest new behaviors or to widen the horizons of our habitual ways of thinking.

In an ecofeminist perspective, prayer has to be rediscovered as a human need. This need is expressed in a variety of forms and circumstances, depending on the particular person or community that is praying. We pray because we need prayer. We pray because we want to pray. We pray because it helps us live better. We pray because we need this contact with ourselves, with our community, and with the entire universe. We pray because of our need to bring to mind the people we love, to reflect on the grace of their lives, to recall their sufferings and joys, and to share with them in their mysterious encounters with us. Prayer reveals the multiplicity and unity we all are. Prayer also opens each of us to his or her ability to draw the world to him- or herself and, at the same time, to be in contact with the world within the confines of our individual subjectivity.

Prayer, then, is not addressed to an abstract "energy flow," as some make the mistake of thinking. It takes place in the light of the concrete materiality of the beings we are, in connection with the materiality of the world that surrounds us, in *relatedness* with that whole of which we are one tiny expression.

Prayer is a moment of gratitude, of silent contemplation of the simple fact of being here, of being part of this immense web of relationships, of breathing within the bounds of the world's breathing, of living this instant within the great evolutionary sweep of life. It is breathing within the orbit of the world's breathing and that of the universe; it is the spirit, the breath of life within us. We breathe because we are breathing beings, beings that inhale and exhale. That is our condition and our situation.

Prayer is our personal and collective preparation for acting in solidarity and respect, for awakening feelings of tenderness and compassion for persons and for all living things.

This position does not amount to a denial of the various prayer forms that have been used in different religious traditions, but it insists on the need to avoid dualistic and hierarchical approaches, which have shown how limited they are in furthering the construction of universal brotherhood and sisterhood. Praying is not just making requests; it is being present, being intimately part of the body of the universe, the human body, and the bodies of those who are dear to us—the bodies we love.

This prayer does not stand in opposition the prayer of Jesus as we find it in the Synoptic Gospels. It does not matter what name we give the mystery: We know that Jesus' experience reveals his open acceptance of the great mystery of life. His moments of solitude were probably deep encounters with himself, powerful experiences that threw him once again into the struggle to restore dignity to the lives of the poor and outcast.

Within an ecofeminist perspective, then, praying is also necessary: praying to remain faithful to the very faithfulness of life in ourselves. It is praying to be able to breathe, in our own human way, the breath of the universe; being thankful for life, for this moment, for this situation, and for this encounter. It is praying for the ability to accept what we neither understand nor accept. It is praying for the strength to fight against the evil that injures and destroys. It is praying to "keep our lamps trimmed" when darkness enters our lives. It is praying to stand with the oppressed, the despoiled, and those who have fallen among robbers, as the Guatemalan poet Julia Esquivel has so beautifully written:

I will remain with my people,
with the despoiled,
the duped,
the afflicted,
the sold out.
Those who have never been looked on as human
but who straighten up always
And survive
and start over once again . . .[5]

WE MUST NOT FALL INTO PANTHEISM

Among Latin American Christians, the word "pantheism" has always had negative connotations. Pantheism smacks of materialism and seems close to paganism. It seems to be a regression to a more primitive and rustic world, one that is less spiritual and less complete. It is ambiguous, obscure, and disorderly. Pantheism is associated with the denial of a God who is above all and above everything. It is associated with a vague negation of human reason, which identifies God as the cause of all beings.

Our fear of pantheism is largely explained by our dualistic, idealistic, and spiritualistic formation within the patriarchal tradition. This formation has always insisted on maintaining a hierarchical relationships among all beings, not only distinguishing between higher forms of life and so-called lower ones, but also distinguishing radically between the Creator and creatures.

Pantheism appears to break down the distinction between spirit and matter, between heaven and earth, between God and humanity, and between humanity and all other beings. The fear of pantheism could even be compared with the fear of communism that has marked the history of some Latin American countries in recent decades. Especially among the popular classes, anticommunist propaganda allowed us to blame communism for all the world's ills: hunger, the deaths of children and the elderly, religious persecution, and so on. All that was evil was said to be a fruit of communism. On the popular level, a similar process has taken place with regard to phenomena that are labeled as pantheism. The process takes various forms, all of which identify pantheism with people who mix everything up and fail to accord an adequate place to God.

We have been afraid to adore the sun, as the Egyptians did, or the earth, as indigenous peoples did. We have been afraid to adore nature or to speak of jungles, seas, rivers, and stars as divine. In our hierarchical worldview, we had to keep all these things carefully pigeonholed. They had to remain submissive to the Supreme Lord of the universe and to obey the order established by God. Pantheism would lead to disorder, the breakdown of hierarchies, and generalized confusion. Thus it is possible to understand the fear we developed in the face of this heresy, which tempted us continually—even when we thought we had gotten rid of it.

Besides this, our theology has always insisted on two important words: "identity" and "otherness." These two words refer to human beings, to all other beings, and to the being of God. All beings were characterized by having their own identity, and by their otherness in relation to all other beings.

Identity

Every being must maintain its identity. Every being has something that makes it what it is and nothing else. This is its own essence, that special constitutive something that is manifest in its concrete existence. This identity is hierarchically organized, so that we should keep carefully in mind the place each being occupies in the hierarchy, which is willed and designated by God. Within this hierarchy, then, each being has its particular identity and value.

Otherness

Once we have affirmed identity, we can also posit the notion of otherness. Every being is different from all the others, and this makes it other, different. Every being has its own place and cannot be reduced to any other. Therefore we affirm that every being is absolutely unique and irreplaceable.

Basing our thinking on the identity and otherness we experienced in created things and in human life, we speak of the identity and otherness of God. God is the being whose identity cannot be mixed up with that of any other, and whose otherness is radical and absolute: God is not only superior to other beings, but absolutely different. On this basis, we can speak of the absolute transcendence of God. Although we also speak of God's immanence, we certainly place more emphasis on transcendence.

According to criticism raised in various courses I have given, ecofeminism appeared not to be taking these two notions into consideration; therefore, it looked like pantheism. Consequently, it was an unacceptable school of thought, especially for those who adhered to the Christian tradition.

The confusions raised by this criticism, which is often rather simplistic, are immense. They have reached not only base communities but many religious intellectuals who work in our churches. People have trouble seeing that the traditional wording of our ideas about identity and otherness refers to a specific way of understanding the structure of the universe and a specific understanding of human beings and of God.

In spite of these confusions, the ecofeminist perspective includes the dimensions of otherness and identity; it affirms them as grounded in the relatedness and interdependence of all with all. We are part of an immense web of relationships, a web that evolves outward in different ways, in continuity with the universe's creative process—of which, of course, we still understand very little. This perspective also points to the uniqueness of this moment and the unique countenance of every being, a countenance that is both a unique face and one that reflects the whole web of life that has gone before it and is contemporary with it. Rather than being pantheistic, the ecofeminist perspective opens us to see the sacred dimension of our Cosmic Body and prompts us to assume a humility that dismisses all our totalitarian pretensions. It opens us to an attitude that seeks community and solidarity among all beings.

Sallie McFague insists that the theoretical model she has developed is not pantheistic but "pan-en-theistic." "Everything that is, is in God and God is in all things and yet God is not identical to the universe, for the universe is dependent on God in a way that God is not dependent on the universe," she says. Later, she goes on: "Pantheism says that God is embodied, necessarily and totally; traditional theism claims that God is disembodied, necessarily and totally; panentheism suggests that God is embodied but not necessarily or totally. Rather, God is sacramentally embodied: God is mediated, expressed, in and through embodiment, but not necessarily or totally."[6]

The distinction McFague proposes requires deeper reflection. To say that in the panentheist perspective God does have a body and is incarnate, but not necessarily or totally, means that the last word on the mystery that enfolds us is not our own. It signifies openness to the possibility of all that is different, unpredictable, and unutterable. It means we should not build a closed discourse, a discourse in which the unknown, the as-yet-unthought, or even the nonexistent has no chance of being included. So we do not seek to protect the philosophical image of God as a "being in itself," thereby maintaining the traditional image of transcendence; rather, we open ourselves to a different or broader perception of the "divine milieu" in which we live and have our being.

I like to say, then, that to speak of pan-en-theism is to consider the potentialities of the universe, the potentialities of life, and the potentialities of human life as always open-ended. Thus we escape from the closed circle of immanence and transcendence, of "being in itself," to become part of the reality we call the process of life, in which transcendence and immanence are mere expressions that point to the dynamics that draw us forth.

The poetry of Ernesto Cardenal, in his extraordinary *Cosmic Canticle*, opens us up to the kind of communion that we fear because it breaks down our hierarchies and our securities:

> The universe lit up
> by thousands of galaxies of thousands of millions of stars!
> I gaze at the universe
> and I am the universe gazing at itself.
> The universe's most subtle retina gazing upon itself,
> that's what we are.[7]

THE POOR NEED CONCRETE IMAGES OF GOD

Without denying all the churches' efforts to help the poor, the marginal, and the excluded, we have to recognize that in Latin American there has been an extremely paternalistic tradition that has unconsciously cultivated dependency among the poor. For instance, even when the church has defended the autonomy of the poor, it has sought to make them dependent on certain religious ideas that are presented as salvific. However, we must also admit that this has been a complex human process, one that would be hard to analyze in the kind of book I am writing. I will limit my remarks to only a few considerations.

We always prefer that the good we do be recognized and emulated. We would like the act of doing good—especially when it is done by an institution—to be adopted as a generalized behavior pattern. We would like to have political, social, and religious influence. This is, of course, a deeply ingrained behavior in Latin America, especially in the case of the Roman Catholic Church and its close relationships with the various Latin American countries. The Catholic church has been present here since colonial times, and its influence on the life of the continent is undeniable.

Given this situation, it is understandable that, because we help the poor, we should want them to move ever more deeply into the world of symbolic meanings offered by the various churches, and especially of the Catholic church, which still predominates over the others. But the symbolic world it offers is patriarchal in structure, and it is also distinctly dualistic and hierarchical. Therefore, despite the progress made by liberation theology, the symbolic world the Catholic church offers remains the same.

There is little doubt that despite some rare exceptions, official representatives of the various churches wield power in the relationships they establish with the poor. The poor are looking for security, identity, and consolation, and the churches offer moralistic preaching, an often literal reading of the Bible, the saints, and so on. We are almost immediately tempted to claim in response that the "product" we offer is one that the poor need in order to go on living. Therefore, we block efforts to change this world of meanings, arguing that the poor need it exactly as it has traditionally been communicated to them. To keep this world in its traditional institutional form is to be faithful to popular religious traditions and, above all, to show respect for popular culture, say some pastoral agents.

A typical example is religious authorities' growing encouragement of popular participation in the maintenance of shrines, the canonization of saints, new sightings of apparitions of the Virgin, the spread of stories of miracles, and so on. Often they argue that this is done out of respect for the people's desires, but little is said of the ways in which they themselves bolster these desires or of the propaganda they put out in order to keep these desires as they are— not to mention these authorities' conscious or unconscious complicity with the political and economic means used to keep poor people dependent. We know how well political and economic power holders like to support this kind of religious practice by means of financial contributions, even by installing banking services in the immediate neighborhoods of shrines and miracle sites. The dependency we see in patriarchal religion is largely an expression of a culture of dependency and exclusion.

What alternatives do we suggest? What new expressions would we be inclined to propose? The ecofeminist perspective does not attempt to offer recipes or radically new solutions; it merely seeks to point out the ways in which we can appear to be social progressives when what we really are is religious conservatives. What we have here is an often unconscious struggle to stay in power, to hold on to a religious power that still has a significant influence in Latin America, especially in the cultural formation of our peoples.

There is a great deal at stake here, and we do not always clearly discern what attitudes will be helpful in encouraging freedom and creativity in religious expression. The important thing, nonetheless, is to avoid stifling creative initiatives, spontaneous cultural expressions, or creative feminist liturgies.

Within the culture of dependency, we claim that the poor need concrete images of God. When we are asked about the meaning of these concrete expressions, we answer, "The people need to feel that God is their Father"—or, in the more progressive sectors, their Mother. "The people need to feel that God has not abandoned them, especially when they are living in situations in which they are spurned and totally disregarded."

Would the concrete image of God, then, be one that makes a radical distinction between God as a being who is, in essence, always good, and God's creatures, who are always in need? Does this concrete image of God not amount to repeating the very contradictions that dog traditional theodicies, in which, despite the growth of evil and destruction, God continues to be good and to desire the good of all human beings? Could the concrete image of

God they speak of really be the preservation of a masculine image of the deity, somehow mitigated by the figure of a patriarchal mother, a powerful virgin, the Great Mother of humanity? As far as I am concerned, to save these so-called concrete images at all cost would be one way of denying all the struggles against idolatry that have marked our prophetic tradition.

The ecofeminist perspective opens itself to the multiplicity of forms reality takes and to reality's amazing interdependence, and in the process it reaffirms the need to avoid reducing the mysterious reality of this Sacred Body to a single image. Therefore, we protest the refusal to accept changes in this image, and identify this refusal as negative ideological behavior—even when it is carried out in the name of the poor. This attitude that underlies this refusal treats the poor as ignorant, as helpless, as nonadult. And although it is true that it is largely the economic system that makes the poor what they are, it is also true that our religious world itself has often contributed to perpetuating this situation.

Far from showing a lack of respect for popular cultural traditions, then, the ecofeminist perspective proposes a reflection on the real interests that are at stake—and on the anthropocentric and androcentric religious ideology that is put forth in the name of respect for these same traditions.

I am aware of the complexity of this topic and of the difficulties that appear when we are deeply involved, as we are in Latin America, in the struggle for survival. But, once again, the task of teachers and writers is to help people reflect on their daily lives, including the everyday things that keep us imprisoned and enslaved to ourselves. Our task is to stir up the waters so that life can be constantly renewed.

THE ECOFEMINIST PERSPECTIVE FAILS TO STRESS THE IMAGE OF A GOD OF LIFE COMMITTED TO THE POOR

One of the most common objections to ecofeminist thinking has been that it fails to focus its concern preferentially on the poor, on their political organization, and on the social changes required for their survival. There is a tendency to identify ecofeminism with "new age" groups, and at the same time to emphasize those groups' more individualistic and alienating features.

I think there are some very significant ambiguities in all this. In the first place, we increasingly need to ask what ecofeminism we are talking about, just as we sometimes ask what Christianity we are talking about. In a pluralist society such as our own, names no longer offer a reliable key either to things or to social movements. Besides this, in Latin America there is a widespread fear of opening up our markedly anthropological and anthropocentric Christianity to its more cosmic, ecological, and feminist dimensions. If we did so, our analyses would have to be more broadly based; they could not be limited solely to the human dimension. We fear that the cosmic dimension could somehow take away from our Christian identity. This fear is rationalized by an appeal to the idea that Christianity is based on a direct revelation from God to a specific human group, and by the argument that this revelation ought to be preserved and defended.

These attitudes offer no critical analysis of the challenges to Christianity at this point in the evolution of the planet and of humanity itself. Questioning our image of God would force us to modify a centuries-old theological edifice; it would mean talking about our tradition in a different way and working more creatively and freely with the legacy of our forebears. Both conservatives and progressives show strong resistance to this kind of change. Deep down, both groups agree that there is an untouchable "revelation," and that if we tamper with it we run the risk of losing Christianity's identity and its public claim to be a religion founded by God. When we ask them what exactly its revealed, untouchable content is, they answer right away that it has to do with the whole dogmatic corpus regarding trinitarian monotheism: the incarnation, the passion, and the resurrection lived out by Jesus for the sake of human salvation. The revealed data are reduced to a certain point of view, a certain interpretation of Scripture, and specific formulations that, although they contain undeniable truths, certainly do not exhaust the whole process through which truth unfolds as we ourselves move along the path of history.

In the face of the new international context in which we find ourselves, the transformations of every sort that are taking place in our world, and the new theological alternatives that certain schools of thought—among them ecofeminism—are proposing, most Christian theologians have a rather closed attitude. An argument frequently put forth, especially by Latin American progressives, is that ecofeminism fails to offer solid religious grounding for popular emancipation struggles, which are regarded as struggles for freedom along the road to the reign of God. Once again, they argue that the image of God offered by ecofeminism is not firmly grounded, not demanding enough, and only vaguely committed to dealing with specific situations. But what they call "grounding" can be reduced to a particular sociological reading of Christianity, especially the one that has been widely hailed in the last twenty-five years. This point of view appears to be in severe difficulty today owing to the widespread crisis being experienced by liberation social movements themselves. What they call a solid foundation is the anthropocentrism and theocentrism that have long marked our thinking. What they call groundedness is the continuation of a theology based on a hierarchical religious system.

In fact, ecofeminists do not base themselves on this or that theological system when we invite others to participate in the process of saving the earth or defending life. On the contrary, we struggle for the dignity of life, and the foundation for this struggle is in the sacredness of the life that is within us and in which we participate. Every being and every moment is unique and extraordinary within this immense Sacred Body, whose boundaries are immeasurable. At every instant, every being maintains its own uniqueness, and in this context every being is worthy to live the fullness of its own existence.

We will not speak of the "God of life," but of life as a divine milieu. We will speak of life as a sacred individual and collective reality that should be loved, respected, and preserved. We will speak of life as a mystery, and of the greatest of mysteries as a reality that is present in life. We will speak of the life that throbs in us, and in the lives that surround us—the lives we love. The "God of life" still appears to be above life—as if there were an ordinary life, the everyday life of the various beings and of nature, and above it all a divinity that presides over and governs that life. Ecofeminism opens the doors to a new understanding of the role of religion in human life.

In this sense, we do not love other persons and the world itself on account of a superior Being who (we are told) creates, loves, and saves all creatures. The invitation to love and mercy does not come from a reality that is external to us; rather, it is an urge that is present in our very humanity. Within our very being, within our flesh, within our "organized energy," there throbs an incredible attraction toward other beings. Although this outward-looking energy can be discharged in destructiveness and hatred, it can also open up in tenderness and mercy. And this is the human enigma, its paradox and its constant challenge.

What we call the divine is within us, and it draws us to open ourselves passionately to other beings. We need to remember, however, that this openness is never total. It always implies a closedness, a denial, an exclusion. Closing ourselves off is as much a part of the dynamic of life as is opening ourselves. Openness and closedness are expressions of all living things, and not merely of the human—despite the fact that in human beings it takes on its own characteristics.

Going beyond a naive stance toward nature and its appeal, women and men in various parts of the world have seriously criticized the patriarchal system's complicity in the destruction of the earth, of women, and of children. Intellectuals involved with the feminist, ecofeminist, and ecological perspectives have repeatedly described the horrors of the destruction we have been creating for ourselves. This is not a romantic approach, but a concrete one that recognizes the reality that men plan and declare wars while women remain behind with their children, struggling for daily survival. In this respect I recall the women of Sicily, who protested against the stationing of nuclear missiles in their territory:

> Our "no" to war is part and parcel of our struggle for liberation. Never before have we so clearly seen the connection between the nuclear arms race and the culture of muscular men; between the violence of war and the violence of rape. In fact, rape is women's historical memory of war. . . But this is also our daily experience in times of peace, and in this sense women are always at war. . . It is no coincidence that the repulsive game of war—in which a good part of the male population seems to take pleasure—goes through the same stages as traditional sexual relations: aggression, conquest, power, and control. There is very little difference between a woman and a territory.[8]

Why has the male God of life so seldom condemned these horrors? Why do his functionaries fail to mention these injustices? Why are they silent in the face of growing violence against women? What side do they choose in life? These concrete situations of struggle and commitment prompt us to affirm the engagement of ecofeminism in struggles for social justice, and, beyond that, in the struggle for ecojustice, which requires a wider and more global perspective.

WHAT DO WE DO WITH BIBLICAL IMAGES OF GOD?

Another frequently heard criticism is that the ecofeminist perspective brings in traditions and forms of discourse that are not integral to the great traditional themes of Christianity. Ecofeminism is accused at times of appearing to forget traditional biblical images of God and of God's liberating intervention in the "history of salvation." Beyond this, it appears to propose significant changes in the traditional expressions of meaning that have been a part of our heritage. "By what authority," the critics ask, "do you seek to change Christianity and still remain within the Christian community?"

In my view, these reproaches express a fear of pluralism right in the heart of what we call "Christian experience." Because of this fear, the critics absolutize one interpretation—the dominant one—as the only means of maintaining our identity. In the process, they fail to see that biblical interpretations and the very images of God found in the patriarchal perspective are plural and circumstantial.

The ecofeminist perspective does not cast the Bible aside; it merely works with it from a different perspective. Ecofeminism gives more attention to texts that seem in closer line with the worldview it is proposing, and attempts to broaden our extremely western reading of the text. Similarly, at every moment in our history, the Christian community has identified more with some texts than with others—and has interpreted them according to its needs.

I think it is of fundamental importance to avoid putting the authority of the Bible above that of life, above everyday struggles and above the scriptures of other cultures and the histories of all peoples. It is not because it is in the Bible that we should do this or that, just as the fact that this or that's not being in the Bible does not mean we should not do it. Our life experience is our first teacher.

In this sense, we no longer call the Bible the "Word of God"; rather, we call it a human word on life and meaning. It is a "word" that continues to inspire us despite the fact that it does not always fit within our cultural horizon. It is a word linked to our religious history, our beliefs, and our very flesh.

The ecofeminist perspective has never abandoned the Bible. This should be clear from the many texts and commentaries by women theologians from various countries. One example is *Ecofeminism and the Sacred,* edited by Carol Adams;[9] another example is the many biblical references found in the Chilean ecofeminist journal *Con-spirando.* Beyond this, groups of women in various Latin American countries are working within the perspective of Brazil's Ecumenical Center for Biblical Studies (CEBI) in an effort to reread the biblical scriptures and rediscover in them the integrity of creation and respect for women.[10]

In the same way, Christian women of other continents and traditions have shown a special interest in reappropriating the Bible in order to rediscover in it the religious experience of our forebears. A more detailed study of feminist writings in the last twenty years is the best answer to the doubts being raised on this particular score.

God: Models and Mystery

Sallie McFague always reminds us that when we speak of God we are speaking of models, not descriptions.[11] Models are categories, frames of reference, and organizations of meaning we construct to speak of that which we live and perceive. We always think in terms of frames of reference, of a given order and organization. There is no thought that does not have a particular logic, a certain sought coherence. The organization of meaning changes, just as do the models we use to understand the world, ourselves, and God. There is no one explanation for the birth, highlighting, or even death of certain models and religious symbols. Everything is a cultural effort, in a given place and time, to express something about the "ultimate reality" that grounds all that is.

As McFague says so clearly, "Models are to be judged not by whether they correspond with God's being (the face is not available to us), but whether they are relatively adequate (in other words, more adequate than alternative models) from the perspective of postmodern science, and interpretation of Christian faith, our own embodied experience, and the well-being of our planet and all its life forms."[12]

For this reason, all that we say about God is an approximation, a model for expressing our perplexed grasp of the mystery that envelops us. "Mystery" is a word I use quite often in this book. I like it despite the fact that it sometimes exasperates some colleagues, such as sociologists, who think it reflects very little efficiency or productiveness. But in order to speak of the meaning of life, which is a reality of which we are more ignorant than knowledgeable, I have to use the word "mystery." Mystery as used here means that which is known and at the same time unknown, a mixture of certitudes and uncertainties; of probabilities, hypotheses, realities that surpass us, and fundamental questions to which we have no answers. Mystery is a word that traverses all things, all words, all lives, and all our yearnings, because it reveals and hides all that is and is not. For anyone who does theology or who reflects on the meaning of life, the word "mystery" is essential. It is one of those words that is indefinable, but that can in the final analysis be part of any definition.

But what is really important is to understand the historical consequences of our imprecise discourse on God, of our "models of God." This is the case because models are not neutral. They betoken a stance, an action in the face of the various problems that arise in our world. God as all-powerful Lord, king over all persons and living things, God as omniscient, omnipotent, and omnipresent, or even God as the avenger of the poor and restorer of justice—all are images or models that imply concrete historical behaviors.

In this sense, the "ecofeminist model" expressed in relatedness is undoubtedly just one more model: It suggests a certain kind of religious sociopolitical action that will be somewhat different from the actions that flow from other models. This is what I have tried to show throughout this chapter.

God: My Hope

God is my hope. This affirmation, despite the patriarchal ring of the word "God," continues to be made by ecofeminist theologians. God is our hope because to say "God" is, in one sense, to say nothing very precise. To say God is to express through a name our admiration and alarm in the face of the mysterious reality in which we are immersed. To say God is to refuse to absolutize any one way as the only way of justice, truth, and love. To say God is to speak of being and nonbeing. To say God is to speak of the all without limits or the all within limits; of the all on the basis of human perception, and of images of nothingness, even if we do not know exactly how to explain what nothingness is.

God is always the greatest reality, a hope that exceeds all our expectations. God is the possibility of paths that open even when some of the paths we hoped for have closed forever.

To say that God is my and our hope is to affirm that we do not set our hopes on "chariots, horses, and horsemen." It is to say that neither political parties nor trade unions, national states, military forces, speeches, countries, sciences, nor churches have the last word on life. They are passing forms immersed in the flux of all things. To say that God is our hope is to affirm that nothing that is made by us can become our ruler, our master, or our tormentor.

"God is my hope" does not imply the infantile attitude of someone who expects everything to come from the all-powerful One, from a being-in-itself that is distinct from all other beings. God is my greatest hope, the mysterious reality that reveals that hope pours forth from every direction: from persons, animals, and vegetables; from the sun, the moon, and the stars; from love poems and loneliness; from today and even from the garbage. . . . In fact, there will always be a tomorrow, even though I as an individual will no longer be here, even if I have never begotten a child or planted a tree.

In consonance with the whole of Christian tradition, we continue to affirm that God is our hope, because this truth relativizes our projects, our judgments, our anthropocentrism, our androcentrism, and our triumphalism. To say, according to Christian tradition, that God is our hope is to open ourselves to the way of Jesus of Nazareth, who drew close to the despised and abandoned and affirmed their dignity far beyond the social conventions of his time. And, grounded in his resurrected journey, he proclaims the need for all things to be resurrected today, in our everyday lives. The proximity of the oppressed to us reveals the crazy stupidity of our hearts, which are capable of rejection and of decreeing that some persons are of value and others are not. The way of Jesus, the way of foolish love, a way that is far from the logic of the established powers, was the way of affirming the struggle for life, and especially for the life of the oppressed—a way of resurrection, and the only way that gives us the right to affirm that "God is our hope."

God is our hope because our wager in this fragile life is a wager against all hope. God is our hope because we want to go beyond the terror, violence, and fear that crush us. God is our hope because we often have no visible hope, because often the haze of fear that envelops us and all things seems terrifying. God is our hope as the ultimate cry for justice: a "no" to unjust killing, to arms and armies, and a "yes" to a dignified life. God is our hope in our despair in the presence of a dying child—of a loss that constitutes a "piece" being torn from oneself—of the companion who has left us, of the soldier who remains, of destruction, and of the fragments of a quilt that needs to be restitched.

To go on hoping for some way out in life, even though it is not the way out we had hoped for, is in a certain sense to continue to affirm that God is our hope. But it is from within the abyss itself that I live in myself, and it is from within the very terror that assails me in the face of machine guns and tanks that I continue to cry out for the Greatest of Mysteries. Therefore it cries out in me as a power that is both within me and outside me, as a last hope even when I perceive that there is no hope. This is "hoping against all hope."

This apparent contradiction dethrones humanity from its anthropocentrism and relocates us, on the basis of our very fragility, within the welcoming Mystery that envelops us and makes up the being of all beings.

For this reason, within the mystery of our lives, God is our *hope*.

4

ECOFEMINISM AND
THE TRINITY

≈≈≈

*Human beings are a part of the whole we call the Universe; they
are a tiny fragment of time and space. However, they regard themselves, their ideas and their feelings, as separate and apart from all
the rest. It is something like an optical illusion in their consciousness. This illusion is a sort of prison; it restricts us to our personal aspirations and limits our affective life to a few people very
close to us. Our task should be to free ourselves from this prison,
opening up our circle of compassion in order to embrace all living
creatures and all of nature in its beauty.*

Albert Einstein

Feelings and Associations Related to the Trinity

When we hear the word "Trinity," we immediately associate it with
an unfathomable mystery that is part of our faith but that we have
trouble relating to.* We have been told that our God is a Trinity
that has overcome all loneliness and isolation. We have also been
told that it is the communion among Father, Son, and Holy Spirit,
a very beautiful and perfect sharing we should imitate in our own
relationships. Today, this whole way of speaking seems more and

---

*This chapter reproduces parts of the author's book on the Trinity and contains
modifications of other parts. See Ivone Gebara, *Trindade, coisas velhas e novas:
Uma perspectiva ecofeminista* (São Paulo, Brazil: Paulinas, 1993).

more difficult to understand. It seems to take place far from us, far from our own flesh and concerns. And besides, it seems to be a sharing among "persons" who are totally spiritual and perfect. It is, after all, a divine communion that barely affects us.

For these reasons, many people find the idea of the Trinity to be of no interest. We hear it mentioned as a relic of religious belief, but one that has little bearing on our everyday lives. Maybe it is helpful to members of religious communities, who have their basic needs taken care of and can afford the luxury of thinking about these things. In their world, there may be room for the search for perfection and for talk of impenetrable mysteries and "otherworldly" things.

Thinking about the Trinity would appear to be superfluous, hardly worth spending time on in the light of the anguished cries of so many, many people threatened by hunger, disease, unemployment, war, and meaninglessness. The Trinity seems to have nothing to do with abandoned children, landlessness, women's oppression, the neglect of indigenous people and blacks, and the extermination of children and young people.

In one sense, people who express no interest in reflecting on the Trinity are right—especially when we use obscure language that refers to traditional, arcane notions unrelated to everyday life, notions that do nothing to help us survive or to build a spirituality capable of sustaining and enlivening us. These seem to be notions that hearken back to former times; they undoubtedly reflect the doubts and struggles of other times and other historical contexts.

Despite our own difficulties with traditional understandings of the Trinity, we also meet many people who are perfectly at ease with the traditional religious notions they were taught as children. They are apprehensive about questioning their faith and do not want to be forever stirring up and rearranging their inner selves. They stick to one tradition and treat it as an absolute; they do not reflect on historical change or on the ways in which their own faith life might need to change. They often identify the essence of the Christian faith with certain religious and cultural practices that have been handed down to them. I know such persons will have great difficulty accepting a different kind of theological reflection, but despite this I must continue to move forward, seeking alternative paths.

I would like to begin experiencing and reflecting on the Trinity by using a methodology that differs from the traditional one. Although I always keep theological reflection in mind, my methodology has much in common with the philosophy of religion. For a clear and engaging theological work that integrates feminism and the formal theological tradition, see chapter 10 of Elizabeth Johnson's *She Who Is*.[1]

For my purposes here, I will not refer to a history of trinitarian theology that begins with the church fathers and surveys later writings. Rather, I will explore the possibility of a different kind of thinking that can stimulate reflection, a kind of thinking based on what are regarded as "givens," or basic assumptions, within our tradition. For this exploration, I propose an itinerary to be pursued using an investigative method that suits the kind of ecofeminism I am developing in this book. The inquiry includes the following lines of inquiry: exploring what, in human experience, is related to trinitarian language; examining religious language and its crystallization in religious institutions; and reconstructing trinitarian meanings and celebrating life.

What Human Experience Is Described by Trinitarian Language?

In this part of my reflection, I would like to move discussion of the Trinity beyond its christological significance within our tradition. As we know, the creation of trinitarian theology is linked to the affirmation of the divinity of Jesus of Nazareth and the consequent affirmation of one divine nature in three persons.[2] Consistent with the ecofeminist epistemology, or way of knowing, and the reflections on the human person and God that I developed earlier, I propose that we seek a logical and existential form of reflection. I would like to detheologize the issue of the Trinity as much as possible, so that we can understand the reasons that originally prompted us to speak of it at all. Nevertheless, the issue is undoubtedly theological, because it touches on the very meaning of our lives. The point is that we need to discover the Trinity's relevance above and beyond a theology based on eternal substances and essences.

THE WONDER OF BEING HUMAN

Before I speak of the Trinity, I would like to offer a few words about the wonder of being human. I want to remind readers that human beings are a fruit of the long process in the evolution of life itself. Life evolved for millions and millions of years before the creation of the species to which we belong and which we call human. Within humanity, life continues to be created. It develops, folds back, and reveals itself in differing cultures and economic, political, social, and cultural organizations. Life itself led humanity to arise from within the whole creative evolutionary process, which is both earthly and cosmic.

The human race itself carries on this creative expression of life, both in itself and in its works. Participating in the creative evolution of life, we re-create ourselves. This is manifested in our ability to reflect and love, in our ethical behavior, and in all the other capabilities that make us what we are.

For this reason, we must not be afraid to affirm that all we "produce," whether it be knowledge, art, or relationships—even when it is destructive or alienating—is part of our effort to understand ourselves, to transform ourselves, and to respond as adequately as we can to the challenges life places in our paths. In the final analysis, these challenges are the very situations in which we find ourselves in the course of our personal and collective history.

Living within the context of nature as a whole, we have gradually accumulated significant learnings. We have responded, for example, to the challenge of rivers that stretched before us, separating one place from another: We learned to build bridges. To move on water, we built boats, then ships. To cross great distances, we built airplanes, and so on. We learned to closely examine our human experience, as well as the lives of insects, animals, and plants; and thus we found ways of living and developing our creativity as we responded to the challenges posed by each new situation.

Our significant learnings led us to discover the social causes of poverty among our peoples, and then to formulate hypotheses aimed at explaining and interpreting history and responding with concrete actions. Our significant learnings also led us to cultivate a sense of wonder and perplexity in the face of the astounding order that marks all of reality, and to speak of creative and organizing deities, of protective spirits. They prompted us to ponder the enigmas of evil, injustice, and hatred, and of the impunity of wrongdoers, and to speak of devils and of hell. And as we very well know, this process continues to unfold in different forms in different cultures, contexts, and eras.

We ourselves continually re-create the life that is within us. Human culture, in its multiple artistic and literary expressions, bears witness to our admirable creativity. This creativity also exists, albeit in a different form, in the vegetable and animal worlds. We have often been taught, however, that these "other worlds" exercise little creativity. The real reason for this attitude is that we always think of creativity in human terms and judge everything else on that basis. It would be helpful if human beings would stop once in a while to reflect on the creativity that is manifest in, say, an orange seed: the memory present in this small, vital center; its ability to develop when conditions are favorable and to adapt to different soils and situations, to become a tree and produce flowers and fruit, and then, once again, seeds. Its creativity is surely not the same as human creativity, but it clearly participates in the ongoing and awesome creativity of the universe.

Within this perspective, I would like to talk about what we human beings are. We did not simply devise ways of better adapting to the environmental conditions surrounding us; we also created belief systems—myths for explaining the universe; rituals, celebrations, and organizations. What I am trying to say, very concretely, is that it was not overnight that human beings came up with the idea of a Supreme Being, or of, for example, the divinity of the sun. These notions arose among various peoples and are the fruit of a slow evolutionary process in which, little by little, human beings thoughtfully worked out a sense of the meaning of their lives. They began by offering tentative answers to questions about their origins, and also began making sense of their fears, formulating explanations for them and redirecting them. They began to seek the causes of all things: They tried out hypotheses, confirming some and discarding others. Our ideas about the things that surround us, about ourselves and the universe, did not appear out of nowhere; they did not drop miraculously out of the sky or spring up magically from the earth. They are the fruit of a slow maturation, of thousands of years of gestation and continual transformation; in their many and complex meanderings, they have often been invisible even to us.

The seed planted in the depths of the earth goes through a complex process of transformation, of changes in life and in death, before it breaks through the soil's surface. And when we discover that the seed has become a small plant, we do not remember the long, arduous process it went through in the bowels of the earth and in its own innermost recesses, nor do we remember its multiple interactions with all the forces of nature.

The same is true of human beings. The things we produce, even the most precious among them—sublime creations such as our religious beliefs—arise from a long maturation process in which our concern for our immediate needs has always been present. Our extraordinary creativity acquired the ability to produce meanings capable of helping us live out this or that situation. But these meanings are not static realities. They are part of the dynamism of life, and thus they change as well. Of necessity, they undergo transformations in order to respond to life's demands and adapt to new situations as they arise.

We do not always reflect on these things. Often we see only the earth's surface and the things it produces instead of pondering other, more radical issues. We fail to reflect on roots: on the possible reasons for this or that belief, this or that hope. At times it is as if we were possessed by a fear of going farther, and we fail to see that if we do not go deeper, if we do not dig into the earth, turn it over, and fertilize it, not even the little plant that has appeared on the surface will be able to sustain itself unaided.

It is important, then, to get a clear sense that the human meanings of things come from ourselves, as does the human meaning of the entire universe. It is we ourselves who construct our interpretations—our science, our wisdom, and our knowledge. It is we ourselves who today affirm one thing and tomorrow correct what we have said. It is we who affirm the image of God as warrior-avenger or as tender and compassionate figure. It is we, through our ancestors and traditions, who have construed the Trinity as "three different persons in one God"; so, too, we can change our way of portraying it as we develop new perceptions.

We are beings who need meaning. We are like the inhabitants of a continent called Meaning, except that this continent is made up largely of constructs and interpretations that come from ourselves. As my poet friend Rubem Alves says somewhere, "People weave the hammocks they themselves lie in."

HUMAN WONDER AND THE TRINITY

Within the perspective developed here, I am ever more convinced that to begin a discussion of the Trinity by referring to the relationships among Father, Son, and Holy Spirit would be pretentious and would keep us in the realm of abstraction. In other words, to limit the Trinity to its Christian meaning alone is to forget the uncounted years of human history and the many cultural traditions that went before it.

Almost always, our temptation is to repeat, with very few modifications, the things we have learned or been told. It is as if this particular way of speaking about God, which was undoubtedly helpful for centuries and centuries, could not change today in the light of the new challenges history offers us. The human experience of relating to God did not begin with the concocting of theologies about the Father, the Son, and the Holy Spirit. It is much broader in scope, and that scope should penetrate ever more intensely into every fiber of our being.

Throughout our history, we have tied the symbol of the Trinity to the Christian world, identified it with the one God (the One and triune God), and regarded it as true both in its content and in its forms of expression. We would do well to remember, however, that other religious faiths use trinitarian symbols. The ancient Celts, for example, recognized both a masculine and a feminine countenance of God. The feminine image of God was for them a Trinity symbolized by three women, each of whom represented an essential aspect of human life.[3]

The Trinity, as well as the words "Father, Son, and Holy Spirit," are like a secret code that needs to be broken and translated anew. When I speak of them as a code, I mean that they do not refer us immediately to our own world of experience; rather, they demand an effort of interpretation and understanding. They are symbols that refer to life experiences, but their symbolism has grown hazy and been absolutized within a closed, eminently masculine, and more or less arcane theoretical system.

It is like a situation in which someone uses a word whose meaning we do not understand because it is not part of the world of our day-to-day experience. We need to find out what it means, what it refers to, and what experience it attempts to communicate. When we are able to break the code, we discover its meaning and understand what it is trying to tell us. We break the code the way we open a letter tightly sealed with beeswax; finally, we can read its concealed message.

In the words of the North American theologian Sandra Schneiders,[4] our religious imagination needs to be psychoanalyzed. It has reduced the Trinity to "an old man, a young man, and a bird." By using this piece of androcentric irony, Schneiders is trying to evoke a broader experience of God, one in which the metaphors we use can be understood as limited and local expressions of our lived experience. Symbol and metaphor are trying to express what we experience directly or only vicariously. Direct experience is always better than what we are told or have seen only in images.

Because the words "Father, Son, and Holy Spirit" are symbols specific to the Christian world's discourse on the Trinity, they need to be decoded. They must be continually reinterpreted so their great richness and meaning can manifest themselves. We need to grasp the fundamental experience that underlies the Christian belief that God is Father, Son, and Holy Spirit. Moreover, we need to ask whether these are the most useful expressions, the closest to our own experience as the community of Jesus' followers and the closest to our own lived experience of the Divine Mystery. This critical stance is not a denial of our Christian past, which did, despite the limitations inherent in all human creations, attempt to forge relationships embodying justice, love, and mercy among individuals and peoples.

According to Rosemary Radford Ruether's deep intuition,[5] the problem seems to be rooted in western culture—especially in those cultures built around a masculine and monotheistic image of God and of that Creator God's relationship with the cosmos and with all that exists. According to Ruether, this image symbolically reinforces men's dominant relationship with women, slaves, animals, and the entire earth.

Today we are entering a new moment in human and cosmic history, and at this new moment we need to reexamine our experience and reconstruct the meanings that are dear to us and help us live out our lives. Once again, I propose that in talking about the Trinity we start from our *experience*. For this reason, I ask, In our experience, what does the number three (trinity) suggest? Or, again, of what experience does it speak to us? These questions are important for the process of detheologizing that I am proposing.

According to sociologists, the number three is the starting point for social life.[6] In this sense, it makes sociology possible, because sociology is the science of social phenomena. The number three indicates plurality; it is the symbol of the inexhaustible richness and multiplex universality that characterize life. It is a convention that points to the fact that we are many, that life is many-sided and amazingly diversified. And there, in the exuberance of multiplicity, we can grasp what we call creativity. If everything were similar, static, and unmoving, we could not speak of creativity, evolution, or art.

The number three is unquestionably a symbolic convention. It could have been four or seven, for example, but in our culture there was an agreement to attribute to the number three the symbolism of unity in multiplicity. When we speak out of our experience, we speak from a starting point that is better known to us and more accessible to our everyday observation. We all experience diversity in our own lives. No flower is quite like any other; neither is any animal exactly like another. No human being is the same as another, and neither is any given behavior identical to any other. We are unquestionably similar, but everyone has his or her own specific traits, idiosyncrasies, and unique way of being and perceiving the world.

This perception of the multiplicity of things is as ancient as humanity; the pre-Socratic philosophers in Greece, who lived in the sixth century B.C.E., spent a great deal of time reflecting on this. They were amazed by the diversity and change found in everything, and sought ways of understanding this reality, which seemed to characterize all beings. For example, Heraclitus of Ephesus was impressed by the incessant flow of all things, and even in the life of the knowing subject. "We step and do not step in the same river twice; we are ourselves and are not ourselves," he said (Fragment 49).[7]

My question about the Trinity, then, refers first of all to human experience. I ask myself, What was or is the concrete human experience that leads me to speak of a Trinity? In other words, To what human experience is the Trinity related?

I see how often, in Christian theology, we use words and expressions that have very little to do with our everyday experience. Perhaps they did relate to lived experience in other times, but now they often seem meaningless. We mechanically repeat certain things we have learned, but we have little sense of what they refer to, or how and why they came into being.

In fact, we often find we have no adequate words to express our religious experience, or else we simply go on using traditional expressions we once were taught and are terribly afraid to give up. We identify these expressions with our personal faith, never realizing that the language of that faith also needs to be brought into harmony with our contemporary language and, above all, with our current, lived experience. We use a rather abstract discourse that has nothing to do with everyday speech or with day-to-day experience, as if religious experience always needed to be expressed in a specially coded language like that used in the sciences. Through acquired habit, we repeat things we do not understand, and we imagine that the things we do not understand are somehow deeper, more religious, and more trustworthy. It all might be part of what we have been told is the "mystery of faith," and this mystery of faith is something rather obscure, which people accept without question.

I think the great challenge we, and above all we women, face today is to achieve an existential understanding of what we are saying: to express, in a simple way that is our own and yet intelligible, the really significant experiences in our lives. We cannot go on being afraid to speak for ourselves, to draw on our own thought and experience, because it is in these that our faith is expressed and that our loves, our commitments, and our solidarity make themselves known.

Faith could be summed up as the essential values that support life: the values we take risks for, values that, in the experience of

Jesus and of his socioreligious movement, are made flesh in behaviors such as solidarity with the poor, defending life in spite of the many threats against it, condemning oppression, sharing, forgiving, and expressing mercy and praise. These are behaviors that could be called resurrection experiences, experiences of returning to life in every sense of the word.

In his book *Trinity, Society, and Liberation,* Leonardo Boff proposes a theological approach that begins with human community in order to speak of the Trinity.[8] In essence, he stays with classical trinitarian theology; but he introduces new elements, such as the feminine dimension within the Trinity. I think this is an important step forward in renewing our theological formulations. Meanwhile, using the ecofeminist perspective, I am setting out on a somewhat different path.

First of all, I would like to recall that although the poor use some religious expressions that refer to the Trinity, we cannot say, except in a few places scattered around the world, that there exists any special trinitarian understanding or devotion. People repeatedly make the sign of the cross, which is a trinitarian symbol, but there is no real trinitarian reflection. It is like a kind of compulsive habit: We make the sign of the cross as a protective gesture in certain specific situations—when we go by a church, for example, or when we begin or end a meeting, approach a dead body, or sense that we are in danger.

A more systematic reflection on the Trinity takes place among members of religious orders and in the more intellectual sectors of the various churches. Here we find a spiritual and theological concern, as well as what we might call trinitarian religious experiences. In these circles, the word "Trinity" is used more frequently.

As I suggested earlier, if we take the number three as a symbol of multiplicity, we will find that, in their lived lives, people experience the awesome multiplicity of things—of their plurality, the great differences among them, their bewildering transformations, their fragility and transience, and the blend of life and death, death and life. This multiple divergence is Trinity: It is symbolized by the number three, by the "three" that means, in practice, thousands and millions—in other words, infinity.

To become a part of society means to leave intrauterine life, marked by osmosis with the mother (a kind of unified duality), and to be faced with a multiform world, rife with differences, in which each of us is one among very many. Our first life experiences, then, are of multiplicity: of conflict among differences, of struggling to adjust to the presence of individuals who cannot be reduced to one's own ego. And this experience is deeply marked by suffering, by the pain of difference, by competitiveness, by the struggle for survival, by the desire to be or have what others are or have, by the masks we gradually put up in approaching our human relationships and through which we create barriers of all kinds. This is our experience. And it is precisely on the basis of this experience that human beings think of God as different, imagining the deity as superior to all the relativity ingrained in our own makeup. And because we experience plurality in pain, in interior division, in fear, in suffering, and in the precariousness of joy, we look for one God who is above the multiplicity that marks us, a God who unifies in one single being all the diversity that is essential to our nature. We imagine that the One is not subject to our painful limitations and is able to overcome and integrate them.

And because we perceive God as God-for-us, or as starting from us, in Christian experience, as well as in other religious experiences, we speak of a Trinity or of divine triads. The Trinity is an expression of our history—of human history, which is both tragic and challenging—but it is a unified Trinity, as if in that unity we were expressing our own desire for harmony and communion with all that exists. It is a communion to which we aspire in the midst of tears, in the midst of the experience of pain and suffering. It is as if that Holy Trinity of which we speak were the expression of a transformed and harmonized plural world, one in which all suffering and pain are overcome, in which separation and division are subdued, in which every tear shall be wiped away; and in the end God, that is, the One, Love, is all in all.

The experience of the Trinity brings multiplicity and the desire for unity into a single and unique movement, as if they were phases of the same breath. "Trinity" is the name we give ourselves, a name that is the synthesis of our perception of our own expanded existence. "Trinity" is a language we build in an attempt to express our awareness of being a multitude and at the same time a unity. "Trinity" is the word that points to our common origin, our shared substance, our universal breathing within the immense diversity that surrounds each and every one of us, each unique and original creation, a path along the great road of life. "Trinity" is also a word about ourselves—about what we know and live out in our own flesh and our life stories.

For this reason, we need to turn to our everyday experience and verify in it the ground of our image of God. God is the ideal of every human person. To speak of God is to speak of every human being both as identical to and as unlike his or her own being, as similar and as different, as simultaneously in the self and outside the self. So our images of God are also multiple; they vary from one human culture to another. Our efforts to express these images are always poor; they are limited and metaphorical. Similarly, we need to see very clearly that we are not a reflection of the Trinity, as if it were a well-defined triune being up above us, existing in itself and for itself, in which we discover qualities and perfection as best we can from our position down below.

The Trinity is not a being in itself, to be portrayed by us as if we were describing the qualities of an apple or a cashew. The Trinity we worship lives in us and we live in it. The fact that we understand it is born of our own human experience, of our own inner being, as if the Trinity is infinitely greater than we are. It unfolds in an ideal of perfection, in life's aspirations, and in the search for meaning. In it, we meet ourselves; in it, we see ourselves; and in it, we are all that is. In speaking of it, we speak of ourselves. In attempting to describe it, we describe ourselves. The Trinity is a language, a metaphor that seeks to explain the unexplainable, the ineffable.

The thread of trinitarian experience and of the language that attempts to express it is born, then, out of our own inner being, like the web is born out of the spider. But unlike the spider, we have become accustomed within patriarchal society to believe that the web does not come from ourselves but exists in itself, outside of us, and that it has revealed its inner pattern to us. To affirm the contrary—to say we are like spiders who weave their own webs and then dwell in them—sounds like blasphemy, treason, a devaluing of the mystery of God. It appears to bring with it a kind of autonomy for which we could be blamed or even could blame ourselves. To say we are spiders, and so is the rest of the universe, would, for many people, be tantamount to falling into the pantheism that is so harshly vilified and condemned in our religious tradition. "But we are not God, and neither is the world God," they vehemently argue. They cannot see that we exist within that great Divine Mystery that unfolds and is revealed in manifold ways, and that what we know of it is only the fruit of our experience and our striving to interpret it by seeking its meaning.

Some people would argue that trinitarian discourse has nothing to do with Jesus' experience, and that, as Christians, we should not use it. Christian language is grounded in Jesus' experience, as when he cried, "Abba, Father," or when he said he and the Father were one, or when he promised to send the Holy Spirit. We might ask, however, what aspect of Jesus' experience coincides with that language. What was the experience out of which he said what he said—granting, also, that we are not sure he did in fact say it? Was this, perhaps, what the disciples or the Gospel writers experienced and what led them to express themselves as they did? They probably never considered the philosophical and theological refinements that would be devised later on. In fact, it is hard to know what really happened; in talking about these experiences, all we have to go on is a great number of hypotheses and interpretations.

We need to recognize that there is a very tenuous relationship between Jesus' experiences and our discourse about them. What we surely understand better about Jesus is his merciful spirit, his compassion for human suffering and the paths to which he pointed, leading us in the direction of sisterhood and brotherhood. And this is what is most important in Christian life.

In this sense, it is not enough to quote a few of Jesus' words in order to formulate our statements on the Trinity. We need to rely on our own experience—on our personal and collective stories, on the values we hold fast, on our tenderness and compassion, and on the questions we ask ourselves today.

This path could open us to find ourselves, to a new birth or a rebirth symbolized by baptism of fire or baptism in the Spirit. Baptism of fire is what we go through as a result of our inner faithfulness to ourselves. It is a reality that envelops us by virtue of our rediscovery of our deepest self. Within that rediscovery we are reborn in God; we are reborn to the earth, to the cosmos, to history, and to service to one another in the construction of human relationships grounded in justice and mutual respect.

Religious Language and Its Crystallization in Institutions

I have suggested that the Trinity is also a language, a way of expressing our characteristic inner and outer experience of unity and multiplicity. Let us explore this idea further.

THE TRINITY AND LANGUAGE

To say the Trinity is a language means that through it we express our shared experience of transcendence by means of our different cultures and linguistic expressions. The Trinity is present to some extent in various religious creeds, expressed in contrasting cultural modalities but constantly embracing the theme of multiplicity and unity. Perhaps this is one of the reasons we do not cast this expression aside, but instead try to give it a more comprehensive meaning.

In our religious formation we were not always trained to respect pluralism or to perceive the similarities within different experiences. It happens that the world of religion, in its organized forms, is a world that looks for stability, that seeks to strengthen itself by winning new converts and tries to impose its will using so-called spiritual power. To some extent it fears change: It fears the true relativity of things, their fragility, their finiteness, and the transformations inherent in all life processes.

The world of patriarchal religion took symbolic language, which expresses all that is deepest in human beings, and eliminated its symbolic, musical, and poetic forms along with its language of inference, of inflection, and of deep aspirations. It petrified this language and went on to endorse the idea that what it says exists in the most literal sense.

Those religious powers have then gone on to condemn or declare among the saved those who are unfaithful or faithful to their formal institutions and their discourse—that is, their formal expression of thought—both of which have become ossified or sclerotic because their language has stagnated. They blame, harass, and torment those who have begun to come together in seeking the unending changeability of life, its exhilarating richness and transformations, and the astounding interrelatedness among all things.

In the world of patriarchal religion, we have turned our backs on the richness of symbolism and seized upon well-defined concepts. We have turned our backs on the present and held to doctrines that have no contemporary meaning. We have turned our backs on the shifting and relational world that characterizes us and defended the stability of ideas and dogmas. We have held back the evolution of meanings, we have imprisoned symbols, and we have tried to dominate the real. We cling to the illusion that, in this way, we can defeat the powers of change, flexibility, and creativity that are inherent in all vital processes.

We are slaves to language, and, above all, consecrated religious language. We behave as if it were the only one all people should adhere to in order to be faithful to God's will. In my view, every time we accept this kind of submission, we drift far from the dynamic meaning of the Trinity. We fall into a kind of coded monism—a view that all phenomena may be reduced to one principle. This monism proclaims domination by an Absolute that ignores the situation of the earth, of history, and of ever-vigorous human freedom.

Unfortunately, throughout Christian history, our faith in the Trinity has been mainly a faith in three set entities, in three persons who, despite their intercommunication, hold fast to their own abstract independence and their enormous power over us. The Trinity has been presented as the absolute, the totally different, the altogether superior, independent, and perfect Being. This teaching is unquestionably the fruit of a dualistic concept of the world and of human beings that is ubiquitous in traditional Christian theology and especially in catechetical teachings.

Today, if we are to recover the dynamism of the Trinity, we need to recover the dynamism of our own existence—even at the risk of not managing to formulate our ideas in clear and precise terms. Our great challenge is to accept the insecurity involved in discussing what is real. We must seek only the fragile security that comes from dealing with the here and now, with everyday life, with our own experience and with our questions, heeding that wise phrase from the Hebrew world that tells us that sufficient to the day is its own task.

From this perspective, then, the Trinity is not three different persons living in a heaven we cannot point to. It is not three persons different from one another the way we humans differ as persons. The Father, Son, and Holy Spirit are not of divine stuff as opposed to our human stuff; rather, they are relationships—relationships we human beings experience and express in metaphorical rather than metaphysical terms.

A simple example: We say that love is a relationship, but we do not make love into a "person" or thing we call "love." If we were to say love is "a being," we would be on the metaphysical level—on the level of philosophical discussion about beings in themselves. Thus we would have to stop thinking about love metaphorically or symbolically.

However, if I should happen to call someone "my love," it would signify that my relationship with that person is tender, kind, and loving, and that his or her actions showed solidarity, readiness to serve, and so on.

Therefore we need to reaffirm that the Trinity is the expression of the Mystery, both one and multiple, that envelops us, that has made us what we are, and in which we participate ceaselessly. We need to get beyond the idealistic and mechanistic thinking we habitually fall into when we speak of the Trinity, thinking that operates as if the Trinity were a kind of "being out there," operating independently of ourselves. The Trinity is relationship, after all: an existential experience in ourselves and in the world.

THE TRINITY: FATHER, SON, AND HOLY SPIRIT

As we have said, the Trinity is a symbol, a metaphor—an image that suggests something other than what literal language can offer. The metaphor refers to a reality we call transcendent, that is, beyond that which can be spoken of. The word "transcendence," as I use it here, is the affirmation that words cannot fully express what we understand and live out.

By using symbolic language and the images appreciated by the ecofeminism we are developing, we can begin to broaden the notions of Father, Son, and Holy Spirit. I wish to point out that the source of life is in all of us, that it is our common origin and dwelling place (Father/Mother); that we are therefore daughters and sons derived from that same source; and that it is out of this same relational energy source that we are linked with all that exists (Spirit) and are able to stand in solidarity and be merciful, tender, just, impassioned, and awestruck in the face of the wonder that has fashioned us.

Father, Son, and Holy Spirit are symbolic expressions; as such they are a language that bespeaks experience. They refer to the profound intuition that all of us participate, along with everything that exists, in the same Breath of Life. We have a common origin. We participate in the same evolutionary process. In order to say that we all share the same breath, it is not necessary to go on using a trinitarian language that is limited to masculine experience. For this reason, we can open out or broaden our notion of Trinity and allow other languages to emerge as the fruit of the experiences we are having at present. I do not want to propose a new way of using the language that speaks of our origins and of our everyday lives, but I do want at least to open the possibility that we can say it using our own style, within our own cultural idiom, and according to the way we feel it.

Despite the undeniable benefits they have afforded us, centuries of Christian catechesis have crystallized and petrified religious experience and its corresponding symbolic language, perhaps to the point of sclerosis. As I use the expression, to crystallize something is to make it rigid and difficult to rejuvenate, to protect it from change and isolate it from our present experience. And it was this process of crystallization, which is a common human phenomenon, that influenced our trinitarian experience and reduced it to a conceptual system dealing only with the relationships among three divine persons in terms historically defined by males.

Today we are called to refashion the meanings of our lives: to simplify them, democratize them, and allow them to be pluralistic. This final reflection invites us to go on to the third step we proposed at the beginning of our journey.

Reconstructing Trinitarian Meanings and Celebrating Life

We use the word "reconstruction" when a piece of land, a human relationship, a city, or even a society needs to remake itself—to re-create itself, to renew its relational life. This becomes necessary because something has happened that has weakened an edifice, a relationship, or a bond of friendship. Although the new construct maintains something of the old, it should still be regarded as new, the fruit of our present efforts and meaningful for our time. I would like to offer you a somewhat tentative effort at rebuilding, in this sense, trinitarian meanings—a reconstruction that is demanded by our current historical situation.

RECONSTRUCTING MEANING

I want to remain on the level of concrete human experience, of our everyday lives. On this basis I will try to offer a more adequate and understandable account of things that are important in our lives. Within this perspective, I would like to offer five reflections on this reconstruction: the Trinity in the *cosmos*; the Trinity on *earth*; the Trinity in *relationships among peoples and cultures*; the Trinity in *human relationships*; and the Trinity in *every person*.

This list undoubtedly suggests that everything is Trinity, that all things are part of that vital and intimate relationship between multiplicity and unity that marks both our character and our makeup. This perspective opens us to realities beyond Christian experience. We generally have tended to base our theories about the Holy Trinity on the Bible, on ancient philosophies, on the debates surrounding heresies and religious conflicts, and on systems of established power. Speaking from the point of view of the philosophy of religion, I cannot, as I explained before, limit my theological work to the traditional trinitarian perspective. I want to carry out this reflection within a broader anthropological perspective that will allow us to see how much the great variety of human groups have in common when they deal with the earth and with the universe. I think this approach is fundamental in today's world.

I want to work toward a better understanding of our experience and of the ways we interpret it, so we can penetrate to the core of human life's religious dimension and quietly leave behind the triumphalism that has characterized our theology and our Christian behavior. For the sake of life's survival and that of human groups everywhere, we have to assume an attitude of humility and deep respect for varying cultural forms and for the different ways in which the mystery of life is articulated.

I am convinced of the importance of our personal and collective experience in recovering our deepest beliefs and the values we hold dear, values that underlie the meaning of our lives and are the foundation for dialogue among different peoples and cultures. I am also convinced that, despite our obvious differences, when we make contact with the deepest level of every human being's experience we will find it is grounded in a single, shared mystery that invites us all to act in ways that express communion, equality, and reciprocity.

The Trinity in the Cosmos

"This universe is a single, multiform energetic unfolding of matter, mind, intelligence and life."[9] So says Brian Swimme, a United States astrophysicist who has worked hard to tell the story of the universe in empirical language. He tries to show that, as we approach the end of this century, humanity has acquired the ability to tell the story of the universe itself. This is a fundamental step in coming to understand our shared history and in the effort to create a new relationship with the earth and the cosmos, and among all peoples.

At this point, I merely want to draw your attention to the unique and multiform structure of the universe. In symbolic and metaphorical terms, we could call it a trinitarian structure. By "trinitarian structure" we mean the reality that constitutes the entire cosmos and all life-forms—a reality marked simultaneously by multiplicity and by unity, by the differences among all things, and by their articulated interdependence. Stars, galaxies, heavenly bodies, planets, satellites, the atmosphere, the seas, rivers, winds, rain, snow, mountains, volcanoes—all are expressions of the manifold creativity of the universe. They are profoundly interdependent and interrelated. They are diversity and unity, existing and interrelating in a unique and single movement of continuing creativity.

This cosmic trinitarian structure is in a certain sense independent of human beings; at the same time, we are the only ones able to name it, to understand it, to stand in awe before it, and to recognize ourselves as an integral part of it. Because of our awareness of our great and extraordinary dependence on the cosmos, then, we are the only living beings capable of calling our bodies cosmic bodies.

The Trinity on Earth

Plants, animals, forests, mountains, rivers, and seas form the most diverse combinations in the most remote and varied places. They attract one another, couple with one another, blend with one another, destroy one another, and re-create themselves in pale or exuberant colors. They grow and feed on one another's lives, transforming and adapting to one another, dying and rising in many ways within the complex life process to which we all belong. In its stunning mutations, the earth sometimes threatens us and sometimes awes us, sometimes makes us shiver and at other times inspires shouts of joy. Spinning around the sun and on its own axis, it creates days and seasons and brings forth the most varied forms of life.

The earth as Trinity! The trinitarian earth is a movement of continuous creativity, unfolding processes of creation and destruction, expressions of a single vital process. We need only think of the succession of geological eras, the birth of the continents, the transformation of seas into deserts, the flowering of forests, and the emergence of manifold expressions of vegetable and animal life in order to grasp the immense creative force in which we are immersed and of which we are an integral part.

In the preceding section, we saw the trinitarian structure of the cosmos; now, using strictly empirical observation, we have gone on to detect the trinitarian structure of the planet earth. We can rightly call ourselves terrestrials, earth-beings. But in calling ourselves terrestrials, we accept the responsibility of knowing and loving the earth as a living being, and of refraining from manipulating its secrets and destroying it.

The Trinity in Relationships among Peoples and Cultures

Whites and blacks, indigenous peoples, Asiatics and mestizos—all with different languages, customs, statures, and sexes—make up the awesome and diverse human symphony in which, once again, multiplicity and unity are constitutive expressions of the single vital process that sustains us all.

In its complex process of evolution, life brings about the variety of human groups and invites us to contemplate the exuberance of our own diversity. If we accept this diversity as part of the trinitarian structure itself, and take it seriously as the basic makeup of all beings, there is no way to justify the idea of any being's superiority or inferiority. What we have now is cosmic citizenship. We are merely "cosmics," terrestrials, members of the cosmos and of the earth; we need one another and can live only on the basis of a community of being and of interdependence among our differences.

I am convinced that if we were to try to develop this idea of cosmic and terrestrial citizenship, we could more easily overcome the different strains of racism, antiracism, xenophobia, exclusion, violence, and sexism that are rife in our cultures. A new sense of citizenship needs to be born and grow in us, without denying the national affiliations that are still part of our history.

The era of national citizenship, understood here as adherence to a specific nationality to the detriment of others, has not yet ended; but it is already heralding the frightening consequences of looking at human beings in terms of systems of mutual protection and destruction. The plurality that makes us a human species is Trinity: It is the symbolic expression of a single and multiple reality that is an essential component of our living tissue. This plurality is essential if human life itself is to continue, and if the different races and cultures are to develop, support one another, and enter into communion.

The Trinity in Human Relationships

Human relationships are marked by the interaction among "I," "you," and "he" or "she." I would say that even in the experience of solitude, my solitude is an interior "multitude," an uproar, a music made up of many tones. In this sense, even solitude becomes a trinitarian metaphor. To understand the multiple solitude that is part of our makeup is to better understand the biological, psychological, and religious processes that are part of our lives.

When monks seek solitude, they are really seeking an encounter with their inner voice. Out of the babble of voices from within and without, they endeavor to listen to their own true selves. They need to be on an unending quest throughout their whole lives, because their and our deepest personal reality is interior, fleeting, and virtually inexpressible. Just what is this reality we call "I"? In fact, the "I" is an extraordinary conjunction of multiple meetings: of persons, experiences, traditions, and stories, put together in more or less unique form. We experience all this multiplicity in the unique personal reality we call "I."

Clearly, the search for our inner self is not the province of monks or sages alone; historically and socially, however, and above all in the past, these have been the people who remained mindful of and symbolized in their lives the fundamental dimension of encounter with oneself and with the whole.

We need to remember also that the feeling of solitude has many meanings, and that a given meaning will have a positive or negative impact on our psyche. Meanwhile, it seems true to say our solitude still implies a certain communion with the air, the sun, the earth, and the multitude of person who pass through—and have passed through—our lives. This communion, which is not always conscious, is the very condition of the possibility of speaking about solitude. Our solitude, then, is in this sense a trinitarian solitude, a solitude beyond our individuality, a personal solitude inhabited by multiplicity. Multiplicity, then, is the indispensable condition for the affirmation of our personal solitude.

Our individualistic society insists on affirming the almost total independence of the ego, and goes on cultivating in us the illusion of our individual omnipotence. On this it bases all its systems of economic competition and social exclusion. Today, many people are beginning to discover the inadequacy of this view. As we know, life is itself an open event. It only subsists when it is open to multiplicity, to diversity; it is only creative and dynamic when its vital components are allowed to come together. If we lacked any element—air, water, heat, minerals, plants, persons, affection, and so on—life could not continue within us.

The trinitarian mystery is also found in intimate, I-Thou relationships. We are I-Thou and mystery—the mystery of our presence to the world, to the universe, and to ourselves. We are the mystery of our stories, our traditions, and our questions. We are I, Thou, and mystery, and therefore Trinity, in the closeness and allure of a profound relationship that leads us to a deeper level of intimacy, of desire to know one another, of tender sharing. For this reason, knowing one another requires not only time, patience, and dialogue, but also a constant and challenging investment of ourselves. We are challenged to enter into a process of shared self-revelation, of unmasking ourselves, of manifesting an ever greater part of ourselves. We will find that what we reveal is drawn from those things that are known and unknown to ourselves, and therefore to others.

To affirm the Trinity as a symbol of our own being, at the same time one and multiple, is to allow diverse human groups and mystical experiences to meet, open up to one another, listen to one another, and discover the amazing similarity between our deepest experiences, even when these experiences are expressed in various languages and cultural contexts and by people who are entirely different from one another. This is an ancient challenge that humanity will have to keep on facing in the coming millennium. And beyond any doubt, the way we accept this challenge will determine the new path taken by men and women of all races and nations of the earth.

The Trinity in Every Person
On the basis of all we have said so far, we can easily see that for each one of us, personal circumstances are related to those of others and of the whole earth and the cosmos in a totally interdependent way. I am I, but at the same time I am thousands of lives and circumstances that have gone before me to weave and prepare for my personal life. I am myself, but I am also the countless lives that went before me. I am my ancestors, with their personal histories; their voices and traditions run through my veins. I am I, but my being goes beyond my individuality, beyond the personal story limited by the years of my own life. This does not mean I cannot call myself "I," as a person who is to a certain extent free and autonomous, who loves and hates and hopes. But it means that my personal reality, my autonomy, is always relational, "dependent on . . ."

For this reason, I can say that our own personal being is trinitarian: It is mysteriously multiple and at the same time it is one. And, most important, this extraordinary reality can be seen in the lives of all peoples; it is present in all biological functions, in all cultural and religious processes. This vision gives us a new worldview and a different anthropology, on the basis of which we see ourselves as persons who are of the earth and of the cosmos, participants in the extraordinary process of life's evolution. "The new heavens and the new earth" are always on the way: They were coming to be yesterday, they are coming to be today, and they will be on the way tomorrow. Heaven is not opposed to earth; it does not present itself as something superior or as the final aim of our efforts, the place in which we will at last enter into a state of divine peace and harmony.

This perspective opens us up to valuing our present life, and to struggling for all living things' right to realize, in themselves and in others, the possibilities that are their due.

Life after death, as we are accustomed to calling it, is part of the mysterious and sacred journey of life itself, a mystery that is beyond ourselves. We can say very little about this. We can only report what we deeply sense: that out of the dissolution of one living form there arise thousands of others; that one life nourishes a sequence of others; and that in the end our living is part of this process, part of the dissolution and recomposition of life.

Some readers may be a bit disappointed that I have not spoken more of heaven, of the angels, of the embrace of the Father who awaits us at the gates of paradise, of that joyful reunion with those we have loved or would like to have known. These dreams belong to the present; they are the dreams of children or adults, dreams drawn from our religious education, dreams that have at some moment consoled or comforted us. But the mystery of life, in its long and sacred journey, will not permit anyone to take possession of its unfathomable ways, of its sequences of transformation or its unforeseen courses of events. People can dream, as they do when they take turns making up stories; but in the long run, very simply, it will be what it will be. Human knowing cannot see beyond the "cloud of unknowing" that envelops us.

Therefore we need to trust, to welcome this reality as a part of the gift of being here, today, participating intensely in this greatest of mysteries and struggling for the dignity of all persons' lives today. For this reason, the "ancient" newness we dimly foresee today needs to gradually become flesh in us. It is like a collective pregnancy—we get a sense of the new life being generated within our own flesh, and we welcome the fact that, on account of this life, the world will never be the same again.

THE TRINITY, GOOD, AND EVIL

In traditional theological discourse on the Trinity, only its absolute goodness was mentioned. Evil was never included: On the contrary, it was inconceivable to juxtapose the goodness of the triune God with human evil.

However, if we develop a more holistic reflection based on *relatedness*, we will be tempted to think differently. There is an inherent logic in the reflection we are developing, even though culturally and existentially we have been accustomed to thinking and feeling in a different way.

If we say the Trinity envelops all as an expression of our single and multiple reality, we will also have to include evil within it. I will attempt to offer only a few thoughts on this, in the conviction that we will have to return to this topic at another time. In this reflection, the issue of evil seems inevitable, not only when we speak of the celebration of the Trinity but also because we are living in difficult times. The powers of evil, as we sometimes call them, appear to have the most energy—and, in fact, to be winning out.

Human cultures have always been able to distinguish immediately between good and evil—to construct moral systems that affirm the superiority of the good and identify it with a superior power—and to see this power as present in the human or even as transcending the human. In the Christian tradition, as we know, evil has always been opposed to good. God made all things good, and evil appeared as an accident. This is the case in all interpretations written, on the basis of Genesis and other biblical texts, of the issue of evil.[10]

The popular religious imagination even created the devil, a being opposed to the infinite goodness of God, and hell, a place of loss and punishment, as opposed to heaven, the place of salvation and reward. Although they have always been present in human life, evil and suffering have been unceasingly combated. It has never been enough to identify evil; it has been necessary to fight against it.

We have always had difficulty reconciling the goodness of God with suffering and injustice. What we might call ethical evil, the evil committed by ourselves, is always reflected in the evil undergone by others in an endless spiral of vengeance and suffering, much of it unnecessary. The presence of evil has always been regarded as absurd, and all moral systems sought ways not only of healing evil and the suffering that flows from it but of preventing people from committing it. Good and evil have their histories, or their sociocultural conditioning, and the various forms of human behavior have been organized on the basis of a certain consensus regarding them.

In the Christian tradition, God has always been on the side of goodness. God is in fact the Supreme Good. Therefore, in those dramatic and inscrutable situations in which evil seems to win out, God is always "cleared" or exempted from any direct responsibility. In some situations, we have gone as far as to admit that God could punish out of love, in order to teach us to follow the path of goodness. This would be God's instructive role, God's task as a good teacher. Meanwhile, the greatest responsibility is attributed to human freedom and God generally remains "innocent." We needed this innocence so that God could still be God.

The ancient problem of evil is with us today as never before, above all because, as I pointed out above, we see an increase in the destruction of persons, of groups, and of the earth itself. Our society seems ever less capable of devising formulas that permit dignified human sharing and the possibility of survival on the earth. We have the impression that our present world, despite its theories, its analyses, and its designs, turns ever more often to violence and exclusion in order to solve its problems. This in turn has brought about a growing wave of destruction, one greater than at any other time in history. No one can ignore the premeditated genocide, the "death squads," or the covert training of armies by great world powers.

Our most usual problem-solving methods have been force, weapons, brutal institutionalized violence, the murderous elimination of others, and an "every man for himself" attitude. Returning evil for evil has become a virtual rule of life for many individuals and social groups. Look, for example, at popular support for the death penalty and, in Latin America, the systematic elimination of prisoners or even delinquent youths. Look at the interventionist behavior of large countries, which leave impoverished countries without the slightest chance of survival with dignity. Look at the encouragement of racism by very powerful white groups.

In this context, even as religions speak of God's goodness and mercy, or perhaps of the punishments of hell, they become ever less capable of mitigating the wave of violence that subsists and seems to grow within us. Our age-old discourse on good and evil no longer touches hearts; it no longer offers the satisfying explanations it once did, and it no longer sustains us in the face of growing depravity. The benign will of God seems irrelevant to the struggle for survival and the spirit of unrestrained profiteering. God "just doesn't help us the way God used to." The rich appeal to God to protect their riches. The wretched of the earth, the hungry, the landless, the unemployed—those who thirst for justice—feel ever more acutely the silence of God even when, "hoping beyond all hope," they continue to speak of God's justice.

Traditional religious discourse seems ever farther from daily needs. Despite this, a variety of Pentecostal groups, mixing fakery with naive credulity and keeping people captive and enslaved to so-called divine powers (and above all to their own representatives), gain more and more adherents among the poor.

An ecofeminist, trinitarian vision of the universe and of humanity does not identify evil, destruction, and suffering as realities that are outside ourselves and need to be eliminated by the use of violence, nor does it say they should be accepted as "God's will." Rather than pointing to "the other" as the source of evil, it recognizes that what we call evil is in ourselves; in a certain sense, evil is also our body. Evil is a relationship we ourselves construct. It leads to the unraveling of the entire fabric of human life.

An ecofeminist, trinitarian view of the universe places us instead at the very energy source of all that exists. At the same time, it makes a distinction: On one hand is the creative-destructive process inherent in the evolution of life itself; on the other is moral evil, evil defined in ethical terms. The latter refers to human evil, the evil worked by ourselves: actions that, when combined with our inherent frailty, can make us murderers of life in all its multiple expressions.

When we speak of human beings, we always speak in terms of good and evil. But when we speak of the cosmos, of the universe, we need to speak of forces that are simultaneously creative and destructive. This constitutive reality of the universe, these positive and negative poles, so to speak (we use these terms with an awareness of the limitations of our language), are inseparable in all the life processes. The birth of our solar system, for example, required the destruction of others. The appearance of a desert region may mean the death of a river. The use of fish as food may require the destruction of many of them, and so on. The life of one animal depends on the death of another on which it feeds.

It is we human beings who refer to the processes of creation and destruction as good or evil, because we always speak in terms of what is good or bad for ourselves. But seeking insight into this essential aspect of life will help us better understand our own human existence. For example, it is we who say a typhoon brought about evil and destruction. It is we who speak of a murderous flood or a death-dealing ray. It is we who say a drought brought about disaster and caused an exodus from the countryside to the large cities. It is we who say that a fox is bad because it ate a chicken. It is we who call a cobra evil when its poison enters our system.

We always speak of evil in human terms, even when we talk about animals or of nature as a whole. The fact that we are the "consciousness," or the thinking process, of the universe leads us to label things as good or evil according to the way they affect us. These kinds of statements were made long ago by ancient Greek philosophers and by many medieval Christian thinkers, although their contexts were different from ours. Today we need to have another look at these reflections in the light of our contemporary historical situation and our more global and articulated sense of the life processes.

Ethical evil, however, is evil wrought by human beings. On one hand, it arises from the dynamics of life itself and from our human condition, which includes weakness, dependence, and interdependence. On the other, the Christian tradition has always taught that evil actions arise out of our selfishness and the excesses of our passions; from our selfishness, greed, and arrogance.

But ethical evil also results from our very limited understanding of ourselves, from our individualistic and anthropocentric relationships with all other beings. We have acquired a highly developed sense of our individuality—of our superiority or inferiority—but we have very little sense of our collective nature, or of the way in which our communion with everything else assures our survival and shared happiness.

Because of our narrow affirmation of our personal, racial, religious, and even class identity, we have ended up creating systems to protect ourselves from one another, systems based on greed or on the perceived superiority of those who regard themselves as "the strongest" or "the finest." These systems have not allowed us to perceive the ephemeral nature of our individual lives and projects. Instead, we exalt the individual and regard the most powerful, wealthy, or brilliant individuals as absolutes, as quasi divinities to be protected against all the ebbs and flows of history. Human intervention has produced imbalances in the whole network of our relationships with the earth, and in recent centuries it has guided our evolutionary process toward a frightening catastrophe.

It is out of this perspective that we have developed the idea of a person who is God above history and who presides over it. This in turn led us to construct an image of a just divinity somewhere outside our world: a powerful deity often fashioned in the image of the powerful of this world. This God, who is also an "individual," is always just, strong, and good—the very opposite of our fragility and depravity. This is the God of theodicy, a God who is very difficult to reconcile with the tragic reality of human history. It is a God whose goodness "in itself" must always be affirmed and defended, as if in defending the goodness of a Supreme Being we could guarantee an escape from our own tragic iniquity.

The idea of this unfailingly good divinity prompts us to ask endless questions in the face of the variety of blind alleys into which it seems to lead us. It makes us think of the book of Job and the discussions of his friends, who seek possible explanations for his suffering.

In the final analysis, there are no convincing answers. Evil continues to be part of the human enigma and the enigma of all living things, part of the enigma of the cosmos itself. In a way, the dramatic historical spectacle keeps repeating itself. The poor continue to bend their knees before this deity (God), begging for mercy, clemency, and help in satisfying their most basic needs, harboring the spark of hope in the midst of their everyday lives. They act toward this God much the way they act toward the powerful of this world, hoping to be treated with consideration and to be left some prospect of earning their livelihoods with dignity. The poor are slaves of many masters, and, by analogy, also of a supreme Master.

Might it be possible to leave behind this crude and highly patriarchal, hierarchical, materialistic, individualistic, dependent, and class-biased understanding of God and of the Trinity? To answer in the affirmative would seem to me an essential step both for the present and for the sake of the future.

This is above all a wisdom path, a spiritual path, a personal and collective empowerment that opens us to a wider and freer perspective. By "spiritual path," I mean a path that transforms our inner convictions, a demanding path that goes beyond adherence to a political party's program or obedience to a code of canon law. It is a spiritual path because it is the path of the Spirit, which blows freely where it will; no one can hamper its movement. It is a spiritual path because it is the path of God as *relatedness*, the breath of life in each and every one of us.

We are constantly being invited to return to our roots: to commune with the earth, with all peoples, and with all living things, and to realize that transcendence is not a reality "out there," isolated, "in itself," superior to all that exists, but a transcendence within us, among us; in the earth, in the cosmos, and everywhere. This is a transcendence that is here and now, among those who are like us and different from us, among plants and animals, rivers and seas. This transcendence invites us to reach beyond the limits of our selfishness and respond to our call to a new collective ethical behavior centered on saving all of life. This transcendence is a canticle, a symphony unceasingly played by the infinite creativity of *life*.

What, then, is evil, in this traditional yet novel perspective? The answer is no more than an approximation, one that involves all the paradoxes that are inherent in this issue, paradoxes that have always tormented us and forced us to reflect.

Within this perspective, what we call human evil is the unbalanced situation in which we find ourselves: our millennial thirst for individual power and our millennial hunger to eat more and more while preventing others from consuming their rightful share. Our species' evil is this excessive desire to take possession of life and make it our own. It is the appropriation of goods—and also of other persons, whom they regard to be of secondary importance—by individuals and groups, the self-appointed proprietors of the earth.

Evil is the growing dysfunctionality in both personal and social life that leads me to the narcissistic cultivation of my own individuality and my ecclesiastical, political, or business interests. Evil is the excess or abundance that is held back and hoarded. Whether it be food, land, power, knowledge, or pleasure, it remains in the hands of the owners of capital: those who, with the support of their direct and indirect accomplices, present themselves as veritable gods upon the earth.

Evil is the idolatry of the individual, of the "pure" race, of the messianic people, of the empire that dominates by insinuating itself into everything—even into people's inner beings—inducing them to believe in their own inferiority. Evil is the ascendancy of one sex over another, its domination over all personal, social, political, and economic realms. Evil is the domination and exploitation of the earth as a source of profit, as capital formation.

Evil is the proclamation and imposition of my gods as eternal and exclusive, capable of saving all of humanity. Evil is the claim that some people know the will of God and are commissioned to teach it as irrefutable dogma, while others are obliged to humbly recognize and accept their own ignorance.

Evil is plural and singular; present, past, and future.

Human evil is the evil that leaves us perplexed. It poses innumerable questions, many of them unanswerable. Cosmic "evil," on the other hand, is the creation-destruction process that is inherent in the universe and frightens us only when we suffer its consequences.

This two-faced evil is part of the Trinity we are and of the humanity and divinity we also are. This evil, then, is the negative aspect, the flow of destruction, of death and life, found everywhere in the universe, on earth, and among human persons. But this evil, which is perceived at the very heart of human experience, also bears extraordinary creative possibilities for the unfolding of our sensitivities and the opening of our inner being to that which is beyond ourselves.

In some way too, things that appear negative are an energy that is capable of developing within us the capacity for loving others: for bending to those who have fallen on the road, for taking in an abandoned child, for replanting a ravaged forest; for cleaning up a polluted river, for feeding animals during a time of drought. Out of the garbage we accumulate, a flower can bloom. Dry bones can return to life; the horror of war can become a cradle of compassion. We ourselves, and the whole universe, are made up of the same energy—an energy that is both positively and negatively charged. This very energy continually creates and re-creates the earth and human life.

Human history bears witness to the fact that the great gestures of mercy and tenderness have been born of dramatic, life-threatening situations. When another's pain becomes unbearable, it becomes my pain, and stimulates the birth of loving gestures. The Buddha, Jesus, Mary, Mohammed, Fātima (the daughter of Mohammed); the thousand Francises, Clares, and Teresas; the ever-present Severinas and Antonios,[11] the Bachs and Beethovens, the van Goghs and the Picassos, turn pain into a source of compassion, mercy, and new prospects for life.

This new vision, which is present in our reflection on the Trinity, helps us leave behind the dualistic and confining anthropocentrism that has characterized our western Christian tradition, a dualism that has not only opposed God and humanity, but also spirit and matter, man and woman, good and evil; throughout the course of our history, it has engendered a thousand and one antitheses.

For this reason we can say evil is part of the Trinity. It is our task to exorcise it and to struggle against its destructive power in order to see that from it, we can learn something new about our own being and about the life of the earth and of all living things. To welcome evil is not to rejoice over the fact that we commit it. Rather, it is a way of appropriating this aspect of our being, of recognizing, in a community setting, who we are, and of following the path to abundant life for all living things. The evil we do comes from our-selves, as does the struggle against it. This reality forms part of the human paradox itself, of that lack of symmetry that dwells within us and leads us to destroy that which oppresses us and build that which gives us life. And this process of construction and destruc-tion, of creation and elimination, is the very pattern of what we are: It is integral to the fabric of our lives, to our everyday lived reality.

The maxim "Love your neighbor as yourself," attributed to Jesus of Nazareth, should be taken up by us and understood as the way back to what we could call a trinitarian balance. If we have excessive love for ourselves, we will fall into a seemingly unlimited narcissism and the virtually implacable destruction of others. We will continue to build empires of Nazism, fascism, racism, classism, machismo, sexism, and all kinds of excesses that end up turning back on us, and, above all, on the poor. Restoring a balance between I and Thou, I and we, we and they, ourselves and the earth, is the way to turn back and allow the human, as well as plants and animals and all the creative energies of the earth, to flourish anew.

Of course, this new vision does not appear to solve our imme-diate problems. Neither does it offer quick and easy solutions. It is still like a new suit that has not yet adjusted to the contours of the body. It is still being stitched and hemmed. In the meantime, this vision insistently calls on us to see the universe as our body, the earth as our body, the variety of human groups as our body. This body is in evolution, in creative ecstasy, in the midst of destructive and regenerative labor, of death and resurrection. Everything is our body, our trinitarian body: it is a continual tension and commu-nion of multiplicity and unity, all within the ecstatic and mysteri-ous adventure of life.

Now, at the close of this millennium, we are beginning to work together as peoples from many parts of the earth to build a new spirituality. It looks, in fact, like a new Pentecost, but it is a slow-moving Pentecost: patient, universal, and at times almost impercep-tible. It is an inner and outer Pentecost that rends our religious boundaries asunder. It begins not only to change our understanding of the world and of ourselves but also to modify our behavior. All this is spirituality—that is, an energy that puts order in our lives, that gives meaning, that awakens in us the desire to help others to discover the "pearl of great price" hidden in our own bodies and in Earth's body. We know that when people find their personal and collective "pearl," they "sell all they have" in order to obtain it. The pearl is the symbolic expression of the new, inclusive spirituality that is growing in our own bodies and is nourished by our human energies, by the earth, and by the cosmos—in the last analysis, by the indissoluble, one and multiple trinitarian energy that is present in all that exists.

Speaking of trinitarian energy makes me think of a beautiful text by Joseph Campbell on the word "aum," the sound that represents the mystery of the word:

> AUM is a word that represents to our ears that sound of the energy of the Universe of which all things are manifestations. You start in the back of the mouth "ahh," and then "oo," you fill the mouth, and "mm" closes the mouth. When you pronounce this properly, all vowel sounds are included in the pronunciation. AUM. Consonants are here regarded simply as interruptions of the essential vowel sound. All words are thus fragments of AUM, just as all images are fragments of the Form of forms. AUM is a symbolic sound that puts you in touch with that resounding being that is the Universe. If you heard some of the recordings of Tibetan monks chanting AUM, you would know what the word means, all right. That's the AUM of being in the world. To be in touch with that and to get the sense of that is the peak experience of all.[12]

5
JESUS FROM AN
ECOFEMINIST PERSPECTIVE

≈≈≈

There is a history of dogmas and speculations, just as there is a
history of States. Very old customs, legal systems and institutions
continue in existence long after they have lost their meaning. That
which once has been does not want to lose its right to eternity;
what was once a good thing wants to be so now and for time
immemorial.

Ludwig Feuerbach, L'Essence du christianisme

Ludwig Feuerbach, who was no ecologist or feminist, prompts me
to speak of Jesus. He reminds me of the need to avoid eternalizing
our religious formulations as if they were requirements of life itself.
He invites me to keep alive the flame of the challenges and questions
that life offers us now, and to seek to express my relationship with
Jesus in the light of the challenges of our time.

How to speak of Jesus in light of the ecofeminist perspective I
am developing? How to speak of him not just with methodological
coherence, but out of my own relational life experience?

I would like to begin by sharing my own journey with Jesus. It
is easier for me to speak in the first person. At certain points in the
journey, questions and answers will appear as the moment calls for
them. There is nothing extraordinary about my story, but I think
that, along the way, some men (and perhaps many women) will
identify with my experiences. To speak of one's own journey is sim-

ply to share some segments of the road one has walked, without trying to construct a full-blown system of thought based on texts published with a pretext of "scientific" rigor. My personal journey is an
expression of my own quest, of things I have experienced in everyday life and of the questions and the need for answers that are part
of any human life. My personal journey is also marked by the questions of many people I encounter. In speaking of their experiences,
they share their own relationships with Jesus within a context far
removed from that of rigorous dogmatic formulations. I will, then,
move along my path of everyday faith life, with all the limitations
this kind of description brings with it.

After this discussion, I will reflect on some aspects of Jesus' life
that seem important to me from an ecofeminist perspective. I want
to open up the possibility of a more thoughtful dialogue, one that
will help us see why it is necessary to speak of Jesus of Nazareth in
a new way.

In practice, these two moments—my everyday faith and an
ecofeminist perspective on Jesus—are not separate in my life, but I
need to distinguish between them methodologically in order to
understand them better. I will not attempt to offer you some new
Christology. Many works have been and are being published on
this subject, some of them within a feminist or an ecofeminist
perspective.[1]

My concern in this reflection is merely to show that logical and
existential coherence is required of us if we embrace the ecofeminist
perspective and identify ourselves as one Sacred Body with the
whole universe. This is not just another formulation we add to the
body of doctrines we have learned in the past. Rather, it requires a
broader understanding of the universe in which we live, a perception that demands of us the task of adjusting our beliefs to the challenges posed by this new moment in the history of life.

As I said, I have neither the desire nor the ambition to build a
new Christology to be discussed by professional theologians, nor do
I want to create a new ecofeminist theological treatise on Jesus. I am
not seeking to weave still another garment in which to dress Jesus so
as to make him more compatible with the contemporary perspective. Rather, I will begin with the experience of people who seek to
remain within the "dialogue" among Jesus' disciples, to share their

current experience and to integrate it with the gospel tradition they have inherited. I would especially like to deal with their discomfort in the face of traditional dogmatic formulas, which they do not find helpful in their deep search for the meaning of life or in their commitment to continue within the discipleship of equals proposed by the Jesus movement.

My question for the Christian faith, and especially for the gospel of Jesus, has to do with the growth of our ecological sensibilities and our struggle against society's patriarchal structures. My question for the gospel has to do with the devastation of the planet, the elimination of so many species, and the destruction of so many human groups, among whom the most directly affected are the poorest of the economically poor. My question for the gospel of Jesus has to do with the manner in which his "way" has been locked within a rigid dogmatic structure that is prepared to exclude those who have doubts or uncertainties and to repress freedom of thought in the name of some monolithic truth. In the final analysis, my questions have to do with the complicity of religious institutions in social injustice and the use of the gospel of Jesus to serve the interests of a privileged elite.

I believe that through simple dialogue, in the perspective of a life of discipleship in which we come to learn from one another, we will recognize one another as sisters and brothers engaged in the same quest. I believe that in becoming aware of what unites us, even if it happens to be the tragic destruction that surrounds us, we will be able to discover once again the meaning of walking Jesus' path, which is pluralistic and welcomes the presence of a variety of different paths.

It is within this perspective that I share with you the first point in my reflection.

The Road I Have Walked with Jesus

Jesus and his teachings have played a central and decisive role for me during most of my life. The person of Jesus was the most basic reference point for all my actions. The question "What would Jesus have done in this situation?" was with me all the time. It was a question I learned as a child, above all in Catholic school. But I soon learned also that if I wanted to make it my guide, the starting point was not always the Gospel itself. Often it was the church's moral teachings and its interpretation of Jesus' life. And sometimes these teachings required me to understand Jesus' way as an arduous one, a way that went against my will and prompted me to obey authorities even when their orders were questionable.

As you might expect, it was not always easy to get satisfactory answers about my actions and choices. I was not always sure whether what I was doing or thinking was in line with Jesus' teachings. But I gave myself over fully to the task. I wanted to do it well, and I often felt guilty as I learned how difficult it was to follow Jesus' will.

My entry into religious life at the age of twenty-two, and my commitment to the struggle for a more just society, also found their justification in my decision to follow Jesus' teachings. Many years later I was able to examine my personal motivations and discern other elements beyond the following of Jesus that could also be regarded as decisive in these choices.

For a long time in my life, when I had to face misunderstanding and persecution (especially political and religious persecution), I explained my suffering in terms of my adherence to Jesus' teachings. Referring to Jesus gave me the support and legitimation I needed to justify my choices. It was as if I were following in the footsteps of someone who, despite differences of space, time, and sex, had a unique universality and an extraordinary ability to draw millions and millions of lives into his own. Jesus' life appeared to illuminate the paths of other lives. His life was an example, a paradigm that sustained those who opted to go through the "narrow gate" of justice and of "bearing one another's burdens."

During the last twenty-five years, in the light of liberation theology, it became even clearer that, for me, there was no other path than that of Jesus. In the last analysis, his stance in favor of the poor and outcast, his firm resistance to oppressive powers, and his lack of dogmatism appeared as fundamental touchstones, essential beacons on my journey. All the values I regarded as fundamental I found in him—in the reading of the Gospel texts and in the witness of the first Christians. The value of the body, especially the bodies of the poor and their basic needs, began to show me the degree to which the following of Jesus required a "religion" that started from the body: an incarnated religion, one rooted in human flesh and in the flesh of the earth. The body of the poor forced me to leave behind metaphysical reflections on the mystery of the incarnation in order to explore its material dimensions. I realized that, in my words and in my life, I could deal only with physical incarnations, the joy and pain made manifest in concrete and specific bodies. I came to realize the degree to which suffering and oppressed bodies, silenced bodies, and ostracized bodies had to do with my faith in God's presence, in the *relatedness* of this unfathomable mystery which is so timidly grasped by human flesh.

When I began to be interested in feminism and to criticize patriarchy, I assumed a stance of systematic suspicion in dealing with traditional theological texts. This sharpened my perceptions, and new questions arose within me. My questions were not specifically about Jesus but about interpretations of his attitudes and behaviors throughout the centuries. I had a problem with intransigent Christologies and dogmas, and with the authoritarian way in which Jesus' image was presented. I had a problem with disdain for bodies, especially those of women and of the earth. Some bodies were more severely battered than others, and some sexes were more oppressed than others; there were persecuted races and "hearts" that were disdained, belittled, and abused.

The option for the marginalized in no way disappeared in my thinking, but it broadened and took on more precise forms. The antidogmatic attitudes, openness to dialogue, and mercy I learned as a follower of Jesus in no way disappeared. But I was still bothered by the triumphalism and dogmatism in which christological reflections were couched. I was bothered by the excessive centrality of Jesus, a centrality that gave little space for personal initiatives—and especially for women's initiatives. It was an exaggerated centrality that ended up treating other religious expressions as secondary or as less important. This centrality was so idealistic in its liberating language that it virtually ruled out alternative religious expressions or contrasting discourses. However, I repeat, my issue was not with Jesus but what they said about him, and what they said often left me feeling suffocated. It oppressed me with its grandiosity. It didn't allow me to breathe deeply, it didn't nourish me, and it didn't satisfy my hunger for meaning. I could make existential sense neither of what I read nor of what I had learned about so many theories on the historical Jesus and on the Christ of faith; on his divinity, his consubstantiality with God, and other such matters. My relationship with Jesus, my discourse on Jesus, and my writings on Jesus began to change.

Today I find that the figure of Jesus still enjoys a special place, but that it has to share that place with other figures. Jesus' figure does not lose its existential centrality, because that centrality in my life has to do with my personal history in the Christian community and the way I express my own hope. But Jesus is no longer the absolute reference in a dogmatic sense, that is, in the way it was presented in the metaphysical Christology that characterized our discourse for centuries. It is a different kind of centrality, one that is more participative, more dialogical, and more open.

To use an analogy, I think the way we refer to Jesus today is like the way we recall favorite dishes of our childhood, those prepared by our mothers or grandmothers. People don't forget those dishes' flavors, and they can always go back to them in their memories or when they enjoy something similar.

"Jesus food" continues to nourish me, but it is the food I find in the Gospels, free of dogmatic refinements. It is the food of the New Testament parables and the stories used by very many human groups. It is the unexpected good food people are served in their friends' and neighbors' homes, or even on benches on busy street corners. It is the food they receive in letters from friends. It is the daily home-cooked meal in which canned goods are rarely used. I seek this food that is free of dogmatic refinements because the christological dogmatics that have come down to us from Nicaea and Chalcedon, along with their later "refinements," took away the good flavor of the Jesus-words, along with his sometimes irreverent, disconcerting, daring, and tender behavior.[2] Dogma took a conversation by a well, a shared meal, a tender gesture, a protest against injustice, an expression of gratitude, or a caress, and turned it into "ordered reason," "systematic reason," and "science." Dogma made a prison out of an invitation to freedom, out of poetry; then it added insult to injury by posting armed soldiers dressed as priests at the doors of paradise so nobody could get out or think differently. Dogma appointed authorized teachers to tell the truth about Jesus, and in this way it killed the creativity of moments of grace, informal meetings, kitchen conversations, and walks along river-banks. When its perspective was radicalized, dogma reduced broth-erly and sisterly relationships to hierarchical obedience; it limited the many paths to one path and the multiplicity of loving exchanges to a single authorized discourse. It went about creating fear: fear of disobeying, of mistaken thinking, of failing to reproduce exactly the right word, the well-formulated doctrine, or the "authentic" tradition handed down from Jesus.

Today I like to say that Jesus is both central and noncentral in my life. I say that he has an open, inclusive, affectionate, dialogical, and provocative centrality. I cannot close him into an absolute rela-tionship, one that excludes others. At first glance, it would seem that I live by an absurd or totally paradoxical logic, but this is more or less my experience. Jesus is as central to me as my own life, as my own aloneness, or as a good friendship; at the same time there are other centers that, so to speak, revolve around my life, or around which my life revolves. For example, if I take the Gospel text in Luke 7:36-50, Jesus' meeting with the so-called sinful woman, I always try to put the central role of Jesus "in parenthe-ses" and listen to the woman as well. How much of her own life she has invested in love! This woman, who is called a sinner, shows us the importance of investing in our own liberation and the importance of loving ourselves, especially for women. We women were trained, in the Christian tradition, to serve "others," to seek to please "others," to deny ourselves for the sake of "others," and to obey authority figures—and we ended up forgetting the need to live the *two* poles of love: love of oneself and love of one's neigh-bor. It was not Jesus who ordered the woman to seek him; it was her initiative and her struggle, and the love that was born of her own heart.

This brings to mind that, in Latin America, we are always depending on somebody to do us a favor so that we can live with dignity. We depend on politicians, bosses, priests, and God. A patri-archal reading of the Gospels has always insisted that we center our attention on Jesus: on his actions, his teachings, and the miracles he worked. It said salvation, the most perfect love, and the solutions to our problems come from him. But why not pay attention to this sinful and nameless woman; why not pay attention to the man with the withered hand, to the paralytic, to the woman with an issue of blood, to the children? Why not imagine instead that it was the women themselves who brought along the bread of the "multiplication," especially since it is they, almost always, who every day carry food for their children?

Why not pay attention to and honor the people's resistance struggles—their endless struggles for liberation and a life lived in dignity? Why not shine spotlights on the insignificant actors, and appreciate their daily struggle to survive and to maintain their dignity? Why not open up our understanding of "salvation" to a broader process, one that is going on consciously or unconsciously in people's daily lives, in the midst of the "ordinary" things that make up the fabric of our lives?

If we do this, we introduce a logic that accents the roles of those actors who are regarded as least important so that they can develop their powers, their creative abilities, and their own style of seeking the paths of salvation.

I would like to believe that this was Jesus' logic, and that it was for this that he was condemned and ostracized by the powerful of his time. He always seemed to insist on the faith, the efforts, and the persistence of ordinary people, and not on favors that the powerful could concede. He seems to have insisted on satisfying the hunger people feel today, on fulfilling the need for wine in today's wedding celebration, on curing the ills that afflict us at this moment—on those very concrete ills that are not named in any existing code of law or dealt with in purely formal intellectual analyses.

From this perspective, it seems that the centrality of Jesus opens us to the centrality of persons, especially the outcast, and to the need to invest in what we could call our "salvation" in the here and now. Thus we move away from an excessive emphasis on the figure of the savior, the hero, the martyr, the king, the saint—as well as the victorious warrior, the only Son of God. We come to speak of the salvation we offer one another when our hearts open up in tenderness and mercy. We leave more room in our lives especially for those oppressed by various ills, for women seeking their dignity, and for children, in order to encourage them to discover in themselves the roots of their own freedom. This is what I call relationships of open centrality.

History is made in many centers, not only in power centers. In this sense, I no longer want to identify Jesus as just one more power center, even though I recognize that his style of acting was different from that of the established powers. Rather, I would like to speak of him as a center of loving energy among us. I prefer to speak of Jesus as someone whose inclusive actions refused to allow his disciples to engage in exclusionary practices, whether they involved sex, race, or class. All can enter into the "wedding banquet," as long as they accept the rules of equal sharing, mercy, service, taking the last place, and washing one another's feet.

If we view the situation from this perspective, not all that was said of Jesus in the past needs to be thrown out. This is our history, our past, our very flesh. At the same time, if we speak of bringing about a new era in our history—a new understanding of the history of the universe and another moment in life of this Sacred Body—then we are required to show a certain consistency.

More and more, we are discovering that imprisoning of Jesus of Nazareth in a specific dogmatic system has done enormous damage in the lives of persons and groups. All the emphasis on the obedience of Jesus to his Father, for example, merely underlined a "culture of obedience" in which women, slaves, and children were always the primary victims. The oppressed were always told they must obey their oppressors, since the latter had received the gift of authority and been entrusted with the exercise of power. This theology of obedience continues to be passed along in our culture, often disguised as freedom and democracy or even as the common good. According to some interpretations, it was this obedience that led Jesus to accept the cross, and it has led women and oppressed peoples to endure a wide variety of holocausts. This obedience generated a complicity with authoritarian regimes, with empires, and with a variety of racist systems. Surely there are many people who would argue that Jesus' sacrifice was freely accepted and therefore cannot be analyzed with the same categories as the so-called culture of obedience. I believe that the obedience of Jesus is of the precise type that does not allow itself to be controlled by any kind of authority system: It is an obedience to the generative source of life within himself and his fellow human beings. This kind of obedience really requires disobedience to the system, and it is because Jesus disobeyed that he was crucified and died. He was, literally, murdered.

Obedience and disobedience can be elements in the power games of imperialist systems. Therefore it is always necessary to ask ourselves about the meaning of obedience: obedience to whom, and to what end? We need to ask the same things about disobedience. Are there some forms of disobedience that cannot be called obedience to freedom, to love for our neighbors and ourselves? We women are raising among ourselves ever greater suspicion about the dogmas concerning Jesus of Nazareth and their flagrant complicity with the processes of exclusion and destruction we all observe.

This whole situation moves me deeply, and leads me, along with many others, to rethink the faith in terms that are more compatible with the agenda of the impoverished, of feminists, and of the planet.

Ecofeminist Challenges to Our Relationship with Jesus of Nazareth

As we have seen in earlier chapters, the ecofeminist perspective I am developing proposes a different way of knowing: a different understanding of the human person, and a different experience of and discourse concerning God. Thus, too, it opens us up to a different understanding of our experience of Jesus and with Jesus. I often insist on the word "experience" and speak of experience within the confines of our bodies and our histories in order to underline the fundamental importance of the physical moment in which we live. To speak of experience is to speak of concrete realities that have to do with our bodies. It is also to speak of our specific ills and pains— and therefore of our need for "salvation," for remedies, and for healing.

In sharing with readers my personal experience with Jesus, I want to make it clear that I do not share the perspective that some people call postchristian. I am not postchristian; rather, I am post-dogmatic and postpatriarchal, even while I am able to understand what traditional dogmatic formulations were trying to say. What those formulations said had its own value and its own historical context, but it cannot be absolutized.

So, in the perspective I am developing, the idea is not to reaffirm traditional dogmas regarding Jesus or to emphasize a salvation beyond history. It is not a matter of rereading the councils of Nicaea and Chalcedon in light of the needs of our own times. Nor is it a matter of having another look at all the ancient christological controversies so as to be able once again to reaffirm Jesus' divinity in patriarchal terms.[3] Rather, I would like to follow the logic of *relatedness* that we have been proposing throughout this reflection, and to dare to free Jesus from the hierarchical and dogmatic apparel in which the church has clothed him for so long.

Along these lines, I would like to think of Jesus as a man who was extremely sensitive to human suffering, who was inspired by the prophetic and sapiential tradition of the Jewish culture to which he belonged, and who tried in various ways to respond to certain forms of human suffering—especially pain, hunger, and various kinds of marginalization. Jesus always insisted that people believe in themselves, and taught that their belief in themselves was an expression of faith in God's power. Jesus' actions were aimed at the recovery of health and dignity, and the recovery of the physical means to health and dignity: food and drink. His actions affirmed that certain physical needs cannot be satisfied by promises or by the future realization of some ideal world. It is this practical wisdom of Jesus that needs to be rediscovered, lived out, and understood in the context of the vital problems we face today. I agree with Sallie McFague that it is precisely the perspective of *body* that will allow us to introduce the issue of ecological salvation.[4] Our economic exploitation projects have enslaved the earth and the powers of nature and made them into an object to be used for unbridled profiteering. It is our actions that have put the earth in bondage, that have damaged it, polluted it, and impoverished it. For this reason, it is the earth that is both the subject and the object of salvation. We need to abandon a merely anthropocentric Christianity and open ourselves up to a more biocentric understanding of salvation. To Jesus' humanistic perspective, we need to add an ecological perspective. This new way of doing things seems to me perfectly justified, because it maintains not only the most fundamental aspects of Jesus' perspective but also the understanding that we are a living body in constant evolution.

Theology has repeated many times that Jesus did not proclaim himself; using an ecofeminist perspective, we could say that he proclaimed respect for the life of every being and abundant life for all. We could say that Jesus' attitudes and behaviors always point Christians toward the building of new relationships, and that today they help us to build a positive relationship between human persons and the earth. It is precisely this that we want to insist on ever more strongly, in order to rebuild the web of human relationships in all its dimensions.

It seems that when we speak of Jesus as a human being—as profoundly human—the sometimes forbidding divine halo we have always attributed to him in Christian tradition seems to disappear. But if we no longer speak of the salvific uniqueness of Jesus the Christ, many feel we give up the power and uniqueness of our faith. A Jesus who can no longer be affirmed as a superhuman being seems to lose his power to move us. As Sallie McFague says,

> The scandal of uniqueness is absolutized by Christianity into one of its central doctrines, which claims that God is embodied in one place and one place only: in the man Jesus of Nazareth. He and he alone is "the image of the invisible God" (Col. 1:15). The source, power and goal of the universe is known through and only through a first-century Mediterranean carpenter. The creator and redeemer of the fifteen-billion-year history of the universe with its hundred billion galaxies (and their billions of stars and planets) is available only in a thirty-year span of one human being's life on planet earth. The claim, when put in context of contemporary science, seems skewed, to say the least. When the world consisted of the Roman Empire (with "barbarians" at its frontiers), the limitation of divine presence to Jesus of Nazareth had some plausibility while still being ethnocentric; but for many hundreds of years, well before contemporary cosmology, the claims of other major religious traditions have seriously challenged it.[5]

Along with McFague, I believe that to affirm the incarnation, or the bodiliness, of the divine does not necessarily require that Jesus have some unique metaphysical character. Jesus is also "our Sacred Body." For this reason, the incarnation, the presence of the greatest of mysteries in our flesh, is more than Jesus of Nazareth. In this sense, we could say that Jesus is for us a metaphor of the divine presence, the unfathomable mystery, the unutterable in the human flesh in which we all are included.

The incarnation refers to our own bodily reality. In other words, we apprehend in our flesh, in our bodily experience, what we call the divine. The place in which we apprehend the mystery that underlies everything is our respective bodies. Therefore, we say we are incarnate, we are beings in the flesh, although we know how complex this affirmation is. In some Christian traditions, the incarnation has often been interpreted in idealistic terms—as if the divine had entered human flesh only at one specific moment, and therefore this moment is made into an absolute.

As we know, we have always been accustomed to thinking of the divine as a being and a power radically different from our own experience. Thus it might appear that "God-with-us," or "Immanuel," who "pitched his tent among us" and "came down from heaven," could be diminished by this new interpretation. However, to speak of Jesus as God's "intermediary," or to speak of Jesus as the expression of the wisdom that dwells within us, is not to deny Jesus' concrete practice as it is set down in the Gospels.

The frame does not change the picture, even if it highlights different elements of it. The picture itself, Jesus' life as it was lived out, has its own integrity—despite the frames in which it has been placed by his contemporaries, by the early Christian communities, by conflicts in the time of the Roman Empire, by later tradition, and by ourselves today. Jesus' actions on behalf of the oppressed, the outcast, the sick, and victims of all varieties are undeniable. That is what shows up in the most vivid colors in the painting of Jesus' life. These actions, then, constitute the picture of Jesus' mission, and for this reason it is always present and always up to date. And this underlying picture, this special painting, should always be displayed—whatever frame is used. Furthermore, the frame can never be more important than the picture. I think this is precisely what has happened in our theology. We have exaggerated the importance of the frame, which is no more than a context, an accessory; often we have forgotten the picture, the painting, the words of life, the actions of Jesus.

Some people might even ask why we need to return today to the figure of Jesus. Why not let it fade away, as any figure from the past does, and seek new reference points for the present? Doing so could even serve the purposes of some feminist and rationalist intellectual groups who find the figure of Jesus to be a stumbling block.

The issue will not be resolved by elimination. We cannot simply get rid of it if it inconveniences us, because our relationship with Jesus is not merely personal but also cultural. Besides (as I said earlier, speaking out of my own experience), the problem is not with Jesus but with what the power brokers have made of him.

In this sense, there are choices to be made. Although there are different positions on this issue, I think we neither wish to nor are able to separate ourselves in an absolute sense from our history. Thus we do not want to stand apart from history or from Jesus of Nazareth as a reference point, because he is woven into the fabric this history. He is part of our personal and social body. Besides, we still find in Christian experience, despite all its limitations, a way of expressing our own convictions.

A tradition only dies when none are left who place their faith in it, when there are no more disciples to keep it alive. This is not the case with the tradition that goes back to Jesus of Nazareth. In my view, this tradition is of fundamental importance. To lose it would be to lose part of an ancient human wisdom—part of its richness, part of its extraordinary expressiveness and beauty.

The figure of Jesus has something profoundly alluring about it. Since the days of our most ancient tradition, Jesus has been the symbol of our hope, and this symbolism has been expressed in many ways and many different languages. Jesus is the symbol of what we seek, of the behaviors and attitudes we judge to be the most fitting in human beings. I think it is in this sense that we could speak metaphorically of Jesus as Savior. He is the Savior inasmuch as he is the symbol of those values that are best able to change our lives, to lead us to goodness and justice. He is the Savior inasmuch as he is a living example with which we identify, in order to conceive of our own lives as salvific. It is the process of salvation he represents that can be assumed by women and men whose hearts are filled with mercy and solidarity.

It follows that, to paraphrase Saint Paul, in Jesus are men and women, Greeks and Romans (Gal 3:27-28); there are white, black, and Asiatic persons. In other words, differences are embraced and respected, because, in Jesus' perspective, it is not a matter of defending masculinity or femininity, or any other just demand. The issue is not dogma but the world of values lived by Jesus and his disciples.

Christian culture has always made Jesus an inclusive symbol who served slaves and free citizens, rulers and beggars, men and women, old and young, prostitutes and public sinners. When we say symbol, we mean a totality that is always open and inclusive, a reality whose immense richness allows it to be continually reinterpreted. Jesus as a symbol is more than a formal signifier with no substance of its own, as some people we meet every day seem to think. They think that to speak of Jesus as a symbol is to diminish him, to fail to recognize his historical character, and to reduce him to something less than real. Many ambiguities in this understanding—or, rather, misunderstanding—need to be clarified.

To say that Jesus is a symbol means that, although he is Jesus of Nazareth, he is really more than Jesus of Nazareth. He becomes the possession of the community of his followers, a collective construct representing a way of life, a path to the meaning of our existence. Jesus as a symbol is in a certain sense greater than Jesus of Nazareth as an individual, because in him millions and millions of persons are encompassed.

When we say Jesus is the symbol who fulfills our dreams, this does not mean that in him everything was worked out or fully accomplished. It is to say we need to entrust our dreams to this man because we need these dreams, and we hope that their fulfillment is possible. We turn over to Jesus, a man, flesh of our flesh, the concrete possibility of a better world and of more just and equal relationships among people. Because of him, we throw in our lot for a world that embodies greater solidarity—but all the while, we know this decision is our own.

We also say that he has achieved what we would like to achieve, although we know that within his concrete historical circumstances he surely could not have accomplished all that has been attributed to him. The word that expresses our dreams and hopes is always colored by our own expectations and by our desire that they be realized.

To use a strained analogy, we could say that when we are very sick we like to know that others who have had the same illness have been cured. When we are "down and out," we like to know that others in the same condition of struggle and suffering have found a place to stay. When we are struggling against racism, we are happy to know that in some other country the rights of the various ethnic groups have been respected. Here, too, there are historical limitations, and surely many of the things we imagine to have been achieved really have not. But all these persons or groups have a real power for us: they symbolize something we are looking for, something that gives meaning to our lives.

What we say of Jesus could be said of Mary as well, who is part of the whole biblical tradition of strong women who were symbols of resistance and of salvation for their people. In them, the life of their people is included and expressed. The degree to which one or another symbol is used will depend in great part on the history of that symbol in this or that cultural community.

All this shows the mysterious power of the symbols and words we use in describing our hope. In these words, we include ourselves along with our ancestors. Through them we live and give life.

So too, Jesus was a person of his time, conditioned by his culture, able to respond only to certain questions; but he is also a symbolic figure who can have meaning far beyond his historical and temporal limitations. So we say that for us, in the Christian community, Jesus is a symbol: a symbol with which we dialogue and in which we include ourselves. And this is so because, as communities of disciples, we make Jesus a symbol of our lives' ideals and values.

In this sense, the centrality of Jesus is not absolute or metaphysical. As I have said before—and I am looking only at the Christian world—other figures such as Mary and Mary Magdalene also have symbolic power. These figures are being rediscovered by various feminist movements, especially in recent years.

Meanwhile, as we know, the patriarchal Christian culture in which we live has placed a greater accent on Jesus. Just how helpful is it to remind ourselves, once again, that our theological culture is not only anthropocentric but also androcentric? The centrality of Jesus cannot be invoked to dismiss prominent figures and symbols from other religious traditions. The ways of justice and love are multiple and varied. Our Sacred Body includes many different expressions of love, mercy, and salvation.

I agree with the words of Sri Lankan theologian Tissa Balasuriya:

> The uniqueness of Jesus is in the depth of his personality; in his total self-giving love that helps fulfill others, and in his message that is uniquely salvific for all who live it. We can think of him as a guru par excellence, who first trod the difficult path up to his death on the cross. He was a humble person who was not concerned about his own greatness but wanted to serve all in truth and in love.[6]

We know that cultural change does not come about in response to decrees, or even as a result of this or that school of thought. It takes time to assimilate not only new values but also new ways of dealing with them. Furthermore, a position that embodies respect for various religious expressions should facilitate the coexistence of different groups that interpret the "Jesus event" in different ways.

At this time, it seems, from an ecofeminist perspective, that what is most important for Christian communities, or communities of followers of Jesus, is neither to try to save christological dogmas out of formal faithfulness to a certain tradition, nor to impose their own interpretations as the only "way" and the only truth about Jesus. These would be attempts to hold on to the same old hierarchical and dualistic perspective in a world that can no longer tolerate dualism or the destruction wrought by the practice of hierarchical exclusion. When we try to hold on to traditional dogma, we also to fail to see the direct or indirect complicity of patriarchal Christologies with the maintenance of an exclusivist system. Many writings have shown the negative effects of imperialist Christologies that present Jesus' lordship in the image of the great lords of this world—not to mention the sacrificial Christologies that insist on the immolation of Jesus, and that are indirect accomplices of the immolation of many different human groups.

It seems to me that the actions and teachings of Jesus can be rediscovered as clues, or as attempts at a response, to the great challenges of today's world. My conviction is shared by all those who work within an ecofeminist perspective. In this perspective, we can speak once again of the openness of Jesus to dialogue, of his mercy, his criticism of oppressive powers, his concern for the sharing of bread and wine, and his delight in the flowers of the countryside. I think these values, which are present in some sense in all humanistic traditions, can be revived in a nondogmatic way by the Christian community.

For the Christian community, Jesus is a symbol of members' dreams, and of their greatest aspirations for humanity and for the earth. But the community of Jesus' followers has changed these aspirations to some degree, as it has responded to the various situations and contexts of human history. We could say that Jesus is not the savior of all humanity in the traditional, triumphalistic sense that has characterized the discourse of the Christian churches. He is not the powerful Son of God who dies on the cross and becomes the "king" who morally dominates the great variety of human cultures. Rather, he is the symbol of the vulnerability of love, which in order to remain alive ends up being murdered, killed . . . and which then rises again in those who love him, in order to revive the vital cycle of love.

Within this perspective, Jesus does not come to us in the name of a "superior will" that sent him; rather, he comes from here: from this earth, this body, this flesh, from the evolutionary process that is present both yesterday and today in this Sacred Body within which love resides. It continues in him beyond that, and it is turned into passion for life, into mercy and justice. In this sense, I am saying that Jesus as an individual person is not superior to any other human being. This is because he is made of the same earth, the same bodily reality that constitutes us all. Meanwhile, on account of his moral qualities, his openness, and his sensitivity, he has come to represent, in a certain sense, the perfection of our dreams and the ideal realization of our desires. And it is precisely this quality that makes the difference. To put it in another way: The difference is not metaphysical or ontological (related to the nature of being) but ethical and aesthetic, because the difference is manifest in his humanity, in the great beauty of the attitudes he expressed and evoked in others. Once again, we can say that Jesus is the symbol of all that we most love. Within this perspective, Jesus can no longer be regarded as the justification for hierarchical power; rather, he is a model of the fraternal and sororal power of communion with all those who claim to belong to his tradition.

Some people will probably argue that you cannot change a hierarchical and patriarchal symbol this way, making it into something democratic, inclusive, and nonsexist. They will say that such an endeavor would be pretentious, because it would offer an image of Jesus that falls outside the patterns to which we have become accustomed over the centuries. But we know very well that all traditions have had their beginnings, even if these beginnings were confused and sometimes unclear. And if they had a beginning, then they also evolved: They are subject to constant transformations. They also appropriate, in their own ways, the life experience of Jesus of Nazareth. They have transformed it, conceptualized it, and turned it into a science and a doctrine. I cannot, therefore, accept positions that refuse to welcome the changes inherent in every tradition, above all when we face, every day, in contact with persons and in the complexities of cultures, the many sufferings and the multiple transformations inherent in life. I cannot accept the idea that we have no authority to speak in our own way of our relationships with Jesus without cutting ourselves off from history. I do not understand why the antiquity of certain dogmatic and conciliar statements or their proximity to Jesus' historical times need to be regarded as the only criteria for the truth of statements about Jesus of Nazareth. I don't want to go into the classical arguments over the Christ of faith and the Jesus of history. My only purpose is to show the possibility of reinterpreting the gospel tradition in the light of the vital issues we are raising today.

Within the ecofeminist perspective I am developing, the criteria of "giving life" and of fostering the "flowering" of life in dignity, diversity, and respect are quite enough to give us the collective authority to speak in different way of our experience as partners of Jesus.

The purist spirit of academia, the universities, and dogma is not a part of concrete, everyday life. The logical coherence of doctrines is constantly undermined by the need to survive, or simply to live. Radical breaks in our basic ways of knowing are only possible in the world of theory. The real world in which we live and share life is always mixed, imprecise, impure, and unexpected. And it is precisely its "mixed" character that allows for the creativity and unpredictability that are able to generate life where there appears to be no more hope.

I want to recall that liberation theology in Latin America insisted for a very long time that the most important thing is not "orthodoxy" but "orthopraxis": acting correctly, with justice and mercy. And it is this acting, feeling, and thinking on the basis of our own experience that has the power and authority to change some aspects of our ancient tradition.

For this reason, the symbol of Jesus can be transformed and is gradually being transformed in Latin American Christian communities, especially among groups of women and among those who are working in ecumenism and ecology. If religious powers impede this vital transformation in our understanding, they surely will be showing little faithfulness to the figure who taught his disciples to take notice of the many occurrences in daily life, of the suffering of marginalized bodies, of the communion among all beings, and of the mystery of life itself.

Jesus is a symbol and an inspiration for the community of his followers, a symbol that is capable of widening its meaning to respond to the needs of our historical moment. It is these not-always-clear paths that ecofeminist insights about Jesus of Nazareth find themselves treading. And it is through them, in the light and darkness of life, that people are learning to understand, within the limitations of our own time, the greatness and simplicity of the life and ethical code of Jesus of Nazareth.

6
THAT ALL MAY HAVE LIFE:
THE WAY TO A NEW
UNDERSTANDING OF RELIGION

≈≈

We are called to affirm the integrity of our personal center of
being, in mutuality with the personal centers of all other beings
across species and, at the same time, accept the transience of these
personal selves.

Rosemary Radford Ruether

Rosemary Radford Ruether's words call our attention to the need to
rethink our lives' religious dimension on the basis of relational
behaviors, and this in turn locates us within the ecofeminist perspective we are developing.[1]

The Issue That Concerns Us

In this chapter following the chapters on Jesus and God, I would
like to open an informal conversation on religion. I am not interested in initiating yet another debate among specialists; I want only
to share some of my own concerns, which flow in large part from
my Latin American ecofeminist convictions.

Some might expect this conversation to be presented as a pre-
liminary reflection to use in defining what religion is, but I am using
a different kind of logic—one aimed at looking at everyday life and
examining the issue of religion from that perspective. I want to ask,
after reflecting on all the issues we've discussed, how we arrive at a

new understanding of religion as a personal experience and as a social institution.

Beyond this, I would like to examine some meanings of our daily, informal, noninstitutional religiosity. This requires us to understand religion outside the context of religious institutions, on the basis of behaviors that appear to be beyond the control of those who exercise religious power. I do not want to offer some facile critique of the religions we find in Latin America. Today the idea is not merely to criticize errors or become voices crying in the wilderness, but rather to find ways of humbly acknowledging that there are errors. Then the most urgent task is to seek alternatives that can restore joy and meaning to our lives.

In this light, I have asked myself whether what we have traditionally called "religion," taken even in its broadest accepted meaning, has really played the role of creating relationships, of "relinking" people with one another, with the earth, and with the powers of nature. I ask whether that which we call "religion" has in fact brought about behaviors that are consoling, tender, and merciful; whether it has helped people live their everyday lives with greater dignity. If we take the examples of certain specific individuals, we can, of course, say that it has; but if we speak of religions as social institutions, the answer might be closer to the negative.

In *The Future of an Illusion*, Sigmund Freud spoke of a triple function of the "gods": to exorcise our fear of nature, to reconcile us with the cruelty of our destiny, and to compensate for the sufferings and privations imposed on us by living life within a given culture.[2] In Freud's view, human beings create religious images in order to make life in society more bearable. That is why we so easily declare that we live this life keeping in mind the next one, in which perfection is promised. Thus, in light of this higher form of life, even death is justified. It is part of the just design of divine providence, or, simply, of God.

The dualistically and patriarchally structured religion described by Freud today seems to be unfolding in so many ways that it is difficult to follow all its contours. But it seems to me important at least to trace the outlines of a phenomenon visible to us today and which some specialists have pointed out from other perspectives.[3] What I am referring to is this: I suspect that there now exists a religion that

stands in opposition to Christian humanist religion, and that is taking on an ever more important role in the life of society. In some
senses, it sticks to the old dualistic mentality, and its discourse
appears to ape the values of humanistic religion. However, this
other religion, which pervades all our behaviors and which is being
sold by the communications media, does not always awaken compassion, justice, or love for our neighbors. It is a "religion" without
religion, without mutuality, and without effective or affective mercy.

My suspicion is based on the conviction that forces much more
powerful than the religious values preached by Christianity moti-
vate societies that are still called Christian. There is a kind of apparent adhesion to religious values, but in fact we can observe personal and social behaviors that are ever more distant from respect for
all persons, solidarity, justice, and the search for equality.

I find myself asking what complex blend of feelings moves the
purveyors of organized violence, whether they be major or minor
actors. I am shocked at the virtually uncontrollable growth of violence and individualism, not only in the world of the rich but also
among the poorest strata of society. Every group uses violence in its
own way to protect itself from other groups. And the "gods" are
useful in offering an ideological justification for this system, in
which some are always defending themselves against others. In the
last analysis, each group has its own particular "god," even if all are
addressed by one generic name.

In Brazil, for example, the campaign to enact the death penalty
for common criminals is gaining increasing support among groups
that call themselves Christian. Nevertheless, the commandment
"Thou shalt not kill" continues to be taught in our schools and
churches, and the value of life continues to be proclaimed in a multiplicity of human rights declarations! In the meantime, what is
happening to our religious principles? Where do we see people living out the values associated with our deepest beliefs?

I repeat, once more, that the purpose of these remarks is not to
point a finger of blame at those alleged to be responsible for this
destructive system, but rather to show how it is presented as virtually the only way of living and surviving. Keeping this in mind, I
want to ask how we can find practical solutions that promote
respect for the life of all. Beyond this, I want to underline the fact

that the various religious systems are all, to one degree or another, accomplices, legitimators, or critics of these systems.

We know it is increasingly true that in order to live, or even just survive, we have to become part of the violent logic of the system. In many parts of the world, religions seem to follow the same violent logic, and in a certain sense they appear to be betraying the basic principles on which their organizations were founded. As institutions, they play the system's power games. They fail to speak out publicly and say what they think if their interests, power, or survival is at stake. The separation in religious institutions between the private and the public spheres continues, despite these institutions' proclamations of support for the struggle against systems that foster injustice. The world of institutionalized religion seems to follow the same hypocritical norms as do other institutions, despite its attempts to present itself as a defender, in God's name, of law and justice.

At this moment I prefer not to mention exceptions to this rule. Exceptions always exist, and still are able to nourish our hope and solidarity, but, as a general rule, religious teachings in Latin America seem ever more ineffectual, ever less able to avert the growing tide of violence. Our religious talk seems more and more distant from the real situations that current social models are imposing on us. One has the impression that the churches propose solutions drawn from a world that is ever more foreign to us, and courses of action that are ever less feasible for the great majority of their members. The churches' recommendations are not being followed even within religious institutions themselves. They invalidate their own solutions by almost inevitably participating in the system's logic. It seems that the difficulties are to be found not only on the level of language or of the messages transmitted by the mass media. Something in contemporary culture quite simply has more power than our sincere will to do good. Something virtually obliges us to accept what we do not want in order to get by as best we can. We are becoming increasingly aware that we are immersed in a kind of "evil" that we have not chosen, or have chosen only indirectly, and that we have no idea how to get out of it. How can we come to an understanding of this problem and the dilemmas it raises? And how can we imagine ways out?

The Destruction of Green Things, of Diversity, and of Our Symbols

Our original religious-symbolic world was constructed on a base that used reference points that communicated something we were already living out deeply and existentially. When we spoke of lilies, flowers, and green things, or of the animals in the jungles, the beauty of rivers, or the breaking of bread, these were all realities that pointed to a certain existential truth, to more or less concrete experiences that all of us were familiar with.

Today, in many places, the "lilies of the field" barely even exist, and we do not often see the blue of the sky. We hardly ever find springs of pure water or breathe air that invigorates us. Pollution and the destruction of plant life are taking over in cities and even in the countryside.

We hardly remember anymore what it is like to break bread in community or to tremble with joy. Many people have almost no bread, and others no longer know what it means to share, to "break bread together." We have virtually forgotten what it means to "be like little children." Today we fear children, those who crowd the streets watching for the chance to violently snatch a crust of bread from us. We live in a society that is afraid of children! This is the most absurd of all absurdities! In Latin American cities, when we pull up at a stoplight and see a group of kids in the distance, we immediately roll up the windows. They frighten us, attack us, and are even capable of killing us. And this is because they themselves are being attacked and killed by the hundreds and thousands by an exclusionary society that prepares a future only for the privileged elites.

Our values and symbols are no longer grounded in concrete, lived experience. They appear to have been reduced to empty phrases, or perhaps to the nostalgic words we still use in order to recall situations that are barely even part of our experience. This is a social problem, but it is also a deeply religious one. The symbols we use to name our dreams have been defiled and are too feeble to impart energy to our lives. The symbols we use to refer to the things that are important to us have become worn out, bankrupt.

How can the truth make us free and allow us to survive if we are forced continually to lie? Almost everything in our world is based on lies. In order to sell our product, we say it's the best, even though we know it's really one of the worst. In order to keep our jobs, we curry favor by praising an incompetent boss. We teach our children not to lie, but we know we need to lie again and again in this society shot through with hypocrisy, manifold futilities, and contempt for those who fail to heed its ways.

Many teachers repeat things they no longer believe, and are afraid to teach out of their deepest convictions, because they would risk losing their jobs or the social recognition they enjoy. We cover our ears to corruption at all levels and in every institution, pretending that it hardly exists in order to hold on to our positions. Cheating, competition, lying, backstabbing, and shameless robbery are the law that governs market morality—and, to some extent, that of the churches as well. All our lands seem to be saturated with the same poison, and all peoples are lumped together in a kind of "gospel of perdition," to use the words of Edgar Morin.[4]

Could this shared perdition, this shared historical destiny, perhaps be the tragic beginning of a new path of solidarity? Religions of instant salvation are growing; they offer miraculous cures, promise jobs, do exorcisms, appear to give people an identity, and generate moments of shared euphoria. But even as these religions play into the hands of the established system, they seem not to see the logic of destruction that is growing visibly in our economically globalized society. They blame all evils on occult powers, demonic possession, and other things that have virtually nothing to do with our collective, historical responsibility.

There is a growing complicity with the dominant political powers on the part of the oldest and most traditional churches. The alliances between "temporal" and "spiritual" powers still have not disappeared, despite the growing autonomy of national governments. Silence, collusion, conniving, and trade-offs seem to be standard institutional behaviors.

And what religion prevails? What is the religion that "reconnects" our world and our relationships? What kind of "reconnection" is going on among us?[5] Are we not dealing with a kind of metareligion, a religion handed down and institutionalized by the international economic market?

This is the religion with which a salvific "new covenant" is being sealed in order to guarantee our survival. The representatives of these divinities are the new "priesthood" with whom we have to conduct our religious sharing. It has all the earmarks of a violent, "warrior" religion that dominates us and governs our relationships. To all appearances, this is the religion we practice in our daily struggle to survive, by means of deceitful relationships, the environmental pollution that makes our air unbreathable, and the overarching lie that envelops us all.

Religion is no longer the "sigh of the oppressed" or the "heart of a world without a heart," as Feuerbach said, because it itself has been absorbed by the consumer market, it itself legitimates political deals, it itself has lost its "essence" and its salvific power, and it itself has ended up with no heart.[6] I feel we are being called to a new kind of reflection, one that leads us to ask ourselves what we mean by "religion." This is a most urgent task, for it is tied to the very survival of the human species on this planet.

Religion and Community Life

Another very practical matter, one that directly concerns the life of women in various parts of Brazil and Latin America, is the issue of community life. How can we build community in the midst of the anonymity of life in big cities? How can we live in community when the TV beckons us to shut ourselves inside with our favorite program? How can we live in community when suspicion and fear begin to threaten our relationships in the neighborhood and on the block?

Various groups with whom I have reflected on ecofeminist theology manifest growing discontent not only with traditional theological content and traditional religious symbols but also with the absence of alternative spaces in which they can express themselves or create alternative celebrations that manifest their deepest beliefs. Such spaces, or communities, would help us discover meaning in our lives and would also support us in reflecting on what to tell our children.

Only rarely can churches and chapels continue to be regarded as alternative community spaces, for they continue to be dominated by the established powers. Besides that, they seem too big, too roomy, and too cold. Yet our homes are too small to serve this purpose.

I have often heard concerned mothers ask how they can speak to their children of God. "What God should I speak of?" they ask. "Will my children grow up in a world without religion?" "Who will offer them guidance so they can behave ethically?"

"The religion taught in Christian schools and parishes is more and more foreign to our children's aspirations and concerns," they go on. "It fails to encourage more loving and merciful attitudes." "Where and how can we live out the more open and integral perspective we dream of?"

Many of these questions reflect the insecurity of mothers who are dissatisfied with traditional Christian ways. These mothers have no new or secure guidelines, nor do they have a human community that supports and upholds them in exploring their incipient questioning and in building new convictions.

The crisis in traditional religious teachings, not to mention the profound crisis in the society in which we live, is being felt in the most diverse groups. And those who are going through this crisis want not to deny it, but to take it on as a challenge for the present and for the future.

I think the most fundamental need many women are feeling is to have a "place," a small community in which their questions and convictions can be shared; a place to which they can, little by little, introduce their children. I believe this felt need expresses the age-old need to live out faith in community. Community appears as a constructive and creative place that not only supports us in living our lives but affirms our convictions, sustains us in moments of doubt, and gives us the energy to persevere. The model of the early Christian communities might be inspiring in some ways, but it has been used so often by the patriarchal world that it is no longer able to generate much enthusiasm for nourishing new communities. Besides that, the ideal they propose seems ever more distant from our real ability to live out the kind of sharing that can ensure that none among us are hungry or needy. Still, in the light of the real problems we face, surely we can salvage these texts and understand the concrete guidelines for action that they offer us.

We could also have a look at the Christian base communities that are so widespread—and so much talked about—in Latin America. It is important to remember, however, that although in some places they retain their organizational (but not doctrinal or liturgical) autonomy, in other places they are totally dependent on the parochial model and are directly or indirectly controlled by priests.

What to do? How to create something that is really the fruit of our dreams, of our wombs, and of the space we need in order to live with greater dignity? These questions haunt us because the answers we have are still not very helpful. Here and there, we witness attempts at the creation of small communities, but what we see so far is that they will require a great deal more work before what most groups are looking for can become even a partial reality.

What we can affirm is that in many groups there is an uneasiness with the traditional Christian theological framework and a felt need for new community settings. At the same time—and this is important—the feelings I have described cannot be said to be widespread. Many groups that call themselves Christian are satisfied with traditional settings and traditional symbolic expressions. For many people, the traditional framework still works, as do parish communities and traditional religious movements. It is not possible to speak of a widespread crisis in the Christian perspective in this sense.

In fact, when examining the situation of religion, we always need to ask ourselves specific questions. For example, Who is in crisis? Who is talking about a crisis, and why? What religion seems to be in crisis? What language is in crisis? and What are people's unspoken hopes?

It is tempting to conclude that the groups suffering the most intense crisis are intellectuals, and especially left intellectuals: participants in social movements who originally got into them through their religious faith. Women are also in crisis, especially those who, prompted by patriarchal Christianity, have participated for years in a variety of social organizations. Today, with the growth of the feminist movement and with increasing criticism of patriarchy, there has been a loss of traditional frameworks alongside an attempt to recover the meaning of life through the struggle to affirm women's dignity.

However, a number of doubts could also be raised regarding the existence of more widespread crisis. We are witnessing an impressive growth throughout Latin America of fundamentalist, Pentecostal, and charismatic religious movements. Worshipers crowd into enormous stadiums, seeking catharsis by loudly praising God, speaking in tongues, wailing, shouting, and so on. Salvation-oriented TV programs are growing by leaps and bounds, and are broadcast not only on Sundays but on weekdays as well. Healings in the name of Jesus, exorcisms (especially of women), and the resolution of economic and emotional problems are "daily bread" on these TV programs and in the various places of worship used by these religions. With all this, how can anyone speak of a crisis in religion, or even of secularization? New gods and new demons struggle in the public forum to separate the damned from the elect, the impure from the pure, and the masters from the slaves.

A Religion That Isn't in Crisis

Never has the Latin American world been so religious, and never has it been so dependent on and enslaved to a model of society that behaves like a "religion" and from which there seems, at first glance, to be no escape. For some people, it seems contradictory to speak of a religious crisis in the very midst of so much religious fervor. It seems absurd to be questioning traditional patriarchal theologies when religions without formal theologies are springing up everywhere. I am referring to the various religious groups that have large media audiences, and that do not begin with doctrinal content, character formation, or a framework of articulated values. Rather, these groups begin with addressing immediate felt needs, the pain that throbs right now: intense emotions, the worries that upset an apparently harmonious life, and the lack of full citizenship that is felt by so many people in our countries.

Religions such as this with no formal theology are growing by leaps and bounds. By responding to immediate needs, they are offering what the state and other social institutions have been unable to provide. At the same time, they reinforce the hierarchical model of society, in which only a few privileged people have the right to a dignified life. For example, the new "media religions" play a role in offering spurious citizenship. For an hour or a day, the individual feels esteemed, has the sense of being the center of attention, or feels that the community is praying for him or her. Orphans have a sense of being sons or daughters; the anonymous, as members of a church, experience the feeling of being known; and the despised enjoy a momentary sense of highly regarded personhood. Instead of abandonment, there is a sense of being a child of God and a member of a paternalistic tradition, and one can anticipate the harmony of heaven.

The social structures upheld by the powerful are not questioned. Indeed, the world of religion seems to take care of just about everything. Solutions to personal problems come from extraterrestrial beings, ahistorical entities who respond only if they are invoked with fervor and insistence.

I am struck by the fact that I see unemployed men in my neighborhood, some of whom are marginalized even within their own families, who dress up in suits and ties on Sundays and go off to worship. They are transformed. For a moment, they are no longer "Joe Blow" but "Mr. Blow." They enjoy an ephemeral taste of dignity and feel like candidates for full citizenship. Later on, the daily grind will return and very little will have changed for the better. But at that moment, something has happened. At that moment, they experience something positive, and perhaps this will be the impetus for some future personal change that we, with our intellectual analysis, are unable to perceive.

I'd like to point out, by way of contrast, that in these religious movements women retain their subordinate social roles. They are not even allowed the opportunity to raise critical questions. Also, because some churches have cautioned women to avoid public scandal and remain silent, situations of conjugal violence cannot be publicly aired.

The search for social identity, full citizenship, and recognition, which is ubiquitous among the impoverished, prompts us to reconsider the feminist or ecofeminist theology project. We see the limitations of our work and of our movements, but still we believe in them. Our effort to deconstruct patriarchal discourse and unmask its ideological and exclusivist character has few supporters, at least in the numerical sense. Is our work, our effort to build a new theological content and to discover new principles in a variety of traditions, threatened by religions with no formal theology? That question is hard to answer.

What we know, in any case, is that there are small groups here and there that believe in our work and are acting in ways that carry through on our convictions. And we want to go on. We have no idea what the future results of our efforts will be. All we know is that these convictions and efforts are fundamental for our own lives in the present, and that, despite all our difficulties, they have helped a number of groups.

Another position that is very common among poor and working people—one that does not appear to be suffering any crisis, least of all in Brazil—is the de facto combination of different creeds or even different ecclesial bodies within a single religious institution. Some groups show a spontaneous attitude of inclusiveness, and members make use of whatever elements they find useful. One can be a practitioner of candomblé, and at the same time a member of the Catholic fraternity of the Lord of Bonfim, of the Franciscan Third Order, or of the charismatic movement. Or one can be a member of the Catholic church, study theology with the Lutherans, and have a guru in the spiritist tradition. These examples show the complexity of religious phenomena in our day, as well as our inability to make absolute and definite statements.

When you come right down to it, the origins and reasoning of the different traditions are of interest only to researchers. The general public has another way of reasoning, on the basis of which it perceives reality and constructs meanings. The central point of this reasoning has to do, on one hand, with the diversity of the traditions that lie at the roots of our culture, and on the other with various sorts of needs, especially those that have to do with economic survival. As we know, political and religious groups are very familiar with our people's problems and are capable of manipulating people's good faith for the sake of elite interests.

In our hour of need, we are likely to call upon anyone who seems able to help us. We also can knock on different doors and get different kinds of help. For this reason, it is ever more necessary to welcome the diversity of groups and the diversity of their needs, expressed or unexpressed. All this makes it still more difficult to understand all religious phenomena within a single analytical frame of reference.

For me, these concrete concerns are one of the signs that we need to rethink religion on the basis of new frames of reference. I make no pretense of offering persuasive answers of my own, but I am convinced that we must not avoid the task of reflecting on them or endeavoring to take new steps, even at the risk of making mistakes.

Religious Biodiversity: A Path in Need of Rediscovery

What, exactly, is religion? This question always returns to haunt us, above all when we struggle to rediscover the meaning of our lives and pursue new forms of action. This question becomes ever more important as religions are recruited into the service of established powers and when they promote alienation or dull our consciousness.

Rubem Alves says that, unlike animals, human beings have refused to be what the past suggested they should be.

They became inventors of worlds. They planted gardens and built huts, houses, and palaces. They constructed drums, flutes, and harps. They transformed their bodies, covering them with inks, metals, marks, and textiles. They invented flags and erected altars. They buried their dead and prepared them for the journey; and in their absence they intoned laments day and night.[7]

This text inspires me to speak of the biodiversity of religions, which goes along with the biodiversity of the cosmos and the earth, and with the diversity of cultures. This is a biodiversity of "rebinding" (re-ligare), of being re-linked or re-bound! Respect for biodiversity and for the organization of life according to the characteristics of every region is an integral component of the ecological creed. If we really believe our lives are related to the places and times in which we live, then there are many conclusions to be drawn.

To speak of the biodiversity of religions is, first of all, to cultivate in ourselves an attitude of respect for diversity among the languages that depict the meaning of life. In this sense, religion is a language. It does not matter whether the meaning has been written down or not. The important thing is to recognize that human beings, men and women, are incapable of simply obeying their biological programming; they seek the meaning of the world though their bodies and beyond them. Biology becomes culture; it is transformed by the great variety of human groups and organized according to the needs of each. In other words, our lives are always more than our own boundaries and always less than the unlimited character we would like to give them. This is simply the paradox that we are.

This vital diversity of meanings has always been present in human history. However, we know how much human groups resist recognizing this reality and tend to absolutize their own truths, attempting to impose them as supreme verities. Religion ends up playing the games of proselytism and power tactics. But religion also appears in our history as an expression of human ingenuity, as a style of "building" worlds and meanings that relate to daily life and give it direction—as well as flavors and colors of its own. Although they have arisen in specific contexts in answer to specific questions, religions have often tended to take on an absolutist, imperialist character. The temptation to dismiss religious languages that are different from our own has become a commonplace behavior.

When a religious language shows signs of claiming imperialist universality and struggles to impose itself and eliminate others, it is guilty of obstructing the flow of biodiversity. It closes itself off within its own truth and can become destructive. And the breakdown of biodiversity affects not only the most immediate human relationships but also social groups: It ends up impinging on physical spaces, which become objects of religious aggression. History has shown us many examples of this. When they appropriated a given territory, colonial systems took over the people as well, destroying traditional beliefs and seeking to impose their own. The destruction of the earth is accompanied by the destruction of the belief systems that link this particular people with this particular geographical area.

Although it takes different forms today, the same process of destruction continues. What is most disturbing is the subtle and aggressive way it is presented in the communications media: people are prevented from asking questions about their hopes, their deepest beliefs, and the directions they want their lives to take. The new divinity, in the image of the "consumer market," seduces us; we allow ourselves to be guided by its dreams and the paradise of happiness it promises. The new divinity demands constant sacrifices, especially on the part of certain groups of people, in order to be allowed to approach its altars from afar, and smell, from the same distance, the aroma of its incense. As we have noted, the new divinity and its priesthood award prizes to some and punish others, subtly reproducing the ancient patterns of dualistic religion.

To speak of religious biodiversity is to open the door to another set of considerations, even though we are aware of their inherent limitations. Biodiversity exists not only among totally different religious traditions, but also within each individual confession. Within confessions, we find not the drama of differing religions, but that of shared human living, with all its joys and adversities. Thus we also find the need to begin weaving qualitative ties among people through small communities with shared interests.

I believe we ought to reflect deeply on the scientific, biological notion of biodiversity, but not, as it might seem, in order to create some new reductionism. This is not a matter of reducing the relationships among humans and the various branches of human knowledge to a biological-ecological paradigm of the diversity of life. We have had enough reductionism! Rather, we need to be aware of the extent to which the universalistic, imperialist attitudes so deeply rooted in the patriarchal world make it hard for us to understand why there is no single, overarching theory that can explain the whole universe and all the situations and relationships within it.

To speak of biodiversity is not, first and foremost, to offer a theory, but rather to call attention to the empirical reality of natural systems, of the arts, of the sciences, of the history of cultures, and of religions. To speak of religious and cultural biodiversity is to attempt to give the human community a structure that will once again allow it to live out relationships that are more personal, closer to nature, and in deeper contact with the dreams and hopes of the great variety of human groups.

Biodiversity can obviously be observed within every family, in the way each child is different, in the variety of likes and dislikes in food, in affinities, in temperaments, and so on. Nothing can be reduced to a single form of expression without incurring the danger that insistence on this single form of expression will kill life itself. To speak of biodiversity is to affirm the fact of process, of the evolution of the cosmos, of the earth, and of all beings—and their need to organize their shared living in a variety of ways. This evolutionary and process-oriented quality also marks our deepest and most ancient beliefs. So, to bring biodiversity into theological reflection is to open ourselves up to pluralism in the expressions of Christian experience, and therefore to change our understanding of what "unity" is. It is not a matter, as some people think, of losing our identity; rather, we seek to make this identity as authentic as possible, as close as possible to the way we in fact live our lives, as close as possible to the domains in which our lives unfold. Thus, biodiversity requires a new effort to form small faith communities that can develop a common language capable of duly respecting every group. What unites us is the desire to reconstruct our human relationships and to develop in ourselves the values of sharing and mercy that are so often forgotten by the current system. What unites us is the need to feel, once again, the warmth of bodies around a common table, the need to be persons and not just numbers among so many others. What unites us is the desire to create a common language, to reclaim symbols that are connected to our history and that evoke the noblest things in us.

As Rubem Alves says in the poetic opening of his book, *O suspiro dos oprimidos,*

> Did you know that religion is a language?
> A style of speaking about the world . . .
> In everything, the presence of hope and meaning . . .
> Religion is the tapestry hope weaves with words.
> And upon these webbings people lie down and sleep.
> And they rest on words interlaced with one another.
> How does one intertwine words?
> Simple words.
> Like desire.
> I know that sometimes the webbings of love turn into shrouds of
>   fear.
> They are webbings that could speak of life or of death.
> And all this is done with words and desire.
> So in order to understand religion, we must understand the ways
>   of language.[8]

And the ways of speaking about the world, of weaving webs, are so varied—and so beautiful in their variety! Why not take this art seriously when we want to give expression to our religious convictions, to our relationship with Jesus, and to all that in fact creates meaning for us? Why not take advantage of the various spaces we still have and propose alternative languages, meanings, and friendships?

Patriarchal religions weave not only shrouds of fear, but also shrouds of death. The extremes of anthropocentrism and androcentrism, which are especially present in Christianity, become accomplices and legitimators of the destruction that is taking place in our midst.

Religious biodiversity gives a heartfelt welcome to the diversity of tapestries. It is an exercise of going beyond our striving to make one single group the herald of a one-and-only truth, the self-appointed bearer of salvific formulas for everybody. Religious biodiversity implies an attitude of humility, which means that there cannot be absolute powers that regulate and dictate the meaning of life, or of the art of weaving meaning, or of the art of evoking presences that are dear to us.

Besides, a tapestry cannot be eternal, atemporal, or valid forever. It will lose its beauty and its aesthetic qualities. Ephemeral things enjoy the eternity of the present moment, and in this resides their evocative and inspirational task. Often the tapestry has to be rewoven, even if some of the old designs are copies—or even though we can manage to reuse some threads that have not decayed. This is re-creation, religious biodiversity, respect for new moments, creative inspiration, and the welcoming of new hands prepared to weave marvelous designs.

Some people may object that not all religions are acceptable, because some of them have been created on the basis of a destructive mentality. They systematically exclude and kill those they judge to be enemies of their beliefs. But barbarity, too, is a de facto characteristic of religions. This observation has been verified throughout this planet, in all times and places. These are the excesses of religion, and when religion begins to generate excesses it no longer preserves its original religious meaning. It becomes dictatorial politics, or imperialism arrayed in the garments of goodness, mercy, and religion.

To respect religious biodiversity is not the same as saying that anything at all is acceptable or that we should give up our struggle against the powers of destruction that make themselves manifest in the religious domain. But who gives us the authority to say that such and such a religious behavior is destructive? I think there is a consensus among the various human groups, a kind of fundamental intuition, that leads us to affirm, despite our disagreements, that certain behaviors cannot be said to promote life. We say this in the awareness that we are always in danger of being in error, of deceiving ourselves, and of failing to exercise wisdom in discerning our chosen paths. However, we have no way of discerning and knowing our world other than our fragile human process.

We are led, on account of this, to admit the paradoxical character of human life. Our certainties are always limited, and so they always need to be contextualized. Our "salvific" efforts are always precarious and limited. Therefore, we need to make bargains in order to live, in order to discern what the common good is; and, in this way, to construct an ethics on the basis of which shared life and solidarity extending beyond my people or my own small group become possible. And this prospect of a wider ethic can begin with a simple reflection on what our bodies need.

As Umberto Eco says in an interview published in the *Folha de São Paulo,*

> [i]t is possible to build an ethics based on respect for the activities of our bodies: drinking, urinating, defecating, sleeping, making love, speaking, listening, etc. . . . To force someone to live upside down is an intolerable form of torture . . . Rape fails to respect another's body. All forms of racism and exclusion constitute, in the last analysis, ways of denying the body of another. We could re-read the entire history of ethics in light of the rights of bodies and the relationship between our bodies and the world.[9]

It is in this sense that to accept religious biodiversity is also to accept a common framework to which all traditions ought to adhere. This common framework is the sole foundation upon which all religions and creeds are born and subsist. This shared framework has to do with the shared responsibility we all need to take upon ourselves in caring for nature, for all human groups, and, in the last analysis, for the living body that evolves and to which we belong. As Eugen Drewermann says, "It is not enough merely to remember that the world is God's creation, or even to speak out, as some politicians do, in favor of or against nuclear energy. We need a fundamental new religious reflection that is able to break with traditional Judeo-Christian anthropocentrism in order to recover a sense of unity and a shared religious experience of the world—notions that in the history of Western ideas have always been combated as anti-Christian, pantheist, or even atheist."[10]

This challenge will open us up to an understanding not only of the Christian experience but of others as well, based on a frame of reference that incorporates a broader understanding of universal brotherhood/sisterhood and a devotion to all the manifestations of this one and multiform Sacred Body.

As Thomas Berry says,

[t]he ecological age fosters the deep awareness of the sacred presence within every reality of the Universe. There is an awe and a reverence due to the stars in the heavens, the sun, and all heavenly bodies; to the seas and the continents; to all living forms of trees and flowers; to the myriad expressions of life in the sea; to the animals of the forests and the birds of the air . . . Our primary need for the various life-forms of the planet is a psychic, rather than a physical, contact.[11]

It is in this last phrase that we find the great challenge to ourselves: the challenge of educating ourselves and the coming generations for the building of a subjective bonding with all beings, a linkage that is capable of halting the process of exploitation and destruction of the planet and its population. We still have not managed to break away from our anthropocentrism, our androcentrism, and, above all, our exaggerated fascination with consumerism. This attitude has in a certain sense become our body, our psyche, and our way of organizing the world.

We have a long road ahead; we cannot lag behind without appreciating the high cost in lives that our position brings about, for, as John Cobb says, it may already be too late.[12] Religions have an undeniable social role in helping us to develop the sensibilities we need in order to love the earth and the human community in the light of the indissoluble communion among all beings.

Although we need to recognize that the various churches and religions have taken few steps toward the necessary and urgent rethinking of their dogmatic pronouncements, we can also affirm that in all of them there are small groups that are increasingly sensitive to these challenges and are opening up alternative ways of living. This growing sensitivity is at the same time nourishing the hope that within patriarchal religions themselves there can be alternative spaces that allow us to avoid complicity with worldwide devastation, spaces that open a way to lives of effective and affective communion. I believe that this is the way in which we will find a new meaning for religion and a new inspiration for our hope.

Alice Walker, the extraordinary U.S. novelist, invites us to think about the beatitudes, or "helpings" (realities that can in fact help us), on the basis of our religious communion, which is related to the earth and to all living things. Her inspiration remains as a "provocation" to a religious faith that is beyond all religions:

> Helped are those who love the Earth, their mother, and who willingly suffer that she may not die; in their grief over her pain they will weep rivers of blood, and in their joy in her lively response to love, they will converse with trees . . .

> Helped are those who find the courage to do at least one small thing each day to help the existence of another—plant, animal, river, human being. They shall be joined by multitude of the timid.

> Helped are those who lose their fear of death; theirs is the power to envision the future in a blade of grass.

> Helped are those who love and actively support the diversity of life; they shall be secure in their differentness.

> Helped are those who know.[13]

EPILOGUE:
AS THE DEER LONGS
FOR RUNNING WATERS

~~~

This epilogue returns to the psalm that inspired its title. Its purpose is to say that there is much left to say. Its purpose is to say that many things I have said could have been said in other, perhaps more "gracious," ways. I conclude by pointing to the tentative character of this song of hope marked by pain and perplexity.

It is the song of an exile who longs for return to her land, to her God, and to her loves.

Let us make this song/lament into our final song as exiles on our own earth, which is divided and plagued by boundaries and by prohibitions on entering and leaving. A strange song of exile, sung within our own body and feeling that it barely belongs to itself . . . the song of one who seeks answers and knows that the few she will find are fragile and ephemeral.

It is the stubborn song of one who seeks, despite everything, the beauty of the ephemeral, of that "something" that always escapes us, even when we insist on trying to hold it fast. It is the song of one who seeks to rediscover arms and embraces, love poems, and reasons for beginning to hope once again. It is the song that is born of the body, and born of the earth. . . .

An earth where the number of displaced persons increases . . . of refugees, prisoners, and the homeless, of those who are hungry for love and for bread. An earth that is burned, robbed, exhausted, devastated, divided up, and poorly loved. It is our land and a foreign land! A land of friends and enemies! A hostile earth and a mother earth, a homeland earth, a brother earth and a sister earth.

A land of pain and hopeful longings . . .

Our longings are expressions of our hope. And when we long for hope, it is because our own ability to hope has fallen ill. Despite this we still have the strength to hope once again.

In the blind darkness of our days, we have little idea how to hope for what we hope for, how to heal our wounds, restore our strength, or quench our thirst. This is why we say that our hope is ailing, that our Sacred Body is ailing.

This is surely not a fatal illness, one that is bound to end in death; rather, it is a serious ailment that brings with it the gravest of risks. It is a sickness that threatens us, because it has already killed part of our Sacred Body. It is an ailment that we ourselves have in a certain sense created, one that is born of ourselves, of our excesses and our violence.

This affliction is both good and bad for us. It is the fruit of our wombs. . . . It began as something good and turned into something evil. It is an affliction that is part of our being, of our daily lives, of our relationships, and of the entire earth.

Our hope is as diseased as we ourselves are! From where shall our salvation come? Who will drag us out of the filth that we ourselves have produced? Who will rescue us from the foul odor that obliterates our sense of smell, from the corruption we unceasingly breathe? Who will put an end to the endless violence in which we have become entangled?

Who will save us from unlimited progress, from the idols of money and power? Who will save us from our own prejudices, from our inability to look for change?

On what doors can we knock in seeking help? Before what altars can we pray? What gods will be willing to lend us a hand?

Even the green things we eat have been poisoned as they grew!

Where shall we go? Who will come to our aid?

Bewildered, we wander about like someone who no longer has a sense of being diseased. Drunken, we no longer sense the excess of drink in which we are awash. Drugged, we no longer recognize our condition or muster the will to drag ourselves away from its stupefying effects. Fascinated by our false images, we no longer know who we are.

And yet the flowers go on budding, and birds and children still come forth. . . . The sun shines again today, and last night the moon swept the sky with its silvery light. . . . Once again, I smell the tempting aroma of the kitchen, and the hope of tender meetings pervades my body.

To seek living waters is to prefigure our hope. . . . And the living water is life itself since its very beginning, since its primordial reality, since its origins still present in ourselves.

To seek living waters is to seek an atmosphere that is propitious for life, and to respectfully permit the development of all forms of life.

This book is no more than an "aspiration," a "con-spiracy," a "breathing with" by one who wants "a new heaven and a new earth" to spring from this very ground.

"As the deer longs for running waters," so we join our longing with hers.

Hungry and thirsty, we expect to see hope spring up once again in our own womb, in the womb of the earth, out of our entrails, out of the Divine that lives within us and renews us. Like the deer, we move forward seeking what will bring us to life, what will enliven our Sacred Body with its thousand and one lives. Like the deer, we have sensed the "living waters" from afar; and now we run toward them, but with no certitudes . . . barely allowing our goal to keep us alive, to keep us dreaming and to prepare us for the next step on the way.

"As the deer longs for living waters," we live in thankfulness for those who carry within them the fragile stubbornness of seeking, of ceaseless searching.

> My body is thirsty for this water . . .
> For the water of life . . .
> the life of water . . .
> When will we go to drink it?
> And to tremble with joy with the multitude of the poor,
> With the trees and flowers,
> With the fishes and birds,

With the stars and the moon,
With the rain and the wind,
With the snow and the dew,
With the sun and the entire earth.
"As the deer longs for running waters . . ."

NOTES

≈

PROLOGUE

1. As Maria Mies and Vandana Shiva say, the word "ecofeminism" is a new term for an ancient wisdom. It was introduced at the end of the 1970s or the beginning of the 1980s. It was first used by Françoise d'Eaubonne and became popular in the context of feminist struggles against the destruction of the environment. Cf. Maria Mies and Vandana Shiva, *Ecofeminism* (Halifax, N.S.: Fernwood Publications; London; Atlantic Highlands, N.J.: Zed Books, 1993), 13.

INTRODUCTION

1. Leila da Costa Ferreira, "A politica ambiental no Brasil," in *Mulier e meio ambiente,* ed. Centro Informação Mulher, São Paulo (CIM) and Centro Ecumênico de Documentação e Informação (CEDI), March 1992, 20, 21.

2. Marcel Gauchet, *Le désenchantement du monde: Une histoire politique de la religion* (Paris: Gallimard, 1985).

3. Leonardo Boff, *Ecologia, mundialização, espiritualidade* (São Paulo: Ed. Atica, 1993); Frei Betto, *A obra do artista: Uma visão holistica do Universo* (São Paulo: Ed. Atica, 1995).

4. See *O rostro indio de Deus* (São Paulo: Coleção Teologia e Libertação, 1989).

5. Rosiska Darcy de Oliveira, *Elogio da Diferença: o feminino emergente* (São Paulo: Ed. Brasiliense, 1991), 103.

6. Bila Sorj, "O Feminino como metáfora da natureza," *Revista de Estudos Feministas*, CIEC, Escola de Comunicação UFRJ o (1992), 149.

7. Nicole Claude Mathieu, "Questions à l'eco-féminisme," *Ecologia, Feminismo, Desenvolvimento,* ed. Maria Inácia d'Avila e Naumi de Vasconcelos, EICOS-UFRJ 1 (1993): 129.

8. Maria Mies and Vadana Shiva, *Ecofeminism* (Halifax, N.S.: Fernwood Publications; London; Atlantic Highlands, N.J.: Zed Books, 1993), 160.

9. Carolyn Merchant, *The Death of Nature: Women, Ecology, and Scientific Revolution* (San Francisco: Harper, 1980), 2.

10. *Con-spirando, revista latinoamericana de ecofeminismo, espiritualidad y teología,* Santiago, Chile, 1 (March 1992): 1.

11. *Con-spirando* 4 (June 1993): 1.

12. Rosa Domingo Trapasso, "Ecofeminismo: revisando nuestra conexión con la naturaleza," *Con-spirando* 4 (June 1993): 3.

CHAPTER 1. KNOWING OUR KNOWING

1. Eduardo Galeano, *The Book of Embraces,* trans. Cedric Belfrage (New York: Norton, 1991), 73.

2. Carlos Mesters, *Paraiso, saudade ou esperança* (Petrópolis, Brazil: Vozes, 1971), 31.

3. Cullen Murphy, "Women and the Bible," *Atlantic Monthly* (August 1993): 50.

4. Ronaldo Muñoz, *O Deus dos cristãos* (Petrópolis, Brazil: Vozes, 1986), 26.

5. Jon Sobrino, *Cristologia desde América Latina* (Mexico City: Centro de Reflexión Teológica, 1977).

6. Gustavo Gutiérrez, *Teología de la liberación* (Madrid: Sígueme, 1970), 250. Cf. *A Theology of Liberation: History, Politics, and Salvation,* trans. Sr. Caridad Inda and John Eagleson (Maryknoll, N.Y.: Orbis Books, 1973), 193–94.

7. Gustavo Gutiérrez, "La opción preferencial por los pobres," in *La religión en los albores del siglo XXI* (Bilbao, Spain: Universidad de Deusto, 1994), 116.

8. Rosemary Radford Ruether, *Gaia and God: An Ecofeminist Theology of Earth Healing* (San Francisco: Harper and Row, 1992), 250.

9. Ibid., 33–34.

10. Seyla Benhabib, *Situating the Self* (New York: Routledge, Chapman, and Hall, 1992), 213.

CHAPTER 2. THE HUMAN PERSON FROM AN ECOFEMINIST PERSPECTIVE

1. Paul Ricoeur, *Histoire et vérité* (Paris: Seuil, 1955), 118.

2. Emmanuel Mounier, *O Personalismo,* 2d ed. (Lisbon: Livraria Morais Editora, 1964).

3. *The Catechism of the Catholic Church* (Vatican City: Libreria Editrice Vaticana, 1994).

4. [The Portuguese language uses the same word to designate both "conscience" and "consciousness." —*Trans.*]

5. Brian Swimme and Thomas Berry, *The Universe Story* (San Francisco: HarperSanFrancisco, 1992).

6. Rosemary Radford Ruether, *Gaia and God* (San Francisco: HarperSanFrancisco, 1992), 31.

7. Jean Ladrière, "Le problème de l'âme et du corps dans la conception classique," in B. Feltz and D. Lambert, *Entre le corps et l'esprit* (Liège: Mardaga,1995), 14.

8. Brian Swimme, *The Universe Is a Green Dragon* (Santa Fe: Bear and Co., 1984).

CHAPTER 3. GOD: AN ECOFEMINIST APPROACH

1. Sallie McFague, *The Body of God: An Ecological Theology* (Minneapolis: Fortress Press, 1993), 20.

2. Emmanuel Levinas, *Le temps et l'autre* (Paris: PUF, 1979).

3. Edgar Morin and Anne Brigitte Kern, *Terre-Patrie* (Paris: Seuil, 1993), 198.

4. Levinas, *Le temps et l'autre,* 28.

5. Julia Esquivel, "Elección," in *Florescerás Guatemala* (Mexico City: Ediciones CUPSA, 1989), 12.

6. McFague, *The Body of God,* 149–50.

7. Ernesto Cardenal, "Cantiga 5: Stars and Fireflies," in *Cosmic Canticle* (Willimantic, Conn.: Curbstone Press, 1993), 39.

8. Maria Mies and Vandana Shiva, *Ecofeminism* (Halifax, N.S.: Fernwood Publications; London; Atlantic Highlands, N.J.: Zed Books, 1993), 15.

9. Carol J. Adams, ed., *Ecofeminism and the Sacred* (New York: Continuum, 1993).

10. See, for example, Coca Trillini, *De la pirámide al arco iris, Cuaderno de trabajo sobre mujer y biblia* (Buenos Aires: Paulinas, 1995).

11. Sallie McFague, *Models of God: A Theology for a Nuclear Age* (Philadelphia: Fortress Press, 1987).

12. McFague, *The Body of God,* 152.

CHAPTER 4. ECOFEMINISM AND THE TRINITY

1. Elisabeth Johnson, *She Who Is: The Mystery of God in Feminist Theological Discourse* (New York: Crossroad, 1993).

2. Karl Rahner, *The Trinity* (London: Burns and Oates/Herder and Herder), 1970.

3. Robert Lentz, "The Celtic Trinity," *Creation Spirituality* (January–February 1991).

4. Sandra Schneiders, "God Is More than Two Men and a Bird: An Interview with Sister Sandra Schneiders," *U.S. Catholic* (May 1990): 20–27.

5. Rosemary Radford Ruether, *Gaia and God* (San Francisco: HarperSanFrancisco, 1992).

6. Michel Maffiesoli, *Le temps des tribus* (Paris: Éd. Méridiens Klincksieck, 1988).

7. Rodolfo Mondolfo, *El pensamiento antiguo, desde los orígenes hasta Platón,* 4th ed. (Buenos Aires: Editorial Losada, 1959), 47.

8. Leonardo Boff, *A trindade, a sociedade e a libertação* (Petrópolis, Brazil: Vozes, 1986).

9. Brian Swimme, *The Universe Is a Green Dragon* (Santa Fe: Bear and Co., 1984), 28.

10. See Paul Ricoeur, *Finitude et culpabilité II: La symbolique du mal* (Paris: Aubier, 1960); Adolphe Gesché, *Le mal* (Paris: Cerf, 1993).

11. ["Severinas and Antonios" refers to poor people who are able to turn their suffering into compassion, love, mercy, poetry, and social action. Severina is the heroine of *Morte e Vida Severina,* a well-known Brazilian poem/novel by João Cabral de Mello Neto, which describes the suffering of poor peasants in northeastern Brazil; Severina and Antonio are very common names among the poor. —*Trans.*]

12. Joseph Campbell, *The Power of Myth* (New York: Doubleday, 1988), 230–31.

CHAPTER 5. JESUS FROM AN ECOFEMINIST PERSPECTIVE

1. Ivone Gebara, "Cristologia Fundamental," *Revista Eclesiastica Brasileira* 48 (1988): 259–72.

2. The Council of Nicaea, held in 325 during the pontificate of Pope Silvester I, proclaimed the Nicene Creed in opposition to the teachings of the heretic Arius. It affirmed the consubstantiality of the Son with the Father. The Council of Chalcedon, held in 451 during the pontificate of Celestine I, proclaimed that Christ had two natures, one divine and one human, in a single person. See Hubert Jedin, *Brève histoire des conciles* (Tournai, Belgium: Desclée, 1960).

3. Louis Bouyer, *Le fils éternel: Théologie de la parole de Dieu et christologie* (Paris: Cerf, 1974); Joseph Moingt, *L'Homme qui venait de Dieu* (Paris: Cerf, 1994); Jon Sobrino, *Cristologia desde América Latina* (Mexico City: Centro de Reflexión Teológica, 1977).

4. Sallie McFague, *The Body of God* (Minneapolis: Fortress Press, 1993).

5. Ibid., 159.

6. Tissa Balasuriya, "Right Relationships: The De-routing and Re-routing of Christian Theology," *Logos* 30 (September–December 1991): 204. (published by the Center for Society and Religion, Colombo, Sri Lanka).

CHAPTER 6. THAT ALL MAY HAVE LIFE

1. Rosemary Radford Ruether, *Gaia and God* (San Francisco: HarperSanFrancisco, 1992), 251.

2. Sigmund Freud, *L'avenir d'une illusion* (Paris: Quadrige/ Presses Universitaires de France, 1995), 18. E.T.: *The Future of an Illusion,* ed. James Strachey (New York: Norton, 1989).

3. Hugo Assmann and Franz Hinkelammert, *A idolatria do mercado: Ensaio sobre economia e Teologia* (Petrópolis, Brazil: Vozes, 1989).

4. Edgar Morin, *Terre-Patrie* (Paris: Seuil, 1993).

5. [In Portuguese, the term *re-ligar* means to re-bind or reconnect. The author makes a play on words here, calling attention to the original Latin etymology of the word "religion." —*Trans.*]

6. Ludwig Feuerbach, *L'Essence du Christianisme* (Paris: Maspero, 1982).

7. Rubem Alves, *O que é a religião?* 2nd ed. (São Paulo: Brasiliense, 1981), 17.

8. Rubem Alves, *O suspiro dos oprimidos* (São Paulo, Brazil: Paulinas, 1984), 16.

9. Humberto Eco, interview, *Folha de São Paulo* (Brazil) (April 1994): sec. 6, p. 7.

10. Eugen Drewermann, *Le progrès meurtrier* (Paris: Stock, 1993), 86.

11. Thomas Berry, *The Dream of the Earth* (San Francisco: Sierra Club, 1988), 46.

12. John B. Cobb, *Is It Too Late? A Theology of Ecology* (Beverly Hills, Calif.: Bruce, 1972).

13. Alice Walker, "The Gospel according to Shug," in *The Temple of My Familiar* (New York: Simon and Schuster, 1989), 288–89. Quoted in Sallie McFague, *The Body of God: An Ecological Theology* (Minneapolis: Fortress Press, 1993), 212.

BIBLIOGRAPHY

≈

I cannot offer a complete bibliography of works that deal directly with ecofeminism. This list merely complements the reference notes, offering a few more books that were present, in one way or another, in my thinking as I wrote this reflection.

Adams, Carol, ed. *Ecofeminism and the Sacred.* New York: Continuum, 1993.

Alves, Rubem. *O enigma da religião.* Petrópolis, Brazil: Vozes, 1975.

———. *O suspiro dos oprimidos.* São Paulo, Brazil: Paulinas, 1984.

Berry, Thomas, with Thomas Clarke. *Befriending the Earth: A Theology of Reconciliation between Humans and the Earth.* Mystic, Conn.: Twenty-third Publications, 1991.

Boff, Leonardo. *Ecologia, Mundialização, Espiritualidade.* São Paulo: Atica, 1993. (Available in English as *Ecology and Liberation: A New Paradigm.* Maryknoll, N.Y.: Orbis Books, 1995.)

———. *O rosto materno de Deus: Ensaio Interdisciplinar sobre o feminino e suas formas religiosas.* Petrópolis: Vozes, 1979. (Available in English as *The Maternal Face of God: The Feminine and Its Religious Espressions.* San Francisco: Harper and Row, 1987.)

———. *Paixão de Cristo, Paixão do Mundo: O fato, as interpretações e o significado ontem e hoje.* Petrópolis: Vozes, 1977. (Available in English as *Passion of Christ, Passion of the World: The Facts, Their Interpretation, and Their Meaning Yesterday and Today.* Maryknoll, N.Y.: Orbis Books, 1987.)

Boff, Leonardo, and Aloysius Pieris, eds. *Poverty and Ecology. Concilium* 5 (1995). English edition from Orbis Books, Maryknoll, N.Y.; French edition from Beauchesne, Paris.

Brown, Joanne Carlson, and Carole R. Bohn, eds. *Christianity, Patriarchy, and Abuse.* Cleveland, Ohio: Pilgrim Press, 1989.

Chung Hyun Kyung. *Struggle to Be the Sun Again: Introducing Asian Women's Theology.* Maryknoll, N.Y.: Orbis Books, 1990.

Clifford, Anne M. "An Ecofeminist Proposal for Solidarity," in *In the Embrace of God: Feminist Approaches to Theological Anthropology,* ed. Ann O'Hara Graff. Maryknoll, N.Y.: Orbis Books, 1995.

Daly, Mary. *Beyond God the Father: Toward a Philosophy of Women's Liberation.* Boston: Beacon Press, 1973.

d'Eaubonne, Françoise. "Feminism or Death," in *New French Feminisms: An Anthology,* ed. Elaine Marks and Isabelle de Courtvron. Amherst: University of Massachusetts Press, 1980.

Facio, Alda. "Cuando el género suena, cambios trae." GAIA, Centro de las Mujeres. Caracas, Venezuela: Fondo Editorial "La Escarcha Azul," 1995.

Feuerbach, Ludwig. *L'Essence du christianisme.* Paris: Maspero, 1982. (Available in English as *The Essence of Christianity.* New York: Harper, 1957.)

Gassner, John. *Mestres do teatro,* trans. Alberto Guzik and J. Guinsburg. São Paulo: Perspectiva, 1974.

Gebara, Ivone, and Maria Clara Bingemer. *Maria Mãe de Deus e Mãe dos Pobres.* Petrópolis: Vozes, 1987. (Available in English as *Mary: Mother of God, Mother of the Poor.* Maryknoll, N.Y.: Orbis Books, 1989.)

Gesché, Adolphe. *Le cosmos.* Paris: Cerf, 1994.

———. *Le mal.* Paris: Cerf, 1993.

———. *L'homme.* Paris: Cerf, 1993.

Gilligan, Carol. *In a Different Voice: Psychological Theory and Women's Development.* Cambridge: Harvard University Press, 1982.

Girard, René. *La violence et le sacré.* Paris: Grasset, 1972. (Available in English as *Violence and the Sacred.* Baltimore: Johns Hopkins University Press, 1977.)

———. *Des choses cachées depuis la fondation du monde.* Paris: Grasset, 1978. (Available in English as *Things Hidden since the Foundation of the World.* Stanford, Calif.: Stanford University Press, 1987.)

Gounelle, André. *Le Christ et Jésus.* Paris: Desclée, 1990.

Grant, Jacqueline. *White Women's Christ and Black Women's Jesus.* Atlanta: Scholars Press, 1989.

Habermas, Jürgen. *La technique et la science comme idéologie.* Paris: Gallimard, 1973.

Hinkelammert, Franz. *Sacrificios humanos y sociedad occidental: Lucifer y la Bestia.* San José, Costa Rica: DEI, 1991.

Hunt, Mary. *Fierce Tenderness: A Feminist Theology of Friendship.* New York: Crossroad, 1991.

Isasi-Díaz, Ada María, "Elements of a Mujerista Anthropology." In *In the Embrace of God: Feminist Approaches to Theological Anthropology,* ed. Ann O'Hara Graff. Maryknoll, N.Y.: Orbis Books, 1995.

Johnson, Elisabeth. *Women, Earth, and Creator Spirit.* New York: Paulist Press, 1993.

Kant, Emmanuel. *Critique de la raison pure,* 4th ed. Paris: Quadrige/Presses Universitaires de France, 1993. (Available in English as *The Critique of Pure Reason.* Chicago: Encyclopedia Britannica, 1989.)

Kolakowski, Lezek. *Modernity on Endless Trial* (Chicago: University of Chicago Press, 1990).

Lovelock, J. E. *Gaia: A New Look at Life on Earth.* Oxford: Oxford University Press, 1979.

Lyotard, Jean-François. *The Postmodern Explained.* Minneapolis: University of Minnesota Press, 1993.

Maffesoli, Michel. *Au creux des apparences: Pour une éthique de l'esthétique.* Paris: Plon, 1990.

"Meio Ambiente," in *Tempo e Presença, Revista Bimestral do CEDI.* Rio de Janeiro, Brazil (January–February 1992): 261.

Merchant, Carolyn. *The Death of Nature: Women, Ecology, and the Scientific Revolution.* San Francisco: Harper and Row, 1980.

Mies, Maria. *Patriarchy and Accumulation on a World Scale: Women in the International Division of Labour.* London: Zed Books, 1986.

Mies, Maria, Veronika Bennholdt-Thomsen, and Claudia Von Werlhof. *Women: The Last Colony.* London: Zed Books, 1988.

Moltmann, Jürgen. *Deus na Criação: Doutrina Ecológica da Criação.* Petrópolis, Brazil: Vozes, 1993. (Available in English as *God in Creation: A New Theology of Creation and the Spirit of God.* Minneapolis: Fortress Press, 1985.)

Moser, Antonio. *O problema ecológico e suas implicações éticas.* Petrópolis, Brazil: Vozes, 1983.

Rae, Eleanor. *Women, the Earth, the Divine.* Maryknoll, N.Y.: Orbis Books, 1994.

Ress, Mary Judith, Ute Seibert-Cuadra, and Lene Sjorup, eds. *Del cielo a la tierra: Una antología de teología feminista.* Santiago, Chile: Sello Azul, 1994.

Ruether, Rosemary Radford. *New Woman, New Earth.* New York: Seabury Press, 1975.

_____. *Sexism and God-Talk: Toward a Feminist Theology.* Boston: Beacon Press, 1983.

Russell, Bertrand. *A History of Western Philosophy.* London: Unwin Paperbacks, 1987.

Russell, Peter. *O despertar da terra, O cérebro global.* São Paulo, Brazil: Cultrix, 1991.

Salisbury, Joyce S. *Padres de la iglesia, vírgenes independientes.* Bogotá: TM Editores, 1994.

Schüssler Fiorenza, Elisabeth. *In Memory of Her: A Feminist Theological Reconstruction of Christian Origins.* New York: Crossroad, 1983.

_____. *Searching the Scriptures: A Feminist Introduction.* New York: Crossroad, 1993.

Shiva, Vandana. *Abrazar la vida: Mujer, ecología y supervivencia.* Montevideo: Instituto del Tercer Mundo, 1991.

Sjoo, Monica, and Barbara Mor. *The Great Cosmic Mother: Rediscovering the Religion of the Earth.* San Francisco: Harper and Row, 1987.

Sölle, Dorothee. *Teología política: Confrontación con Rudolf Bultmann.* Salamanca: Sígueme, 1972.

_____. *The Window of Vulnerability: A Political Spirituality.* Minneapolis: Fortress Press, 1990.

Támez, Elsa, ed. *Through Her Eyes: Women's Theology from Latin America.* Maryknoll, N.Y.: Orbis Books, 1989.

Thompson, William Irwin, ed. *GAIA: Uma teoria do Conhecimento.* São Paulo: Gaia, 1987.

Trible, Phyllis. *God and the Rhetoric of Sexuality.* Philadelphia: Fortress Press, 1978.

_____. *Texts of Terror: Literary-Feminist Readings of Biblical Narratives.* Philadelphia: Fortress Press, 1984.

Whitehead, Alfred North. *Science and the Modern World.* New York: Free Press, 1967.

Williams, Delores. *Sisters in the Wilderness: The Challenge of Womanist God-Talk.* Maryknoll, N.Y.: Orbis Books, 1993.

INDEX